LOS .
RAILWAY
WALKS

Collins

An imprint of HarperCollins Publishers
Westerhill Road, Bishopbriggs, Glasgow G64 2QT

Copyright © HarperCollins Publishers Ltd 2016
Text © Julian Holland
Maps and photographs © as per credits

First edition 2016

PB ISBN 978 0 00 816358 7
TBP ISBN 978 0 00 817266 4

10 9 8 7 6 5 4 3 2 1

Printed in China by RR Donnelley APS Co Ltd

Collins ® is a registered trademark of HarperCollins Publishers Ltd

A catalogue record for this book is available from the British Library

If you would like to comment on any aspect of this publication, please contact us at the above address or online.
e-mail: **collinsmaps@harpercollins.co.uk**

www.harpercollins.co.uk

 facebook.com/collinsmaps

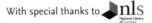 @collinsmaps

With special thanks to

MIX
Paper from
responsible sources
FSC www.fsc.org **FSC™ C007454**

FSC™ is a non-profit international organisation established to promote the responsible management
of the world's forests. Products carrying the FSC label are independently certified to assure
consumers that they come from forests that are managed to meet the social, economic and
ecological needs of present and future generations, and other controlled sources.

Find out more about HarperCollins and the environment at
www.harpercollins.co.uk/green

FRONT COVER: *Built to serve Lord Beaumont Hotham of nearby Dalton Hall, Kiplingcotes station
has been well preserved with its station building, goods shed, platforms and signal box providing an
interesting stopping-off point alongside the Hudson Way Rail Trail.* © Julian Holland

LOST
RAILWAY
WALKS

JULIAN HOLLAND

**Explore 100 of Britain's
lost railways**

CONTENTS

*Please note that all historical maps in this book are from Bartholomew's Half Inch Series from the 1950's and 1960's. As they are for illustrative purposes only they should not be used as a substitute for up-to-date Ordnance Survey maps.

INTRODUCTION

I have a confession to make! Yes, I used to be a trainspotter. I've said it now. However, this all-consuming hobby that took up all my spare time and pocket money in the early 1960s wasn't just the writing down of locomotive numbers in a notebook. I travelled far and wide around Britain's then still extensive railway network, meeting like-minded people, visiting places that most people had never heard of (Thornton Junction, where's that?) and travelling on lines that were soon to be confined to the dustbin of history – many of which feature in this book. Sadly, my fun was short-lived thanks mainly to motorway-mad Ernest Marples and his overpaid lackey, Dr Beeching, as, by the late 1960s, the sun had set on Britain's 150-year-old golden age of steam and the executioner's axe had fallen on many of the country's rural railways. It was Desolation Row indeed so, to take my mind off this senseless destruction, I enrolled at Hornsey Art College in North London – actually I was in a former air-raid shelter up on the North Circular Road next to the Hertford Loop. Probably in sympathy with the students at the Sorbonne in Paris, many of my fellow budding artists (clutching unread copies of Mao Tse Tung's Little Red Book) decided to stage a sit-in and so I was locked out of college for months on end with my local authority refusing to pay my grant. I could never fathom out what it was all about, despite being addressed by Jack Straw at a student mass meeting in Crouch End Town Hall. Woe is me, I thought, but eventually the whole sorry saga finally came to an end and I returned to college much wiser, having spent my lock-out time

working as an X-ray porter at Whittington Hospital and in the underground deep-freeze at the old Billingsgate Market.

So, what, you may be asking by now, is this to do with Lost Railway Walks? Well . . . the first time I came across a 'lost' railway was actually in North London of all places. As an art student, I rented a room in a large house in Muswell Hill Road – behind me were Queen's Woods while opposite were Highgate Woods. Quite a salubrious address for just £4 a week. One of my fellow students who lived at the same address was having a nightmare of a time with his then girlfriend, and he decided to end it all by throwing himself off a bridge on to what he thought was an electric railway line. The location of this bridge? Cranley Gardens. Well, unknown to him, the line, the branch from Highgate to Alexandra Palace, had closed to passengers many years before and despite plans by the London Passenger Transport Board in the 1930s to link it in with the London Underground network, its electrification had been scuppered by the onset of World War II. I suppose my student friend had much to thank Adolf Hitler for! Anyway, I digress, as the Finsbury Park to 'Ally Pally' line is now one of many 'lost' railways that have in recent years seen a renaissance, albeit without trains and tracks, and in this particular instance without any cyclists either.

Contrary to popular myth, railway closures in Britain were not a new phenomenon when the 'Beeching Report' was published in 1963. The dark economic clouds of the post-war years had

Ex-SR 'Q' Class 0-6-0 No. 30539 heads into Broadstone station with local train in 1956.

brought closure to around 3,000 miles of railways around the country even before the good doctor appeared on the scene. Dr Beeching's 'Axe' was just the *coup de grace* on another 4,500 miles of deliberately run-down railways in an era of 'You've never had it so good', gleaming new motorways and a powerful road transport lobby – the exhortation by rail users' groups of 'Use It, or Lose It' just fell on deaf ears. Since those dark days Britain's remaining railways have been reborn and the thousands of miles of 'lost' railways have found a new life, giving enjoyment to walkers, cyclists and even horse riders in a peaceful, traffic-free environment. And it doesn't stop there either, as they are all, without exception, wildlife corridors in which butterflies, birds, small mammals and wild flowers flourish.

There is also much to discover for the keen-eyed lost railway sleuth, although Southern Railway concrete fence posts may not be everybody's cup of tea. Overgrown platforms, platelayers' huts, over and under road bridges, soaring viaducts, menacing rusty girder bridges, long and dank tunnels, old railway coaches masquerading as tea shops and B&B accommodation, restored signal boxes, goods sheds and stations (many of them private residences) all bring the lost railway

journey back to life. Not forgetting the beautiful scenery as well!

In **Lost Railway Walks**, I have selected 100 of what I consider to be the best 'lost' railway routes in Britain. Some are just a few miles long while others are quite lengthy, but whether you are a jogger, dog walker, buggy pusher, bike rider, hiker, marcher or stroller you are pretty well guaranteed to have a great time away from all the hustle and bustle of modern life.

Julian Holland

KEY TO MAP SYMBOLS

Route open as footpath/cycleway

Route now inaccessible

Nearby heritage line of interest

Railway line open (selected only)

Footpath/cycleway alongside open railway

Footpath/cycleway alongside heritage railway

○ Station open

● Station closed

S. and D. Railway Station, Highbridg

SOUTHWEST ENGLAND

Camel Trail

ORIGINAL LINE
18 miles

LENGTH OPEN TO WALKERS & CYCLISTS
17½ miles

ORIGINAL ROUTE OPERATOR
Bodmin & Wadebridge
Railway/London & South
Western Railway

LINE OPEN TO PASSENGERS
Padstow to Wadebridge:
1899–1967;
Wadebridge to Bodmin North:
1834–1967
(Note Dunmere Halt to
Wenfordbridge never carried
passengers)

OS LANDRANGER
200

NATIONAL CYCLE NETWORK
Route 32

REFRESHMENT POINTS
Padstow, Wadebridge, Bodmin

CAR PARKING
Padstow, Old Town Cove,
Wadebridge, Dunmere
Bodmin, Scarletts Well
Bodmin, Grogley Halt, Shell
Woods, Wenfordbridge

HERITAGE RAILWAY
Bodmin & Wenford Railway

OPPOSITE LOWER:
*The only major engineering
structure on the Camel Trail is
the three-span girder bridge
which crosses Little Petherick
Creek, east of Padstow.*

PADSTOW ⇢ BODMIN
AND WENFORD BRIDGE

One of the earliest railways in Britain and the first in Cornwall to use steam locomotives, the Bodmin & Wadebridge Railway opened between Wadebridge and Wenfordbridge, with a branch to Bodmin, in 1834. Its main purpose was to transport stone, and later, china clay, from quarries on the edge of Bodmin Moor to a quay on the River Camel at Wadebridge with sea sand for farmers going in the opposite direction. Passenger-carrying was initially minimal as the railway only owned one carriage, operating a sporadic service between Wadebridge and Bodmin. The railway was purchased by the London & South Western Railway (LSWR) in 1847 but remained isolated from the country's growing rail network until 1888 when the line from Bodmin Road (now Bodmin Parkway) to Boscarne Junction opened.

Padstow was only reached in 1899 when the LSWR finally completed its line from Halwill Junction via Wadebridge – the final part of the company's meandering 259¾-mile route from London Waterloo via Exeter and Okehampton. With the coming of the railway, the small harbour village of Padstow soon became a popular destination for holidaymakers and, in 1927, the Southern Railway introduced the 'Atlantic Coast Express' from Waterloo. This popular multi-portioned train last ran in September 1964 by which time all the railways in North Cornwall had been listed for closure in the 'Beeching Report'. Passenger services to Bodmin and Padstow ended on 30 January 1967 although china clay traffic from Wenfordbridge continued to operate to Bodmin Road until 1983.

Following closure, the entire route between Padstow and Wenfordbridge along with the branch from Dunmere to Bodmin was reopened by Cornwall Council as a footpath and cycleway known as the Camel Trail. Virtually the entire 18-mile level route is traffic-free making it popular with cyclists, both young and old. The Trail, which is used by an estimated 400,000 people each year and contributes £3 million to the local economy, is easily cycled in one day. It also has much to offer lovers of wildlife as it passes through a Site of Special Scientific Interest and a Special Area of Conservation.

Starting at Padstow, where the station buildings and platform have survived, the Trail follows the south shore of the Camel Estuary, crossing Little Petherick Creek on a fine girder bridge, to reach Wadebridge. Here, the station building is known as the Betjeman Centre, so named after the Poet Laureate John Betjeman who loved to travel by train to North Cornwall. The railway route has disappeared in the town, so the Trail makes use of local roads before regaining the trackbed on its route up the winding and wooded river valley past the sites of Grogley Halt and Nanstallon Halt to Boscarne Junction. Here it meets the Bodmin & Wenford Railway which operates mainly steam-hauled tourist trains to Bodmin and Bodmin Parkway between February and October.

Beyond Boscarne Junction, the Trail splits with one branch heading off into Bodmin town and the other continuing up the valley through Dunmere Woods to Hellandbridge, Poley's Bridge and Wenfordbridge.

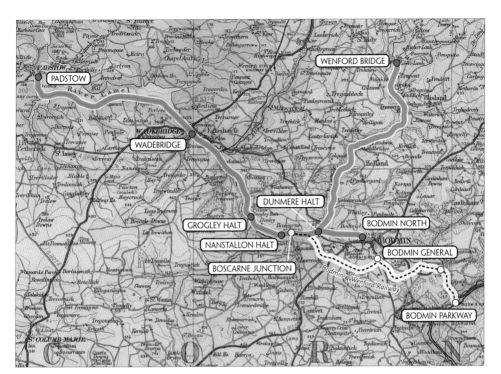

PADSTOW
PADSTOW
WADEBRIDGE
WADEBRIDGE
WENFORD BRIDGE
DUNMERE HALT
GROGLEY HALT
NANSTALLON HALT
BOSCARNE JUNCTION
BODMIN NORTH
BODMIN GENERAL
BODMIN
Bodmin & Wenford Railway
BODMIN PARKWAY

BARNSTAPLE →→→ MEETH

Ilfracombe
Barnstaple
Meeth
Okehampton

Tarka Trail

ORIGINAL LINE
24¾ miles

LENGTH OPEN TO WALKERS & CYCLISTS
24¾ miles

ORIGINAL ROUTE OPERATOR
London & South Western Railway/North Devon & Cornwall Junction Light Railway

LINE OPEN TO PASSENGERS
Barnstaple to Bideford: 1855–1965;
Bideford to Torrington: 1872–1965;
Torrington to Meeth 1925–1965

OS LANDRANGER
180/191

NATIONAL CYCLE NETWORK
Route 27

REFRESHMENT POINTS
Barnstaple, Fremington Quay, Instow, Bideford, Torrington

CAR PARKING
Barnstaple, Fremington Quay, Instow, Bideford, Torrington

NATIONAL RAIL NETWORK STATION
Barnstaple

The first railway to be built in North Devon was a freight-only horse-drawn tramway which opened between Barnstaple and busy Fremington Quay in 1848. It was taken over by the North Devon Railway in 1851; steam locomotives and a passenger service were introduced and the line extended to Bideford in 1855. Originally built to the broad gauge of 7 ft 0 ¼ in, the line was absorbed by the London & South Western Railway (LSWR) in 1865, extended to Torrington in 1872 and then converted to standard gauge in 1876. Also served by trains from Exeter, the original station at Barnstaple became a busy junction station following the opening of the Ilfracombe branch line in 1875 and the extension of the GWR's line from Taunton in 1885.

South from Torrington, a 3 ft-gauge tramway had opened to serve clay works at Peter's Marland in 1880, and its 5½-mile route was incorporated into the standard-gauge 20½-mile North Devon & Cornwall Junction Light Railway which opened between Torrington and Halwill Junction in 1925. This Government-backed line was engineered by Colonel Holman F. Stephens and was one of the last railways to be built in Britain during the 20th century. Clay from Peter's Marland, milk from a large creamery at Torrington and 'imported' coal from South Wales via Fremington Quay kept the route busy, but the 'Beeching Report' of 1963 soon put an end to passenger traffic. Both the Barnstaple to Torrington and Torrington to Halwill Junction lines lost their passenger services in 1965 although milk traffic continued until 1978 and clay traffic until 1982. Today only the 'Tarka Line' from Exeter to Barnstaple remains open for passenger traffic.

Since closure, the former railway route between Barnstaple station and Meeth has been reopened as a footpath and cycleway by Devon County Council. Forming part of the 180-mile Tarka Trail, the section from Barnstaple to Bideford opened in 1991 and was then extended in stages via Torrington to Meeth by 1997.

Starting at Barnstaple station where there is a café and cycle hire shop, the Trail follows the south shore of the Taw Estuary to Fremington Quay where the station is also home to a café and cycle hire shop. After crossing one of the many original railway bridges along this route and following in the footsteps of the BBC 2's 'Great Train Race' organized by James May in 2011, the Trail reaches Instow station where the restored signal box, level crossing gates and platforms are but a short distance from the beach. From here, the level route follows the east shore of the Torridge Estuary to the restored Bideford station and signal box where a converted railway carriage acts as a café.

Crossing several old railway bridges, the Trail continues southwards along the wooded Torridge Valley from Bideford to Torrington station, which is now home to a public house and where the goods shed is a cycle hire shop. The final delightful section southwards from Torrington still features many of the original basic halts opened in 1925, including those at Watergate and Meeth, the current end of the rail trail.

FREMINGTON

BARNSTAPLE TOWN

BARNSTAPLE JUNCTION

INSTOW

BIDEFORD

TORRINGTON

WATERGATE HALT

YARDE HALT

DUNSBEAR HALT

PETROCKSTOW

MEETH HALT

13

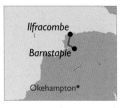

BARNSTAPLE ⇢→ ILFRACOMBE

Tarka Trail

ORIGINAL LINE
15 miles

LENGTH OPEN TO WALKERS & CYCLISTS
8½ miles

ORIGINAL ROUTE OPERATOR
London & South Western Railway

LINE OPEN TO PASSENGERS
1874–1970

OS LANDRANGER
180

NATIONAL CYCLE NETWORK
Route 31

REFRESHMENT POINTS
Barnstaple, Braunton, Ilfracombe

CAR PARKING
Barnstaple, Braunton, Willingcott Cross, Lee Bridge, Ilfracombe

NATIONAL RAIL NETWORK STATION
Barnstaple

W hile the North Devon market town of Barnstaple was first served by rail from the outside world in 1854, it took another 20 years before the small harbour town of Ilfracombe to the north became rail connected. Sponsored by the London & South Western Railway (LSWR), the Barnstaple & Ilfracombe Railway received Parliamentary approval in 1870 for a line to connect the two towns. Constructing the line was beset with problems and obstacles including a shortage of railway navvies, building a bridge over the River Taw at Barnstaple, surmounting steep gradients north of Braunton and tunnelling south of Ilfracombe.

The single-track railway eventually opened on 20 July 1874 and was an immediate success, but its lightweight rails and steep gradients – 1-in-36 south of Ilfracombe and 1-in-40 north of Braunton – led to the line being doubled and relaid to main line standards by 1891. The coming of the railway brought a massive increase in holidaymakers to Ilfracombe during the summer months with most trains being banked or double-headed between Braunton and Ilfracombe. The town was not only served by through coaches from London Waterloo on the 'Atlantic Coast Express' between 1927 and 1964 and the 'Devon Belle' Pullman train between 1947 and 1954, but also by through trains during the summer months from the Midlands and the North via the GWR line from Taunton to Barnstaple.

This rosy picture for the Ilfracombe line all but came to an end in the early 1960s – falling passenger numbers brought about by increased competition from car ownership and cheap foreign holidays all conspired to its eventual demise. Listed for closure in the 'Beeching Report', the line struggled on until 5 October 1970 when it closed for good. A preservation scheme came to nothing and the track was lifted in 1975.

Two distinct sections of the Ilfracombe line have in more recent years each been reopened by Devon County Council as a footpath and cycleway. Forming part of the 180-mile Tarka Trail, the southern section starts at the restored former Barnstaple Town station adjacent to Barnstaple Quay. This 5¼-mile stretch first hugs the north shore of the Taw Estuary before heading inland past Wrafton station (now a private residence) to Braunton. Here both the station building and goods shed have survived. Northwards from Braunton the Tarka Trail follows lanes to Willingcott Cross before rejoining the trackbed of the railway at Mortehoe & Woolacombe station, the summit of the line and now converted to private residences.

The very pleasant 3¼-mile northern section first passes a small car park at Lee Bridge before making the descent down to Ilfracombe, past the two Slade Reservoirs and through the short single-bore Slade Tunnel – the other bore has been bricked up. En route there are reminders of the railway in the form of a Southern Railway concrete signal post, concrete fence posts and concrete permanent way shelters. The route ends at the once extensive site of Ilfracombe station, set high above the harbour town, which is now an industrial estate.

OPPOSITE TOP:
An early view of the railway looking down the Slade Valley towards Ilfracombe

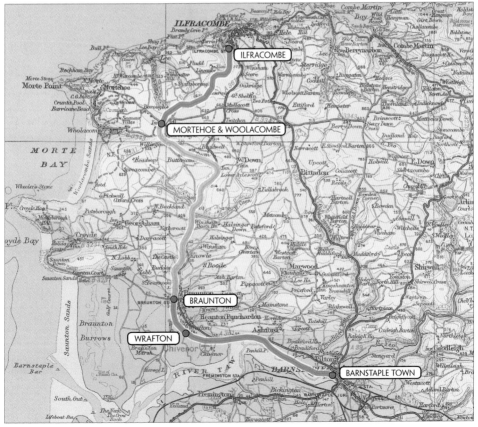

PLYMOUTH »→ TAVISTOCK

Tavistock
Yelverton
Plymouth

Drake's Trail

ORIGINAL LINE
13 miles

**LENGTH OPEN TO
WALKERS & CYCLISTS**
10 miles

ORIGINAL ROUTE OPERATOR
South Devon &
Tavistock Railway

LINE OPEN TO PASSENGERS
1859–1962

OS LANDRANGER
191

NATIONAL CYCLE NETWORK
Route 27

REFRESHMENT POINTS
Clearbrook, Yelverton,
Horrabridge, Tavistock

CAR PARKING
Marsh Mills, Plym Bridge,
Clearbrook, Tavistock

HERITAGE RAILWAY
Plym Valley Railway

The lower Plym Valley had been a centre of industrial activity for many decades before the opening of this railway. Locally mined slate and china clay from Dartmoor had been transported down river to Plymouth via the Cann Quarry Canal, opened in 1829, and a horse-drawn tramway and rope-worked incline, opened in 1830.

Supported by the South Devon Railway (SDR), the 13-mile South Devon & Tavistock Railway (SD&TR) between Tavistock Junction, east of Plymouth, and the historic market town of Tavistock was built to Brunel's broad gauge of 7 ft 0¼ in and opened in 1859. Engineered by Brunel, the single-track railway followed four meandering river valleys – Plym, Meavy, Walkham and Tavy – and required the building of three tunnels and six timber viaducts. A 19-mile broad-gauge extension was opened between Tavistock and Launceston in 1865.

The SD&TR was soon absorbed by the SDR which in turn was absorbed by the Great Western Railway in 1876. In the same year the Tavistock and Launceston lines (southwards from Lydford) were relaid as mixed gauge so that London & South Western Railway standard-gauge trains could reach Plymouth. This arrangement ended in 1890 when the LSWR started using its new route via the Tamar Valley. The GWR converted its Tavistock and Launceston lines to standard gauge in 1892, and Brunel's timber trestle bridges had been rebuilt as masonry or steel structures by the early 20th century.

Although popular with day-trippers from Plymouth, the line suffered from the duplication of routes between Launceston, Tavistock and Plymouth and was listed for closure in the 1963 'Beeching Report'. However, British Railways pre-empted this by closing the line during a blizzard on 31 December 1962. All that remained was a short section from Tavistock Junction to Marsh Mills which continued to be used for china clay traffic until 2008.

Since closure, much of this picturesque route has been reopened by Devon County Council as a footpath and cycleway, today forming an integral part of the Drake's Trail between Plymouth and Tavistock. At its southern end, the Trail shares its route with the Plym Valley Railway which operates tourist trains between Marsh Mills and Plym Bridge. North of this beauty spot, the Trail parallels the old Cann Quarry Canal and heads through the National Trust-owned Cann Woods to cross Cann Viaduct. Continuing northwards through Great Shaugh Woods and across the lofty Bickleigh Viaduct, the Trail reaches Shaugh Bridge Platform with its wide road overbridge before entering the unlit and curving Shaugh Tunnel.

North of the tunnel, Drake's Trail temporarily leaves the old railway route at Clearbrook, close to the popular Skylark Inn, before following country roads and tracks to Yelverton and on to Horrabridge. The trackbed is rejoined here before crossing the Walkham Valley on the recently built Gem Bridge – this replaced the 1910-built steel lattice truss railway viaduct which was demolished in 1965. The dark and dripping confines of Grenofen Tunnel follow before the Trail continues on through Whitchurch to end in Tavistock.

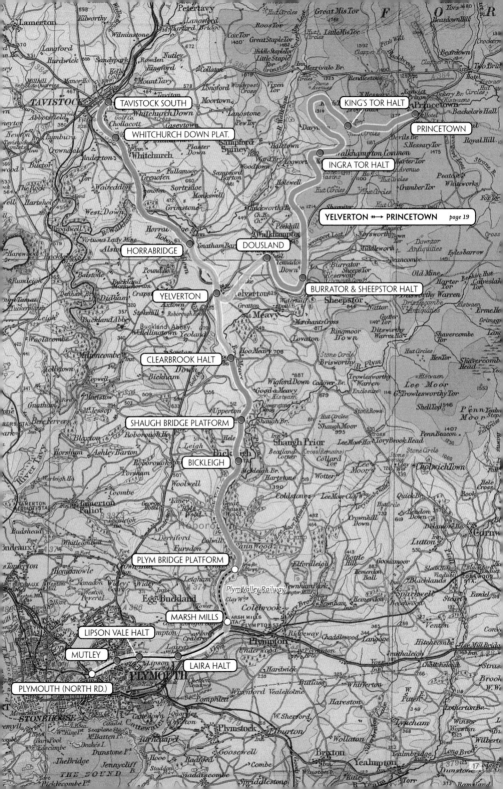

TAVISTOCK SOUTH

WHITCHURCH DOWN PLAT.

KING'S TOR HALT

PRINCETOWN

INGRA TOR HALT

YELVERTON »→ PRINCETOWN   page 19

HORRABRIDGE

DOUSLAND

BURRATOR & SHEEPSTOR HALT

YELVERTON

CLEARBROOK HALT

SHAUGH BRIDGE PLATFORM

BICKLEIGH

PLYM BRIDGE PLATFORM

MARSH MILLS

LIPSON VALE HALT

MUTLEY

LAIRA HALT

PLYMOUTH (NORTH RD.)

17

Princetown
Yelverton
Plymouth

Dousland to Princetown Railway Track

ORIGINAL LINE
10½ miles

LENGTH OPEN TO WALKERS & CYCLISTS
9 miles

ORIGINAL ROUTE OPERATOR
Great Western Railway

LINE OPEN TO PASSENGERS
1883–1956

OS LANDRANGER
191, 201, 202

REFRESHMENT POINTS
Princetown

CAR PARKING
Burrator Reservoir, Princetown

For route map see page 17

LEFT TOP:
PLYMOUTH TO TAVISTOCK
This Staffordshire blue-brick viaduct north of Plym Bridge replaced Brunel's timber viaduct in 1905 and now carries Drake's Trail over the River Plym.

LEFT LOWER:
A group of walkers make their way along the Princetown branch trackbed on the Dartmoor slopes below the 643-ft-high transmitting station on North Hessary Tor.

YELVERTON
⇛
PRINCETOWN

The first railway to reach remote Princetown on Dartmoor was a horse-drawn tramway – the 4-ft 6 in-gauge Plymouth & Dartmoor Railway opened in 1826 to transport granite from a quarry at King's Tor down to Sutton Pool in Plymouth. In 1865, the South Devon Railway opened its broad-gauge line between Tavistock Junction, east of Plymouth, and Tavistock, serving en route the village of Yelverton. It was from here that the Great Western Railway built a 10-mile branch line to Princetown with much of the route following the course of the closed tramway around the contour lines of Dartmoor. Climbing to a height of 1,300 ft above sea level, the standard-gauge line opened in 1883. Much of the traffic generated consisted mainly of granite from various quarries along its route, and it also served Dartmoor Prison, which had opened in Princetown during the Napoleonic War of the early 19th century, and the one intermediate station at Dousland.

Basic wooden halts were later opened on the line. Burrator & Sheepstor opened in 1924 to serve a new reservoir being built; King's Tor and Ingra Tor were opened in 1924 and 1936 respectively to serve quarries. Passenger traffic was always light – most trains consisted of just one coach – although walkers took advantage of the remote and otherwise inaccessible halts during the summer months. Inevitably this delightful but loss-making line had no future under British Railways' ownership, and closure was announced in 1955. The last train, packed with curious passengers, ran from England's highest station on 3 March 1956 and a year later the track was lifted.

Known today as the Dousland to Princetown Railway Track, much of the scenic route of this long-lost railway can be explored either on foot or by mountain bike. Offering wide-ranging views from the slopes of Dartmoor on a clear day, it is seen at its best during the summer months – at other times of the year the mist-shrouded moor can be a daunting place. Meandering around the moorland contours, the trackbed can be clearly followed between Princetown, the site of Burrator & Sheepstor Halt where there is a car park close to Burrator Reservoir (between these two points there is no road access) and Dousland. The remains of the junction station at Yelverton now lie on private property, but the tunnel immediately to the north is still passable with care. At Dousland the station building is now a holiday let, but while the rudimentary wooden halts have long -since disappeared there are still a few poignant reminders of the railway and the quarrying industry along the clearly defined trackbed – a few granite bridges built to last forever and the old quarry workings around Ingra Tor and King's Tor are dwarfed by the high moorland landscape. At Princetown the station has long disappeared, but there are still reminders of the railway in the names of Station Road and the Railway Inn.

OKEHAMPTON »→ LYDFORD

The London & South Western Railway's route into Devon and towards its final goal of Plymouth took an important step in 1866 when the company-backed Devon & Cornwall Railway opened from Coleford Junction, on the Exeter to Barnstaple line, to the market town of Okehampton. The line was extended westward across the 120 ft-high wrought- and cast-iron Meldon Viaduct to a summit of 950 ft above sea level and around the northern edge of Dartmoor to Lydford in 1874. Standard-gauge LSWR trains for Plymouth initially used mixed-gauge track along the GWR's broad-gauge route from Lydford via Tavistock until 1890. In that year a new railway was completed between Lydford and Devonport that allowed the LSWR to run its trains independently to Plymouth. This duplication of routes led to Lydford, Tavistock and Launceston all having two stations each serving competing routes to Plymouth.

Plymouth was then not only served by GWR trains from Paddington, but also LSWR trains from Waterloo – both companies competing with each other for the lucrative trans-Atlantic Ocean Liner traffic between the two cities. For a short period after the Second World War, the former LSWR route was also used by a portion of the 'Devon Belle' Pullman train which was introduced in 1947 but withdrawn only 3 years later. Through services from Waterloo ended in September 1964 when the circuitous route around Dartmoor became part of the Western Region of British Railways. By then the writing was on the wall as the section from Okehampton to Plymouth had been listed for closure in the 'Beeching Report'. The end came on 6 May 1968 when the line closed completely between Okehampton and Bere Alston – the latter station remains open today, served by the Plymouth to Gunnislake service. Despite not originally being listed for closure, Okehampton lost its passenger service from Exeter in 1972 although the line remained intact for granite ballast traffic from Meldon Quarry until 2011.

The Dartmoor Railway operates heritage tourist diesel trains between Sampford Courtenay and Meldon via Okehampton, while First Great Western operates a summer Sunday service between Exeter and Okehampton. Walkers and cyclists can now follow much of the railway route from the beautifully restored station at Okehampton (where a Youth Hostel is housed in the goods shed) to Lydford along what is known as the Granite Way. The route parallels the Dartmoor Railway to Meldon, then crosses the magnificent Meldon Viaduct to skirt the northern slopes of Dartmoor. Highlights beyond here include Lake Viaduct which gives far-reaching views from the Dartmoor slopes into Cornwall – the nearby thatched Bearslake Inn offers refreshments for thirsty walkers and cyclists.

Continuing from Lake Viaduct along the Granite Way, a picnic site at Southerly Halt marks a temporary end to proceedings. From here, the busy A386 road has to be crossed with care before following country lanes to Bridestowe. Here the railway route is rejoined at Bridestowe station, now a private residence, for the final leg to Lydford and its welcoming Castle Inn.

Granite Way

ORIGINAL LINE
9¾ miles

LENGTH OPEN TO WALKERS & CYCLISTS
7¾ miles

ORIGINAL ROUTE OPERATOR
London & South Western Railway

LINE OPEN TO PASSENGERS
1874–1968

OS LANDRANGER
201

NATIONAL CYCLE NETWORK
Route 27

REFRESHMENT POINTS
Okehampton, Sourton Down, Lydford

CAR PARKING
Okehampton, Lydford

HERITAGE RAILWAY
Dartmoor Railway

NATIONAL RAIL NETWORK STATION
(summer Sundays)
Okehampton

OPPOSITE LOWER:
Despite closure in 1968 the viaduct at Meldon still stands today while in the foreground is Meldon Reservoir.

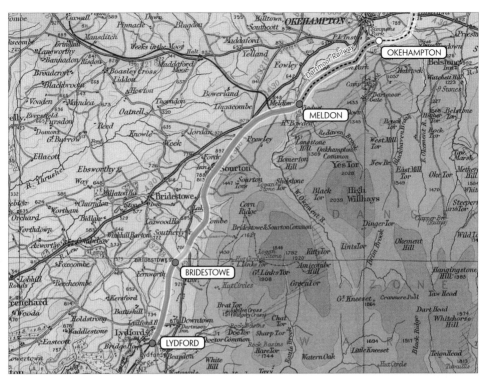

WATCHET
⇥→
BRENDON HILLS

West Somerset Mineral Railway

ORIGINAL LINE
13½ miles

LENGTH OPEN TO WALKERS & CYCLISTS
6¼ miles

ORIGINAL ROUTE OPERATOR
West Somerset
Mineral Railway

LINE OPEN TO PASSENGERS
1865–1898

OS LANDRANGER
181

REFRESHMENT POINTS
Watchet, Washford,
Ralegh's Cross

CAR PARKING
Watchet, Brendon Hill,
Langham Hill

HERITAGE RAILWAY
West Somerset Railway

Iron ore had been mined on the Brendon Hills in West Somerset for centuries but only on a small scale. However, in 1853, the owners of the Ebbw Vale Ironworks in South Wales formed the Brendon Hills Iron Ore Company, and industrial activity took a major leap forward with new mines being opened at several locations. Initially the iron ore was transported by horse and cart to Watchet Harbour for transhipment across the Bristol Channel but this was a slow business, and a railway seemed the only answer. Construction of the West Somerset Mineral Railway started in 1856, but it took until 1864 before the 13½-mile single-track line had been completed. It consisted of two level sections – the lower linking Watchet Harbour with Comberow and the upper serving mines at Ralegh's Cross, Eisen Hill, Lothbrook and Gupworthy – linked by the ¾-mile 1-in-4 Brendon Hill Incline. At the top of the incline was a winding house where a stationary steam engine hauled empty wagons up or lowered loaded wagons down.

Passenger services were introduced in 1865, but travelling up or down the incline in an open wagon fitted with benches was a risky business. Iron ore production peaked in 1875, but from then on there was a rapid decline in demand caused by a major recession and cheap imports. With falling traffic, the railway closed in 1898, but this was not quite the end as it was reopened by the Somerset Mineral Syndicate in 1907 – 3 years later the company had gone bankrupt and the line closed again. Despite the lower section being used between 1912 and 1914 to demonstrate automatic train control, the railway was finally abandoned in 1919 and sold off lock, stock and barrel at an auction in 1924.

Today, thanks to the efforts of the Exmoor National Park Authority, three distinct sections of this fascinating railway can be explored on foot. From Watchet Harbour, where some original track has been revealed on the harbour wall, a footpath parallels the heritage West Somerset Railway to Washford, en route passing the station building (now flats) and well-preserved goods shed in Watchet. Between Washford and Roadwater the trackbed lies on private property as it passes the ruins of Cleeve Abbey. The well-preserved station and platform at Roadwater station is now a private house and the girders of the river bridge and one level crossing gate still survive intact. From here the trackbed has been rebuilt as a road as far as Comberow. A steep path leads up the Brendon Incline to the roofless engine house from where there are fine views across the Bristol Channel to South Wales. The final short section of the railway which can be followed on foot can be reached along a road, ½-mile west of Brendon Hill. A permissive footpath from Naked Boy's Bridge follows the top of a beech-lined railway cutting for ½-mile to the Burrow Hill Farm Mine where the roofless engine house was conserved by the Exmoor Park National Authority in 1990.

OPPOSITE TOP:
WSMR Neilson 0-4-0
locomotive at the top of the
incline at Brendon Hill, 1889.

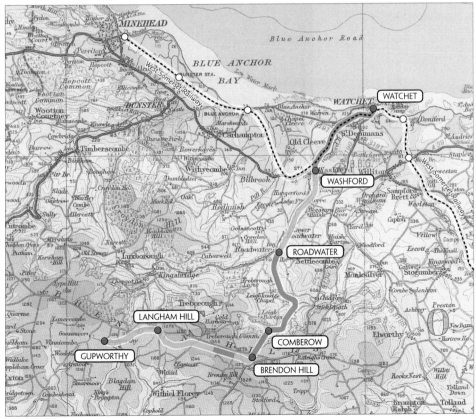

TAUNTON »→ CHARD

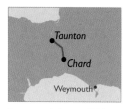

Stop Line Way

ORIGINAL LINE
12¾ miles

**LENGTH OPEN TO
WALKERS & CYCLISTS**
4 miles

ORIGINAL ROUTE OPERATOR
Bristol & Exeter Railway

LINE OPEN TO PASSENGERS
1866–1962

OS LANDRANGER
193

NATIONAL CYCLE NETWORK
Route 33

REFRESHMENT POINTS
Ilminster, Donyatt, Chard

CAR PARKING
Ilminster, Chard

The Somerset town of Chard got a pretty raw deal in 1860 when the London & South Western Railway's (LSWR) new main line between Salisbury and Exeter bypassed the town 3 miles to the south. The town had once been served by the now-bankrupt Chard Canal, but a plan to build a railway along its route from Taunton had failed to materialize. Chard's first railway connection came in 1863, when a short branch line was opened between Chard Junction, on the LSWR main line, and Chard Town station.

Fearing an LSWR incursion northwards into its territory, the Bristol & Exeter Railway acted fast and bought the moribund Chard Canal with the sole purpose of closing it so that a railway could finally be built along its route. The B&ER's single-track broad-gauge line finally opened from Creech Junction, east of Taunton, via Hatch and Ilminster to Chard Central station in 1866. The latter joint station was connected to the LSWR branch, but although it was served by both railways, the two rival companies led very separate existences well into the 20th century.

In 1871, a station was opened at Thornfalcon and 5 years later the B&ER was amalgamated with the Great Western Railway. This rural line led a fairly quiet life – small halts were provided at Ilton and Donyatt in 1928 – until the Second World War when it became part of the 'Taunton Stop Line', a 50-mile anti-tank obstacle built by the Army in 1940 to contain any German invasion of southwest England. Sadly, the post-war years saw a rapid decline in traffic on the line, and it closed to passengers, along with the connection from Chard Junction, on 10 September 1962. Goods services continued between Taunton and Chard until 1964 and between Chard Junction and Chard until 1966.

Following closure, the trackbed between Ilminster and Chard was purchased by Somerset County Council and in 2000 was reopened as a footpath and cycleway known as The Stop Line Way. Well-signposted along its 4-mile route, the trail starts in Ilminster town close to the Chard Canal and heads west to join the trackbed of the railway at Donyatt Cutting where it heads south under a large road bridge before reaching Donyatt Halt. Superbly restored with timber platform, waiting shelter, nameboard, distant signal and a statue to child evacuees who arrived here from London during the Blitz, this little station has reminders of the wartime invasion scare in the shape of a large number of anti-tank concrete blocks.

Beyond Donyatt Halt, the trail heads south to Knowle St Giles where there is a splendid road overbridge and an adjacent concrete gun emplacement that once housed an anti-tank gun. The remains of the Chard Canal are never far away, and the trail skirts the Chard Reservoir – built in 1842 to feed the canal – on the approach to the town. The trail ends at the site of Chard Central station where the original 1866 stone-and-brick Grade II-listed building and its covered roof have been expertly converted into a warehouse shop.

OPPOSITE TOP:
The restored platform and waiting shelter at Donyat Halt features a statue remembering child evacuees who arrived from London during the Blitz.

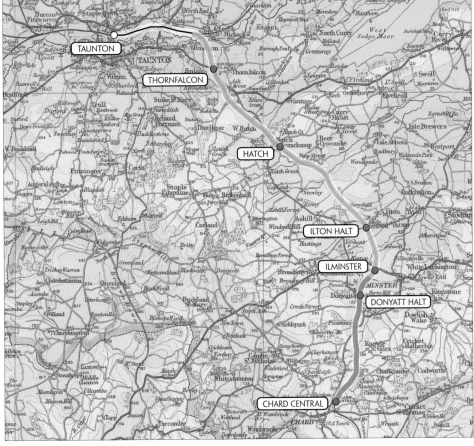

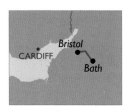

BRISTOL ⟫→ BATH

Bristol & Bath Railway Path

ORIGINAL LINE
15 miles

LENGTH OPEN TO WALKERS & CYCLISTS
13 miles

ORIGINAL ROUTE OPERATOR
Midland Railway

LINE OPEN TO PASSENGERS
1869–1966

OS LANDRANGER
172

NATIONAL CYCLE NETWORK
Route 4

REFRESHMENT POINTS
Bath, Saltford, Bitton, Warmley, Bristol

CAR PARKING
Bath, Bitton, Bristol

NATIONAL RAIL NETWORK STATIONS
Bath, Bristol

HERITAGE RAILWAY
Avon Valley Railway

OPPOSITE TOP:
Warmley Station before it closed in 1966.

The Midland Railway (MR) reached the city of Bath rather late in the day despite it taking over the nearby Bristol & Birmingham Railway in 1845. With intermediate stations at Warmley, Oldland Common, Bitton, Kelston (for Bath Racecourse) and Weston, the 10-mile line from Mangotsfield finally opened to a temporary terminus in Bath in 1869. A permanent two-platform terminus with overall roof and a grand frontage was opened in Bath in 1870 and was known as Bath Midland station until 1951 when it was renamed Bath Green Park.

The opening of the Somerset & Dorset Railway's Bath Extension from Evercreech Junction to Bath Green Park station in 1874 transformed the MR's branch line from Mangotsfield, which soon saw through trains running between the North of England and the Midlands and Bournemouth via a triangular junction at Mangotsfield. Of these the most famous was the 'Pines Express' which was introduced in 1927 and continued to use this route until 1962. The MR branch from Mangotsfield was upgraded to main line standards in the 1930s, and traffic over the route was particularly heavy during the Second World War. In 1958 the S&D route north of Templecombe came under Western Region control, and four years later all through trains over the Mangotsfield to Bath Green Park line and thence over the S&D were withdrawn leaving just a local stopping service. Listed for closure in the 1963 'Beeching Report', the end for passenger services came on 7 March 1966. The former MR line was then singled and used by coal trains to Bath gas works until 1971. In the meantime, the former MR main line between Bristol Temple Meads and Mangotsfield had closed in 1969 with trains being diverted via Filton and Yate.

Since closure, the former MR route between Bristol and Bath via Mangotsfield has seen a renaissance as a traffic-free footpath and cycleway. By the 1990s, almost the entire route was reopened by the cycling charity Sustrans as the first green traffic-free route for cyclists in Britain. Since then, the National Cycle Network has grown to over 10,000 miles across Britain, much of it along disused railway routes. Much of the railway infrastructure remains in place including Staple Hill Tunnel, several bridges over the River Avon, the old platforms at Staple Hill, Mangotsfield and Warmley stations (all featuring modern sculpture) and the 3-mile Avon Valley Railway which shares the tarmacked route between Oldland Common and Avon Riverside via its headquarters at the restored station at Bitton. A proposal to convert part of the path in the Bristol area into a concrete guided busway has met with much opposition from cycle users. Last but not least is the beautifully restored terminus at Bath Green Park – with its grand frontage and graceful curving overall glass roof, it now provides cover for car parking for the adjacent Sainsbury's store as well as for stall holders and events. Various shops have also taken up residence in the station building. It is well worth visiting Bath just to see this station!

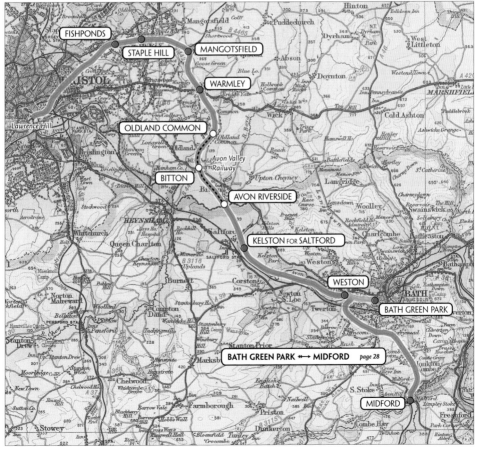

FISHPONDS
STAPLE HILL
MANGOTSFIELD
WARMLEY
OLDLAND COMMON
Avon Valley Railway
BITTON
AVON RIVERSIDE
KELSTON FOR SALTFORD
WESTON
BATH GREEN PARK

BATH GREEN PARK ⟷ MIDFORD   page 28

MIDFORD

BATH GREEN PARK ⇥ MIDFORD

CARDIFF Bristol
Bath
Midford

Two Tunnels Greenway

ORIGINAL LINE
4¼ miles

LENGTH OPEN TO WALKERS & CYCLISTS
2½ miles

ORIGINAL ROUTE OPERATOR
Somerset & Dorset Railway

LINE OPEN TO PASSENGERS
1874–1966

OS LANDRANGER
172

NATIONAL CYCLE NETWORK
Route 244/24

REFRESHMENT POINTS
Bath, Midford

CAR PARKING
Bath

NATIONAL RAIL NETWORK STATIONS
Bath, Oldfield Park

For route map see page 27

Providing an important link between the Midlands and Bournemouth, the Somerset & Dorset Railway's (S&DR) 26½-mile single-track 'Bath Extension' over the Mendip Hills between Evercreech Junction and Bath Green Park opened in 1874. The line was costly to build and featured seven large viaducts and five tunnels, including the single-bore Devonshire and Combe Down tunnels south of Bath. At Bath the line met the Midland Railway's branch from Mangotsfield (see pages 26–27), which had opened in 1869, thus providing a link via Gloucester to the Midlands and the North of England. The construction of the line had virtually bankrupted the S&DR, but it was saved by the Midland Railway and the London & South Western Railway who jointly leased the line for 999 years in 1876, and so the Somerset & Dorset Joint Railway (S&DJR) was born.

The new mainline from Bath to Broadstone saw a steady increase of through passenger and freight traffic. Soon the single-line sections could not cope with the increased traffic, and the line was eventually doubled between Midford and Templecombe and between Blandford and Corfe Mullen Junction. The section between Bath and Midford via the two single-bore tunnels remained single track, and working heavy freight and passenger trains up this bottleneck from Bath required double-heading or a banking engine at the rear. Heavy passenger traffic on Summer Saturdays was always a logistical nightmare for the railway's operators, but this ended, along with the famous 'Pines Express', in 1962 when all through traffic was withdrawn. Under the control of British Railways Western Region, the S&DJR was deliberately rundown so that closure became inevitable. Despite some reprieves, this much-loved railway finally closed completely on 7 March 1966.

Since closure 50 years ago, many parts of the S&DJR have come back to life: a preservation group at Shillingstone have transformed the station which is now open to the public; the delightful Gartell Light Railway runs along the trackbed south of Templecombe; the 27-arch curved Charlton Viaduct now forms the backdrop of the Kilver Court Gardens in Shepton Mallet; the preserved Midsomer Norton station is owned by the Somerset & Dorset Railway Heritage Trust; the Colliers Way footpath and cycleway uses part of the trackbed between Midford, Wellow and Radstock.

Last but not least is the Two Tunnels Greenway which opened as a footpath and cycleway between Bath and Midford in 2013. Access to the railway path in Bath is a short distance to the west of Oldfield Park station, and from there the 1-in-50 climb out of Bath begins to the 447-yd Devonshire Tunnel which is soon followed by the 1,829-yd Combe Down Tunnel, the longest walking and cycling tunnel in Britain, if not Europe, which would have taxed drivers of steam locomotives to the limit in its choking confines. Emerging into daylight, the railway path continues along Lyncombe Vale and over Tucking Mill Viaduct to reach Midford. Here it joins the Colliers Way which continues over Midford Viaduct to Wellow, Radstock and Frome (see pages 31–33).

YATTON ⤏ WITHAM

Strawberry Line Trail

ORIGINAL LINE
31¾ miles

LENGTH OPEN TO WALKERS & CYCLISTS
12 miles

ORIGINAL ROUTE OPERATOR
Bristol & Exeter Railway

LINE OPEN TO PASSENGERS
1870–1963

OS LANDRANGER
200

NATIONAL CYCLE NETWORK
Route 26

REFRESHMENT POINTS
Yatton, Winscombe, Axbridge, Cheddar

CAR PARKING
Yatton, Winscombe, Axbridge, Cheddar

HERITAGE RAILWAY
East Somerset Railway

NATIONAL RAIL NETWORK STATION
Yatton

For route map see page 30

Railways first came to the small Somerset city of Wells in 1859 when the Somerset Central Railway (later to become the Somerset & Dorset Railway) opened its standard-gauge branch line from Glastonbury to Priory Road station. The second railway to reach Wells was the broad-gauge East Somerset Railway (ESR) which opened from Witham in 1862. The third railway to arrive was the broad-gauge Cheddar Valley & Yatton Railway which was completed by the Bristol & Exeter Railway (B&ER) between Yatton and Tucker Street station in 1870. The ESR was purchased by the Great Western Railway GWR) in 1874, and the B&ER was absorbed by the GWR in 1876.

Although Wells possessed three railway stations, they were all unconnected. Only when the East Somerset and Cheddar Valley lines were converted to standard gauge by 1875 was it possible to run through trains between Yatton and Witham via a short section of the S&DR's line at Priory Road station. In Wells, the East Somerset station was then closed and Tucker Street became the main GWR station. Located between these two was the S&DR station at Priory Road, but GWR services inconveniently did not stop here until 1934.

Serving Cheddar and Wookey Hole, the Cheddar Valley line became popular with day-trippers from Bristol. Local milk and seasonal strawberries were also important sources of revenue. Sadly, with increased competition from road transport, all this traffic declined after the Second World War. The S&DR's line from Glastonbury to Wells closed in 1951, and the Yatton to Witham line lost its passenger service on 9 September 1963. Freight continued between Yatton and Cranmore for another year, but the Witham to Cranmore section remained open for bitumen traffic until 1985. Most of that section is still used by stone trains from nearby Merehead Quarry while the short section from Cranmore to Mendip Vale, east of Shepton Mallet, was reopened by David Shepherd heritage East Somerset Railway in 1973.

Since closure, around 12 miles of the Cheddar Valley line has been reopened as a mainly traffic-free footpath and cycleway known, appropriately, as the Strawberry Line Trail. While the longest section currently runs between Yatton station and Cheddar, there are shorter sections open between Draycott and Rodney Stoke and between Haybridge, Wells and Dulcote. Future proposals include reopening the missing links so that the Trail extends from Yatton to Shepton Mallet and westwards from Yatton to Clevedon along the trackbed of a 3½-mile branch line that closed in 1966.

Highlights between Yatton and Cheddar include the restored Sandford & Banwell station, now a retirement complex that is open to the public on summer weekends, a picnic site at the restored Winscombe station platform and Shute Shelve Tunnel. At Axbridge, where the station buildings have survived albeit now alongside a busy bypass, the Trail diverts eastwards through the pretty village before regaining the trackbed near Axbridge Reservoir. This section of the Trail ends close to the well-preserved Cheddar station, which is now used by the stonemasons of Wells Cathedral.

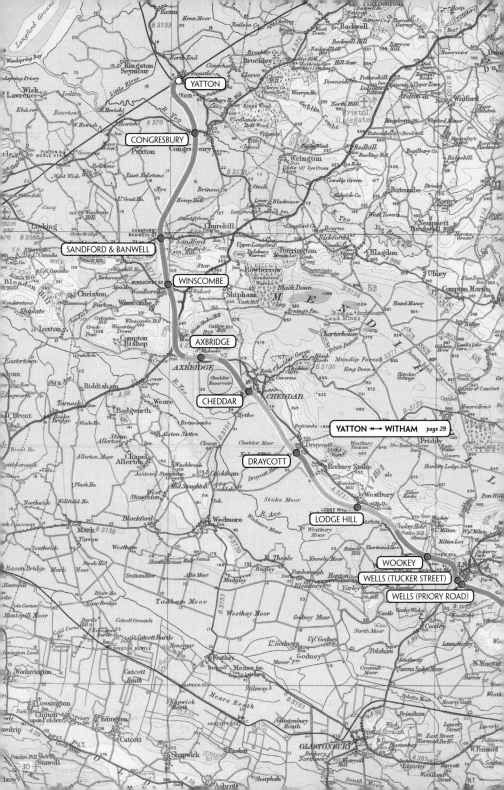

YATTON

CONGRESBURY

SANDFORD & BANWELL

WINSCOMBE

AXBRIDGE

CHEDDAR

YATTON ⟩⟩⟩ WITHAM   page 29

DRAYCOTT

LODGE HILL

WOOKEY

WELLS (TUCKER STREET)

WELLS (PRIORY ROAD)

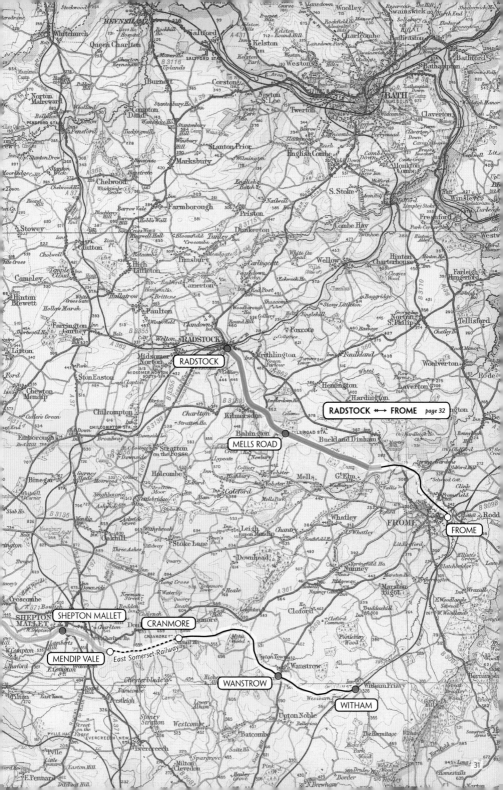

RADSTOCK

RADSTOCK ➤➤ FROME *page 32*

MELLS ROAD

FROME

SHEPTON MALLET

CRANMORE

MENDIP VALE   East Somerset Railway

WANSTROW

WITHAM

31

RADSTOCK ⤚→ FROME

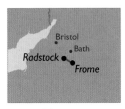

Bristol
Bath
Radstock
Frome

Colliers Way

ORIGINAL LINE
8¼ miles

**LENGTH OPEN TO
WALKERS & CYCLISTS**
5½ miles

ORIGINAL ROUTE OPERATOR
Great Western Railway

LINE OPEN TO PASSENGERS
1854–1959

OS LANDRANGER
183

NATIONAL CYCLE NETWORK
Route 24

REFRESHMENT POINTS
Frome, Kilmersdon, Radstock

CAR PARKING
Frome, Radstock

**NATIONAL RAIL
NETWORK STATION**
Frome

For route map see page 31

OPPOSITE:
*A broad gauge overbridge on
the Colliers Way at Mells. Much
of the track is still intact but
has long disappeared into the
undergrowth.*

Built to serve the North Somerset coalfields, the first section of what became the Great Western Railway's (GWR) 24¼-mile single-track railway across the Mendip Hills between Bristol and Frome was an 8-mile broad-gauge colliery line which opened between Frome and Radstock on 14 November 1854.

The northern section of the steeply graded route between Bristol and Radstock was opened by the Bristol & North Somerset Railway (B&NSR) on 3 September 1873. The B&NSR was worked from the outset by the GWR and was absorbed by that company in 1884. At Radstock there was a break of gauge until June 1874 when the colliery line to Frome was converted to standard gauge, allowing for the first time a direct GWR passenger service between Bristol and Frome. Following a drastic cut in services in 1958, this loss-making line closed to passengers on 31 October 1959.

With the closure of many North Somerset collieries, a decreasing number of coal trains continued to run between Radstock and Bristol until an embankment collapsed at Pensford in 1968. After that date, coal traffic travelled via Frome following the reopening of the section between Radstock and Mells Road which had been closed completely in 1966. Following the closure of the Somerset & Dorset Joint Railway in 1966, a short spur was opened between the two lines at Radstock to serve Writhlington Colliery. This traffic lasted until the end of 1968, and all coal traffic ceased in November 1973 following the closure of the last North Somerset pit at Kilmersdon.

Despite the end of the coal traffic, the section from Frome to Radstock was kept open to serve a wagon repair facility for several more years, and in 1974 a new connection was built between Mells Road and Frome to serve ARC's enormous Whatley Quarry – this section of the line is still open today.

Since closure, much of the disused Radstock to Frome railway has been reopened as a footpath and cycleway, forming part of the Colliers Way which starts at Dundas Aqueduct on the Kenney & Avon Canal near Limpley Stoke and meets the Two Tunnels Greenway (see page 28) at Midford. From Midford, the Colliers Way follows the course of the Somerset & Dorset Joint Railway to the outskirts of Wellow then reaches Radstock along a mixture of steep country lanes and the old railway route. Easily recognized by its pit head wheel, Radstock Museum tells the story of the North Somerset Coalfields. Following the Colliers Way signs from here, the level railway route to Frome is soon regained, continuing southwards to Kilmersdon, then past the site of Mells Road station to Great Elm. En route the disused track of the line remains in situ, lost in the undergrowth, while a series of etched and enamelled copper plate signs set into boulders highlight the planting of a linear orchard of Old English apples and pears. From Great Elm, the Colliers Way leaves the railway route to avoid the working Whatley Quarry and reaches Frome along country lanes.

Bristol
Burnham-on-Sea   Bath
Taunton   Evercreech
              Junction

ORIGINAL LINE
24 miles

**LENGTH OPEN TO
WALKERS & CYCLISTS**
4¾ miles

ORIGINAL ROUTE OPERATOR
Somerset Central Railway

LINE OPEN TO PASSENGERS
1854/1862–1966

OS LANDRANGER
182

NATIONAL CYCLE NETWORK
Route 3

REFRESHMENT POINTS
Glastonbury, Ashcott

CAR PARKING
Glastonbury, Ashcott,
Shapwick

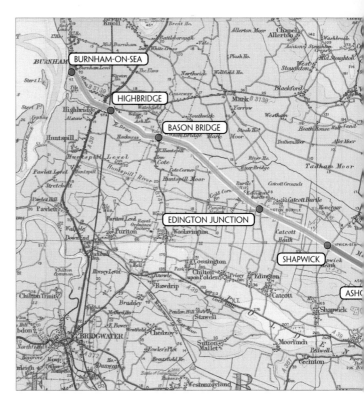

EVERCREECH JUNCTION
⟫⟶
BURNHAM-ON-SEA

Backed by local businessmen and the Bristol & Exeter Railway (B&ER), the Somerset Central Railway (SCR) opened its broad-gauge line between Highbridge Wharf and Glastonbury in 1854. Much of it was built along the course of the moribund Glastonbury Canal which had already been purchased by the B&ER. The line was extended westward to Burnham-on-Sea in 1858 and a branch opened from Glastonbury to Wells in 1859. The SCR's main line was extended eastward from Glastonbury to Cole in February 1862 where it met the standard gauge Dorset Central Railway which had opened from Templecombe at the same time. To facilitate through running the SCR's routes were relaid with mixed-gauge track and in September of that year the two companies merged to become the Somerset & Dorset Railway (S&DR). The completion of the line between Wimborne and Templecombe in 1863 gave the S&DR its through route between the Bristol Channel and the South Coast.

The story of the Bath Extension, which opened between Evercreech Junction and Bath Green Park in 1874, and the formation of the Somerset & Dorset Joint Railway (S&DJR) in 1876 is told on page 28, but it is suffice

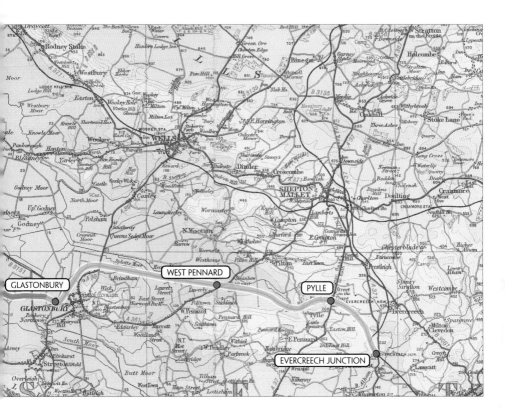

to say that the Evercreech Junction to Burnham-on-Sea line effectively then became a sleepy branch line. A branch line was opened between Edington Junction and Bridgwater in 1890 but this had a short life, closing to passengers in 1952. Meanwhile, the S&DJR's locomotive works at Highbridge closed in 1930, and regular passenger services between Highbridge and Burnham-on-Sea had ended in 1951.

In 1958, all the S&DJR north of Templecombe came under the control of the Western Region of British Railways, and the rundown of the system was soon implemented with through trains being withdrawn in 1962. The S&DJR network was listed for closure in the 1963 'Beeching Report', but despite vociferous opposition and a final 2-month stay of execution was closed completely on 7 March 1966, steam-operated until the end.

Since closure, nearly 5 miles of the Highbridge branch across the Somerset Levels between Glastonbury and Shapwick has been reopened as

a footpath and cycleway. In Glastonbury, the island platform canopy from Glastonbury & Street station is now in a town centre car park while a replica level crossing gate has been erected near to the site of the station. The headquarters building of the Somerset Central Railway now houses the offices of a builder's merchant. The trackbed is joined just to the west of here and soon crosses the River Brue on the original railway bridge. A short detour along a lane follows before it is re-joined alongside the moribund Glastonbury Canal to the site of Ashcott station. En route are old peat workings at Ham Wall – once with their own narrow-gauge railways – which have more recently become nature reserves. Ashcott station was some distance from the village it served, but the nearby Railway Inn is open for refreshments. From here, the railway trail continues alongside the old canal for almost 2 miles through the Shapwick Heath National Nature Reserve to end at the site of Shapwick station.

Chippenham to Calne Railway Path

ORIGINAL LINE
5¼ miles

LENGTH OPEN TO WALKERS & CYCLISTS
5 miles

ORIGINAL ROUTE OPERATOR
Great Western Railway

LINE OPEN TO PASSENGERS
1863–1965

OS LANDRANGER
172

NATIONAL CYCLE NETWORK
Route 403

REFRESHMENT POINTS
Calne, Chippenham

CAR PARKING
Calne, Chippenham

NATIONAL RAIL NETWORK STATION
Chippenham

OPPOSITE LOWER:
A GWR steam rail motor and trailer at work on the Calne branch line in the early 20th century.

CALNE
⟫——▸
CHIPPENHAM

For nearly two centuries the small Wiltshire town of Calne's main claim to fame was the Harris company's pork processing business, which by the early 20th century employed around 20 per cent of its population. Before the coming of the railway to the town, the main transport link for Harris's products was the Calne branch of the Wilts & Berks Canal – shipping out vast amounts of bacon, sausages and pork pies was a slow business by canal boat. To solve this logistical nightmare, the Calne Railway was born in 1860 to link the town with the GWR main line at Chippenham. With no major physical obstacles to overcome, construction of the 5¼-mile line was straightforward, and it opened to great rejoicings in the town on 3 November 1863. The line was worked from the outset by the Great Western Railway, but the Calne Railway Company remained independent until being taken over by the GWR in 1892.

Apart from Lord Lansdowne's private station at Black Dog Siding – from where His Lordship of nearby Bowood House would transport his race horses to meetings in railway horse boxes – there was no intermediate station until 1905 when Stanley Bridge Halt opened. The opening of the railway soon led to a massive expansion of the Harris company, and goods handling facilities at Calne were much enlarged by the GWR in 1895. At the end of the First World War, the Harris company built two enormous factories and a cattle market next to Calne station as well as building its own power station to provide electricity to its business and the townspeople. The Calne branch became even busier during the Second World War when two RAF bases were built nearby but the post-war years saw much of the Harris traffic lost to road transport. Despite the introduction of diesel multiple units in 1958, the branch was losing money at an alarming rate and it was listed for closure in the 1963 'Beeching Report'. Freight services ended in 1964 and passenger services on 18 September 1965. The Harris factory in Calne closed in 1981.

Today, much of the Calne branch line is a traffic-free footpath and cycleway known as the Chippenham to Calne Railway Path. The 5-mile traffic-free route starts at Station Road in Calne close to site of the town's long-demolished station and follows the valley of the River Marden to the outskirts of Chippenham, en route passing the delightfully restored Black Dog Halt, from where there are views of Bowood Lake, before crossing the A4 on a newly-built bridge. Continuing its journey along the pretty Marden Valley, the Path passes under several small road overbridges and the site of Stanley Bridge Halt before heading off in a straight line across farmland towards the River Avon. After crossing the river on a bridge, the Path continues along the old railway trackbed to end close to the national rail network station in Chippenham.

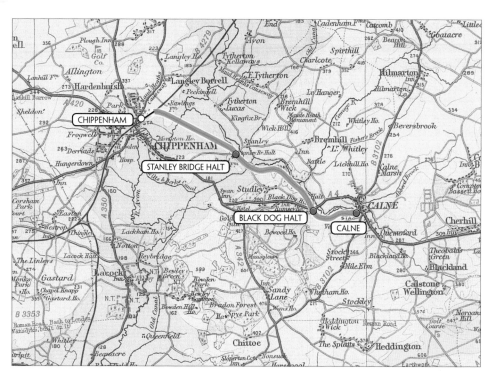

WEYMOUTH ⟫→ EASTON

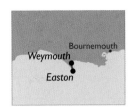

Rodwell Trail

ORIGINAL LINE
9 miles

**LENGTH OPEN TO
WALKERS & CYCLISTS**
2¼ miles
(6 miles for walkers
to Easton)

ORIGINAL ROUTE OPERATOR
Great Western Railway/
London & South Western
Railway

LINE OPEN TO PASSENGERS
1865/1902–1952

OS LANDRANGER
194

NATIONAL CYCLE NETWORK
Route 26

REFRESHMENT POINTS
Weymouth, Wyke Regis,
Portland

CAR PARKING
Weymouth, Portland

**NATIONAL RAIL
NETWORK STATION**
Weymouth

The Isle of Portland, connected by a shingle bank to the Dorset mainland, was for centuries an important centre of limestone quarrying and, from 1848, the home of one of HM Prisons. An inclined plane and horse-drawn tramways linked the quarries to piers, but the island remained unconnected with the growing rail network in Britain until the mixed-gauge Weymouth & Portland Railway opened in 1865. The 5-mile line was operated jointly by the Great Western and London & South Western railways with passenger services running between Weymouth and Portland Victoria Square via the intermediate station at Rodwell in 1870. The broad-gauge rail was removed in 1874, and a short railway was opened in 1878 to serve the Royal Naval dockyards. A new torpedo factory at Wyke Regis was also rail-connected in 1891.

The railway was extended 4 miles beyond Portland station around the north and east coast of the island to Easton by the Easton & Church Hope Railway in 1902. Most of its route was on a ledge cut into the cliffs, and it was also operated jointly by the GWR and LSWR. Passenger services were improved on the line in 1909 when a new station was opened at Melcombe Regis to take pressure off Weymouth station. At the same time, halts were also opened at Westham and Wyke Regis while Sandsfoot Castle Halt opened in 1932. Rodwell and Portland stations were damaged by German bombing in the Second World War, but the post-war years saw a decline in passenger traffic and these services ended in 1952. Freight trains, including Portland stone from the island's quarries, continued until complete closure on 9 April 1965. The two viaducts on the line – over Radipole Lake and over the Fleet Lagoon at Ferry Bridge – were demolished in the 1970s.

Following years of being used as an unofficial footpath, the 2¼-mile section of the line between Westham Halt in Weymouth and Ferry Bridge was reopened as a traffic-free footpath and cycleway known as the Rodwell Trail in 2000. Much of the railway infrastructure has survived including halts with their nameboards at Westham, Sandsfoot Castle and Wyke Regis. The Trail passes through a short tunnel north of Rodwell station where both platforms at this passing place have also survived. Here the route lies in a wooded cutting, but south of Sandsfoot there are fine views across Portland Harbour. The Trail ends at Ferry Bridge, but walkers can rejoin the trackbed on the other side of the Fleet Lagoon and follow it across the causeway to Portland.

On Portland's east coast, the trackbed of the line to Easton can be followed on foot between Balaclava Bay and Church Ope Cove, a distance of around 2 miles. Built on a ledge, this coastal section offers wide-ranging views across Weymouth Bay to the Dorset coast. To complete a circular walk around the island, walkers can take the South West Coast Path from Church Ope Cove then around Portland Bill and up the west coast to Weymouth.

*OPPOSITE TOP:
Built on a ledge high above the
sea, the railway to Easton was
opened in 1902 and closed
in 1965.*

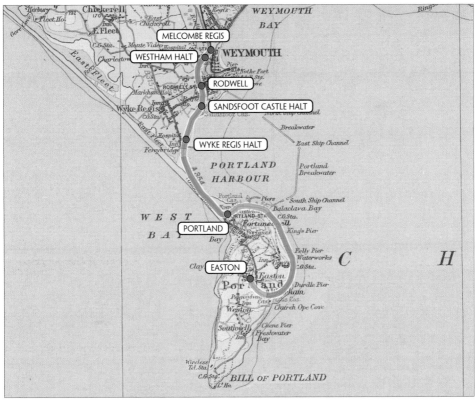

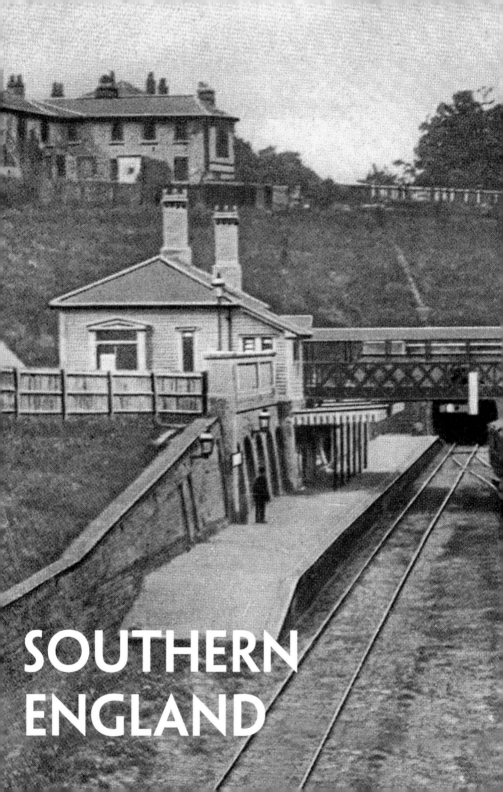

SOUTHERN
ENGLAND

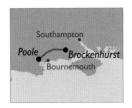

Poole · Southampton · Brockenhurst · Bournemouth

BROCKENHURST »→ POOLE
(VIA RINGWOOD)

Castleman Trailway (Ringwood to Hamworthy)

ORIGINAL LINE
26½ miles

LENGTH OPEN TO WALKERS & CYCLISTS
Lymington Junction to Ringwood: 9 miles/
Ringwood to Poole: 16½ miles

ORIGINAL ROUTE OPERATOR
Southampton & Dorchester Railway

LINE OPEN TO PASSENGERS
1847–1964

OS LANDRANGER
195/196

NATIONAL CYCLE NETWORK
Routes 256 (Ringwood to Wimborne)/
Route 25 (Wimborne to Poole)

REFRESHMENT POINTS
Holmsley, Ringwood, Wimborne, Poole

CAR PARKING
Holmsley, Ringwood, West Moors, Wimborne, Upton Country Park (Hamworthy), Poole

NATIONAL RAIL NETWORK STATIONS
Brockenhurst, Poole

The Southampton & Dorchester Railway was seen as the first step in opening a direct route from London Waterloo to Exeter and the southwest via the Dorset coast. Dubbed 'Castleman's Corkscrew' after the Wimborne solicitor who promoted it, the meandering route across the New Forest via Brockenhurst and Ringwood was opened to Dorchester in 1847. A year later the railway was absorbed by the London & South Western Railway, but any hopes of extending westward from Dorchester came to nothing. Instead, the Dorchester (West) to Weymouth line was opened by the broad-gauge Great Western Railway in 1857 – it was laid with mixed-gauge track which allowed LSWR trains from Southampton to reach Weymouth via a connection at Dorchester.

However, the need for a railway to serve the growing coastal resorts of Christchurch and Bournemouth led to the single-track Ringwood, Christchurch & Bournemouth Railway being opened throughout in 1870. Opened in 1874, a branch from Broadstone also allowed long-distance trains that had travelled from the Midlands and North of England via the Somerset & Dorset Railway to reach the new Bournemouth (West) station. Neither of these new lines were ideal for travellers to the two resorts as

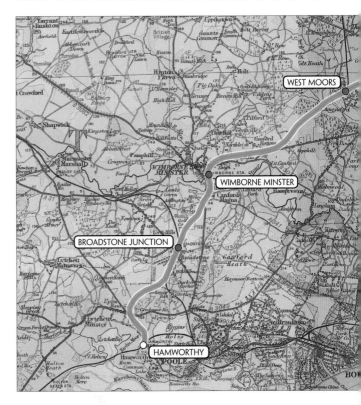

they involved either a lengthy roundabout journey or a change of train at Ringwood. This was only resolved in 1888 when the LSWR opened a double-track main line from Brockenhurst to Christchurch and Bournemouth (Central). The opening of a new line between Branksome and Hamworthy Junction in 1893 completed the main line as we know it today, and 'Castleman's Corkscrew' between Brockenhurst and Hamworthy was relegated to secondary status. From then until its closure on 4 May 1964, it was only used by local stopping trains and Waterloo to Swanage and Weymouth trains on summer Saturdays.

Since closure, much of the 'Castleman's Corkscrew' route between Lymington Junction, west of Brockenhurst, and Hamworthy has been reopened as a footpath and cycleway. Apart from a flooded cutting, the 9-mile section between Lymington Junction to the outskirts of Ringwood provides an excellent route for walkers, mountain bikers and horse riders through the open heathland of the New Forest National Park. Car parks and picnic sites are provided along the route while 1 mile east of Holmsley the straight trackbed has been rebuilt as a road. Holmsley station, complete with platforms, is now home to a café and restaurant. It is interesting to note here that the Association of Train operating Companies has proposed reopening the line between Ringwood and Brockenhurst – watch this space.

Although the railway has disappeared in Ringwood, to the west of the town in Bickery Road the trackbed forms the 16½-mile Castleman Trailway, a mainly traffic-free waymarked route for walkers and cyclists through heathland and forestry plantations that ends at the car park in Upton Country Park near Hamworthy – the concrete platform and nameboard of Ashley Heath station is passed en route. From Upton, a footpath and cycleway runs along the shore of Holes Bay to Poole railway station.

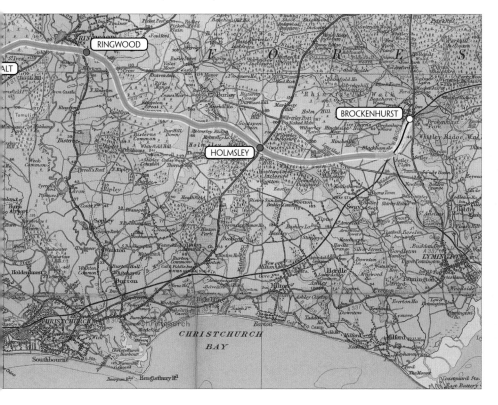

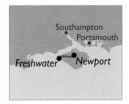

Southampton
Portsmouth
Freshwater • • Newport

ORIGINAL LINE
12 miles

**LENGTH OPEN TO
WALKERS & CYCLISTS**
2 miles

ORIGINAL ROUTE OPERATOR
Isle of Wight Central Railway

LINE OPEN TO PASSENGERS
1888/1889–1953

OS LANDRANGER
196

NATIONAL CYCLE NETWORK
Regional Route 67

REFRESHMENT POINTS
Freshwater, Yarmouth

CAR PARKING
Freshwater, Yarmouth

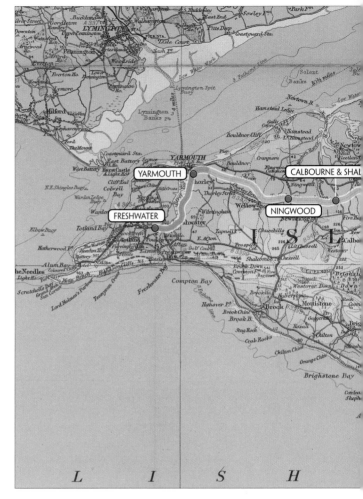

FRESHWATER ⇢ NEWPORT

Receiving authorization in 1873, the 12-mile Freshwater, Yarmouth &
Newport Railway (FY&NR) had a few false starts before it was
completed. Nothing initially happened, and the company was dissolved in
1877. The second attempt came in 1880 when the company was
reincorporated with the blessing of the London & South Western Railway
which was planning on improving its steamer service between Lymington,
on the mainland, and Yarmouth. The railway finally opened to passengers
in 1889, and was initially worked by the Isle of Wight Central Railway
(IoWCR). The arrangements at Newport were far from satisfactory as
trains to and from Freshwater had to reverse out of or into the IoWCR's
station in the town. In 1913, the FY&NR became master of its destiny and
took over operations but this proved too much and it soon went bankrupt,

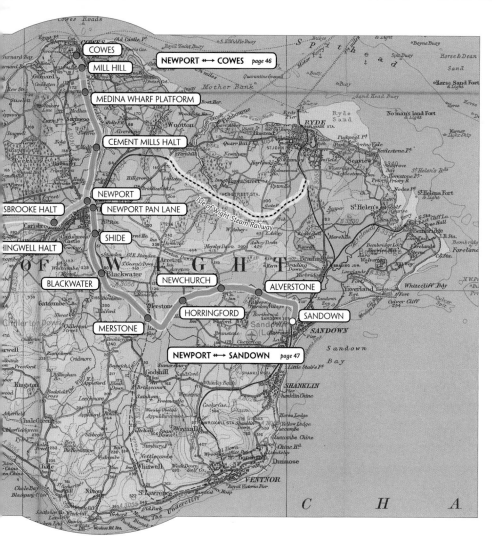

NEWPORT »→ COWES page 46

COWES

MILL HILL

MEDINA WHARF PLATFORM

CEMENT MILLS HALT

NEWPORT

NEWPORT PAN LANE

SBROOKE HALT

SHIDE

HINGWELL HALT

BLACKWATER

NEWCHURCH

ALVERSTONE

HORRINGFORD

SANDOWN

MERSTONE

NEWPORT »→ SANDOWN page 47

after which it was run by an Official Receiver. Reluctantly absorbed by the new Southern Railway in 1923, the new owners introduced the only named train to operate on the island – 'The Tourist' was a through train running between Ventnor and Freshwater via Newport during the summer months. It was particularly popular with holidaymakers, but was withdrawn when the Freshwater line closed. With increased competition from road transport, the post-war years saw a decline in traffic on this loss-making line and it closed on 21 September 1953.

Since closure, the 2-mile section of the line between Freshwater and Yarmouth has been reopened as a footpath and cycleway. From Freshwater, where the End of the Line Café with its mock station canopy marks the start of the path, the route closely follows the unspoilt banks of the tidal western Yar River in an Area of Outstanding Natural Beauty. At Yarmouth, the station building is now a cycle hire centre while in the grounds of a nearby mill the body of a Victorian railway coach has been converted into living accommodation. The railway path continues eastward for ½-mile through Rofford Marsh to end on the B3401.

NEWPORT »» COWES

For route map see page 45

Incorporated in 1859, the 4¼-mile Cowes & Newport Railway (C&NR) became the first railway on the island when it opened between those two towns in 1862. It remained isolated until the Ryde & Newport Railway (R&NR) opened in 1875. Three years later, a railway wharf was opened on the River Medina, south of Cowes, and it was through here that all coal, timber and building materials were 'imported' from the mainland. In 1887, the C&NR amalgamated with the R&NR and the Isle of Wight (Newport Junction) Railway to form the Isle of Wight Central Railway (IoWCR), eventually becoming part of the newly formed Southern Railway in 1923.

With changing holiday habits, the post-war years saw a decline in passenger numbers on all the island's 'vintage' railways and the Ryde to Cowes line, along with the Newport to Ryde line and the Ryde to Shanklin line, was recommended for closure in the 1963 'Beeching Report'. Steam-hauled by Class 'O2' 0-4-4Ts until the end, the line closed on 21 February 1966.

Since closure, almost the entire route of this line along the west bank of the River Medina has been reopened as a well-surfaced, traffic-free footpath and cycleway. At the southern end of the railway path, Newport station, built by the IoWCR in 1887, has been wiped off the map to make way for the town's bypass. There were three intermediate stations between here and Cowes – Cement Mills Halt, Medina Wharf Halt and Mill Hill – but little now remains although the 208-yd-long tunnel at the latter is used as a gun range. The station at Cowes has also been wiped off the map, being demolished long ago to make way for a car park and supermarket.

RIGHT:
Class 'O2' 0-4-4T No W26 enters Cowes station with a train from Ryde on October 1965.

NEWPORT ⇢ SANDOWN

For route map see page 45

The 9¼-mile Isle of Wight (Newport Junction) Railway (IoWNJR) opened between Newport and Sandown via Merstone in 1875. It was connected to the Ryde & Newport Railway (R&NR) at Newport via a viaduct in 1879. This bankrupted the company which was then run by an Official Receiver until amalgamation with the R&NR and the Cowes & Newport Railway to form the Isle of Wight Central Railway in 1887. Becoming part of the Southern Railway in 1923, the line was closed by British Railways on 6 February 1956. In its latter years, it was served by through trains to and from Cowes and during the summer months by a through service between Freshwater and Shanklin. This latter train, the only named 'express' train on the Isle of Wight, was known as 'The Tourist' but it ceased to run following closure of the Freshwater line in 1953.

Since closure, much of the Newport to Sandown line has been reopened as a footpath and cycleway known as the Perowne Way. The starting point near Newport is at the site of Shide station – there were once seven intermediate stations along this line but most of them have been demolished. The only exceptions are at Horringford, which is now a well-screened private residence, and the island platform at Merstone (junction for the line to Ventnor West 1900–1952), which is adorned by a work of art in the shape of a concrete suitcase and a station nameboard. Here there is a car park for users of the Way. En route to Sandown there is the occasional road overbridge and even restored level crossing gates. This pleasant and peaceful walk or ride ends at Sandown station which is still served by 1930s vintage ex-London Underground trains running between Ryde Pier Head and Shanklin.

RIGHT:
A busy scene at Merstone Junction in 1951 with a train for Sandown on the left, hauled by Class 'O2' 0-4-4T No W27 'Merstone', and a train for Ventnor West on the right hauled by Class 'O2' 0-4-4T No W35 'Freshwater'.

ALTON »→ FAREHAM

Meon Valley Trail

ORIGINAL LINE
22¼ miles

**LENGTH OPEN TO
WALKERS & CYCLISTS**
11 miles

ORIGINAL ROUTE OPERATOR
London &
South Western Railway

LINE OPEN TO PASSENGERS
1903–1955

OS LANDRANGER
185/196

REFRESHMENT POINTS
West Meon, Meonstoke,
Droxford, Wickham

CAR PARKING
West Meon, Wickham

HERITAGE RAILWAY
Mid-Hants Railway

Closely following the meandering River Meon along much of its route, the 22¼-mile Meon Valley Railway was opened between Butts Junction, Alton, and Knowle Junction, north of Fareham, by the London & South Western Railway in 1903. The railway was built to accommodate double track but the hoped-for traffic from London to Gosport and Stokes Bay failed to materialize; neither did the military traffic between Aldershot and Portsmouth. By the First World War through services between Waterloo and Gosport had been withdrawn, and the heavily engineered line became a sleepy country backwater served by two-coach push-pull passenger trains. As the line was built to main-line standards it featured grand Mock-Tudor 'Arts & Crafts' style stations with 600-ft platforms capable of accommodating lengthy trains. Tunnels were built at Privett (S-shaped 1,056 yd) and West Meon (560 yd), and at the latter village a 62-ft-high steel viaduct carried the line over the Meon Valley. The railway's only claim to fame came during the Second World War when a special train carrying Winston Churchill, General Eisenhower and other Allied leaders to a meeting to finalize the D-Day landings was parked secretly at Droxford station for several days in 1944.

This bucolic rural railway obviously had no future under British Railways' management, and it closed to passengers on 7 February 1955. Goods traffic continued to operate between Fareham and Droxford until 1962 and between Alton and Farringdon until 1968. Plans to reopen the southern part of the line by preservationists came to nothing, but an isolated stretch at Droxford was used to test the Sadler Rail Coach – a new lightweight railbus designed by inventor Charles Ashby – until 1975 when the track was lifted.

Today there are many reminders of this short-lived railway between Alton and Fareham. The 11-mile southern section of the railway between West Meon and Wickham is a footpath, bridleway and cycleway known as the Meon Valley Trail – during periods of heavy rain the unsurfaced path which is also used by horse riders is muddy and requires a mountain bike or good walking boots. Although West Meon Viaduct was demolished 50 years ago, the tunnels north of here survive and are used for storage and are inhabited by colonies of bats. Both East Tisted and Privett stations have been lovingly restored as private residences.

Reminders of the railway along the Trail include the platforms of West Meon station hidden in the undergrowth close to the unsurfaced car park and the superbly restored station at Droxford which is now a private residence – its platform, canopy, station building and other railway artefacts are, understandably, obscured by a high fence. Nearby a post box has a green plaque commemorating the meeting of the Allied leaders here in 1944.

From Droxford, the wooded Trail continues southwards through delightful Hampshire countryside to Wickham where roadside parking and refreshments are available in the village. The Trail continues on to the site of Knowle Junction, but here walkers and cyclists need to retrace their journey back to Wickham.

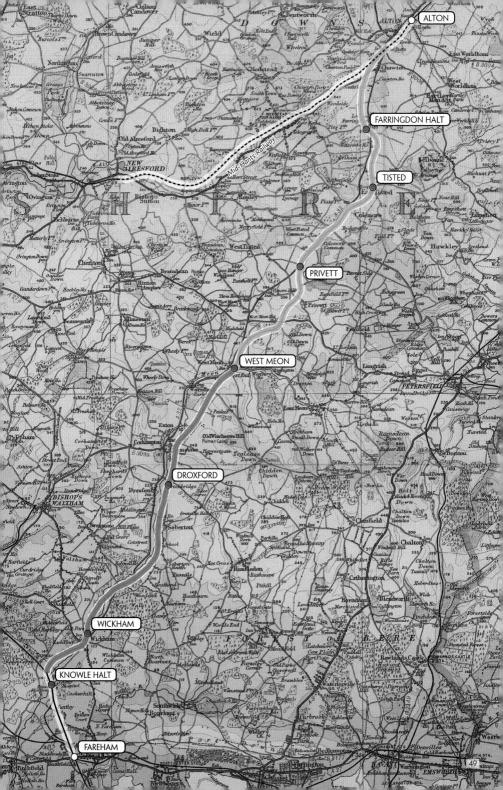

ALTON

FARRINGDON HALT

TISTED

PRIVETT

WEST MEON

DROXFORD

WICKHAM

KNOWLE HALT

FAREHAM

Mid-Hants Railway

49

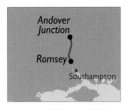

ANDOVER JUNCTION
➤➤ ROMSEY

Test Way

ORIGINAL LINE
18 miles

**LENGTH OPEN TO
WALKERS & CYCLISTS**
8½ miles

ORIGINAL ROUTE OPERATOR
London &
South Western Railway

LINE OPEN TO PASSENGERS
1865–1964

OS LANDRANGER
185

NATIONAL CYCLE NETWORK
Route 246

REFRESHMENT POINTS
West Down, Stockbridge,
Horsebridge, Mottisfont

CAR PARKING
West Down, Stockbridge,
Horsebridge

**NATIONAL RAIL
NETWORK STATION**
Mottisfont & Dunbridge

What became known as the Sprat & Winkle Line between Andover and Romsey was built along the course of the Andover Canal, which had opened along the Test Valley between Southampton and Andover in 1794. Early proposals for the railway involved the Manchester & Southampton Railway, Great Western Railway (GWR), London & South Western Railway (LSWR) and the Andover & Redbridge Railway. Backed by the GWR, the latter company started work on a broad-gauge line but soon went bust, and the unfinished route was finally taken over by the LSWR in 1863 and opened as a standard-gauge single-track line in 1865. Built along the course of the canal, the new railway negotiated many twists and curves which inevitably led to operating difficulties.

In 1885, the LSWR opened a new double-track line from Hurstbourne, on their Basingstoke to Salisbury main line, to Fullerton on the Sprat & Winkle Line. The latter was also straightened out and doubled, and a new station at Fullerton Junction was opened, replacing the original slightly to the north. The line to Hurstbourne had a short life, being singled in 1913, closed to passengers in 1931 and closed completely in 1956.

The opening of the Midland & South Western Junction Railway's north–south route between Cheltenham and Andover Junction in 1894 brought additional traffic to the Sprat & Winkle, with a daily service between the Cotswold spa town and Southampton running over the line until it was closed as a through route in 1961. The Sprat & Winkle passenger service lingered on, kept alive by a regular-interval service between Andover Junction and Southampton until it was listed for closure in the 1963 'Beeching Report'. The end came quickly, and the line closed completely – apart from freight between Andover Junction and Andover Town – on 7 September 1964. The track was lifted in 1968.

Since closure, Hampshire County Council has reopened the trackbed between West Down, close to the site of Fullerton Junction, and Mottisfont as part of the Test Way Long Distance Path. Now a private residence, Fullerton Junction station, its platforms and bridge over the Test have survived and the twin-arched road bridge at the start of this walk is a reminder of the doubling of the railway in 1885. Closely following the River Test to the northern outskirts of Stockbridge, the path southwards can be very muddy at times – the railway's route through the town has disappeared beneath road improvements but is soon rejoined in the water meadows to the south.

South of Stockbridge, the railway path reaches Horsebridge where the station buildings, platforms, canopy, signalbox and 1922 LSWR carriage on a length of track have been beautifully restored and are open to the public for teas on a few weekends each year – at other times it is used as a wedding venue. The final stretch of the railway path is sandwiched between the Test and the A3057 before reaching Mottisfont station (now a private residence). The village, with its National Trust-owned Abbey, is but a short walk from here.

ANDOVER JUNCTION

ANDOVER TOWN

CLATFORD

FULLERTON

STOCKBRIDGE

HORSEBRIDGE

MOTTISFONT

ROMSEY

51

HAVANT »→ HAYLING ISLAND

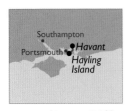

Hayling Billy Trail

ORIGINAL LINE
4½ miles

**LENGTH OPEN TO
WALKERS & CYCLISTS**
4 miles

ORIGINAL ROUTE OPERATOR
Hayling Railway

LINE OPEN TO PASSENGERS
1867–1963

OS LANDRANGER
197

NATIONAL CYCLE NETWORK
Route 2

REFRESHMENT POINTS
Havant, Hayling Island

CAR PARKING
Havant, Langstone Bridge,
North Hayling, South Hayling

**NATIONAL RAIL
NETWORK STATION**
Havant

Promoted by local businessmen in their bid to transform Hayling Island into a holiday resort, the 4½-mile Hayling Railway finally opened for passenger traffic in 1867. Its opening had been delayed due to the building of a timber bridge with a swinging section across Langstone Harbour and an embankment on mud flats to the south of here. Although completed in 1865 when goods services started, passengers had to wait another 2 years due to the poor state of the track discovered by a Board of Trade inspector. During its early years of operation, the Hayling Railway made do with vintage 4-wheeled carriages hired from the London & South Western Railway. In 1872, the London, Brighton & South Coast Railway (LB&SCR) took over running the line before leasing it in 1874.

With intermediate wooden halts at Langstone and North Hayling, the line was kept busy carrying holidaymakers and daytrippers during the summer months but in the winter saw little traffic. Due to weight restrictions imposed on Langstone Bridge, the only locomotives allowed to operate the line were the LB&SCR's diminutive 'Terrier' 0-6-0 tank locomotives – known locally as 'Hayling Billies' – and these remained in service until the line's closure.

Despite the branch line turning in a modest profit, it was still listed for closure in the 1963 'Beeching Report' – the reason being given was the cost of replacing the ageing timber bridge at Langstone. The summer of 1963 saw the line working at full capacity and there was often standing room only for passengers, but its popularity with the public did not save it. Closure came on 4 November 1963, the track was lifted soon afterwards and Langstone Bridge was demolished in 1966.

Closing the railway was rather short-sighted as there is only one road on to Hayling Island, and traffic on this is often reduced to a crawl on hot summer weekends – but there is an alternative. Apart from the missing swing bridge over Langstone Harbour, the entire route between Havant station (still served by trains on the Portsmouth Direct Line from Waterloo and the West Coastway Line between Southampton and Brighton) and Hayling Island is now a traffic-free footpath and cycleway known as the Hayling Billy Trail. At Langstone, walkers and cyclists must use the modern road bridge to access the northern and southern sections of the route. With car parking nearby, the piers of the old swing bridge can be seen clearly at low tide, while a lonely signal post still stands as a reminder of this popular railway.

Heading south and with fine views across Langstone Harbour to Portsmouth, the Trail reaches the site of North Hayling station from where oysters were once dispatched by train to London. This coastal stretch which the Trail passes through is home to a wide variety of protected species of wildfowl, wading birds, butterflies and plant life. The Trail ends at the site of Hayling Island station where there is car parking. Here the 1900-built goods shed has been converted into a theatre while seaside attractions are but a short walk from here.

OPPOSITE LOWER
*The rusty remains of this
signal stand guard at the
southern end of what used to
be Langstone Bridge.*

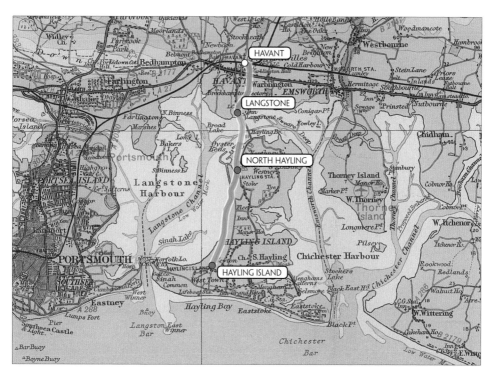

GUILDFORD
⇛
SHOREHAM-BY-SEA

Downs Link

ORIGINAL LINE
29 miles

**LENGTH OPEN TO
WALKERS & CYCLISTS**
31 miles

ORIGINAL ROUTE OPERATOR
London, Brighton & South
Coast Railway

LINE OPEN TO PASSENGERS
1861/1865–1965/1966

OS LANDRANGER
186, 187, 198

NATIONAL CYCLE NETWORK
Route 22/223

REFRESHMENT POINTS
Bramley & Wonersh,
Cranleigh, Rudgwick,
Southwater, West Grinstead,
Henfield, Steyning, Shoreham

CAR PARKING
Bramley & Wonersh,
Cranleigh, Rudgwick,
Southwater, West Grinstead,
Steyning, Shoreham

**NATIONAL RAIL
NETWORK STATIONS**
Christ's Hospital, Shoreham

Although originally seen as a through route from Guildford to the South Coast, this cross-country railway across Surrey and Sussex was effectively operated as two separate entities. The first section to be built was the London, Brighton & South Coast Railway's (LB&SCR) line from Itchingfield Junction, south of Horsham, to Shoreham-by-Sea. Opening in 1861, it served intermediate stations at Southwater, West Grinstead, Partridge Green, Henfield, Steyning and Bramber.

To the west, the Horsham & Guildford Direct Railway had already started to build its single-track line between Peasmarsh Junction, south of Guildford, and Stammerham Junction, south of Horsham. Construction was slow, and before it was completed the company was taken over by the LB&SCR in 1864. A triangular junction was built at Itchingfield to allow the through running of trains between Guildford and Shoreham, and the line via Cranleigh opened in 1865, effectively bringing about the demise of the Wey & Arun Canal. The hoped-for through traffic along both routes never materialized, due mainly to the intransigence of the London & South Western Railway at Guildford, and the spur at Itchingfield Junction was closed in 1867. Thereafter the two lines led completely separate existences apart from meeting at Stammerham Junction for the final 2½ miles into Horsham. The grand station of Christ's Hospital was built at the junction in 1902 to serve the nearby relocated public school.

Between the wars, the Cranleigh Line was also used during the summer months by excursion trains from further up country, but it was badly damaged by German bombing during the Second World War. Contributing to their later downfall, both lines missed out on third-rail electrification in the 1930s and 1940s and were listed for closure in the 1963 'Beeching Report'. Closure for the Cranleigh Line – steam-worked until the end – came on 14 June 1965 while the Steyning Line with its diesel-electric multiple units struggled on until 7 March 1966.

Today, nearly all the former railway route forms part of the 37-mile Downs Link footpath, bridleway and cycleway that links the North Downs Way at St Martha's Hill, southeast of Guildford, to the South Downs Way near Steyning and on to the coast at Shoreham-by-Sea. Railway highlights include: Bramley & Wonersh station with its car park, restored platforms, canopy, concrete station name signs and level crossing gates; restored Baynards station (now a private residence) where apart from the lack of track very little has changed at this delightful rural spot; the unique 'Double Bridge' over the River Arun southeast of Rudgwick; Slinfold station is now a private residence; the 'vandalized' station at Christ's Hospital, which is still served by trains between London Victoria and Bognor Regis; the idyllic site of West Grinstead station with platforms, signal, BR Mk 1 coach, car park and picnic site. While there is splendid scenery to the south of here, all the station buildings have long since disappeared to be replaced by new roads, housing and industrial estates. At the southern end of the Downs Link the West Coastway Line still serves Shoreham-by-Sea station.

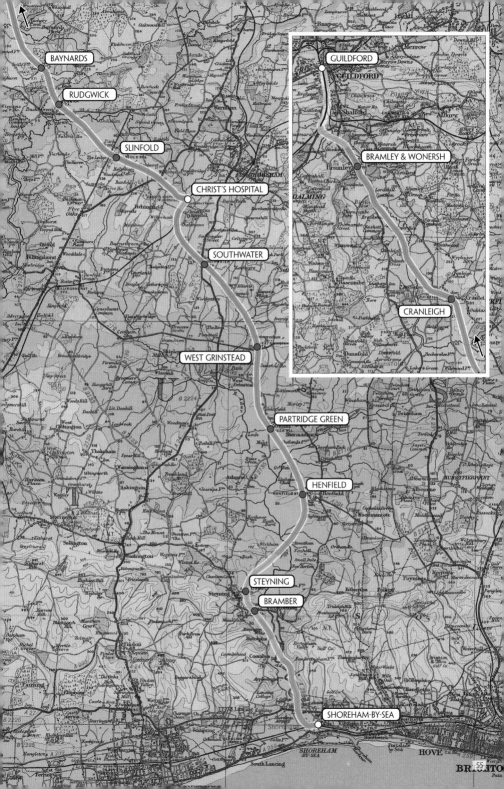

BAYNARDS

RUDGWICK

SLINFOLD

CHRIST'S HOSPITAL

SOUTHWATER

WEST GRINSTEAD

PARTRIDGE GREEN

HENFIELD

STEYNING

BRAMBER

SHOREHAM-BY-SEA

GUILDFORD

BRAMLEY & WONERSH

CRANLEIGH

RYE ⤏→ CAMBER SANDS

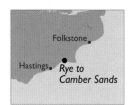

Folkstone

Hastings • Rye to
Camber Sands

Rye & Camber Tramway

ORIGINAL LINE
1¾ miles

LENGTH OPEN TO WALKERS & CYCLISTS
1½ miles

ORIGINAL ROUTE OPERATOR
Rye & Camber Tramway

LINE OPEN TO PASSENGERS
1895–1939

OS LANDRANGER
189

REFRESHMENT POINTS
Rye

CAR PARKING
Rye

NATIONAL RAIL NETWORK STATION
Rye

The ancient hilltop town of Rye was first served by a railway in 1851 when the South Eastern Railway opened its line across Romney Marsh between Ashford and Hastings. A short branch line to Rye Harbour opened 3 years later. Although the latter closed in 1962, the Marshlink Line, as it is marketed today, remains open between Ashford and Hastings despite being listed for closure in the 1963 'Beeching Report'.

Towards the end of the 19th century, the game of golf was becoming increasingly popular in Victorian England, and the town of Rye eventually got its own golf course in 1894 when Rye Golf Club opened. The location of the club in sand dunes on nearby Camber Sands was not ideal, so some local businessmen came up with the idea of building a tramway to convey golfers from Rye to the club house.

The 3ft-gauge single-track line was built by Colonel Holmen. F. Stephens, the leading proponent of light railways in Britain. The Rye & Camber Tramway was his first project, and by the time of his death in 1931 he controlled many light railways in England and Wales. The tramway opened between Monkbretton Bridge in Rye and Rye Golf Club on 13 July 1895 and was an immediate hit with golfers. Services were handled by the diminutive 2-4-0 tank locomotive *Camber*, built by William Bagnall of Stafford, hauling one covered coach. In 1908, the line was extended across the golf links to a new terminus at Camber Sands. A tea room was opened here, and this new destination proved popular with day-trippers during the summer months. However, the tramway depended on a subsidy from the golf club to keep operating during the leaner winter months.

In an effort to reduce operating costs, a petrol rail tractor was purchased in 1925 and this diminutive machine kept the tramway operating until the outbreak of war in 1939. Sadly, the tramway never reopened after the war although the section from Monkbretton Bridge to Golf Links Halt was used by the Admiralty in connection with the building of a jetty.

Despite closure over 75 years ago, much of the route of this little tramway can still be followed on foot today. At Monkbretton Bridge in Rye, nothing now remains of the terminus buildings, but the trackbed south from here is now a well-trodden footpath as far as Broadwater Bridge. After a short deviation, it is rejoined along a concrete road that leads to the inshore rescue station and harbourmaster's office. Amazingly the 3ft-gauge track remains embedded in the concrete which was added by the Admiralty during the Second World War. Beyond here, and even more astonishing, is the well-preserved corrugated hut of Golf Links Halt – the original terminus of the tramway – that is still used as a storeroom by the golf club. The route of the tramway extension to Camber Sands continues through the golf links as a footpath to the site of the 1908 terminus although the platform and tea room have long-since disappeared.

OPPOSITE LOWER
Three foot gauge track embedded in concrete at Golf Links Halt, more than 75 years since closure of the Rye & Camber Tramway.

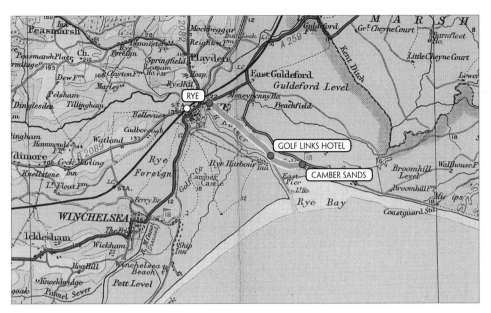

ERIDGE »—» POLEGATE

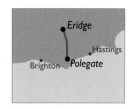

Eridge

Hastings

Brighton · Polegate

The Cuckoo Trail

ORIGINAL LINE
20½ miles

LENGTH OPEN TO WALKERS & CYCLISTS
11 miles

ORIGINAL ROUTE OPERATOR
London, Brighton & South Coast Railway

LINE OPEN TO PASSENGERS
1849/1880–1965/1968

OS LANDRANGER
199

NATIONAL CYCLE NETWORK
Route 21

REFRESHMENT POINTS
Heathfield, Horam, Hellingly, Hailsham, Polegate

CAR PARKING
Heathfield, Horam, Hellingly, Hailsham, Polegate

NATIONAL RAIL NETWORK STATIONS
Polegate, Eridge

Built in two sections 31 years apart, the 21½-mile railway across the South Weald in Sussex between Eridge, Heathfield and Polegate was affectionately known as the Cuckoo Line – it was given this name by locomotive drivers from a centuries-old tradition that the first cuckoo was heard each year at Heathfield Fair. At its southern end Polegate station had been opened by the London & Brighton Railway in 1846, while at the northern end Eridge station was later opened on the Uckfield line by its successor, the London, Brighton & South Coast Railway (LB&SCR), in 1868.

Meanwhile, the LB&SCR opened a 3-mile branch line from Polegate northwards to Hailsham – this was the first section of the Cuckoo Line to open. Proposals to extend northwards across the South Weald from Hailsham to Eridge first came to nothing, and it took until 1876 when the LB&SCR eventually received Parliamentary approval to build the single-track line. With intermediate stations at Hellingly, Waldron & Horam Road, Heathfield, Mayfield and Rotherfield & Mark Cross, the line opened for business in 1880. As part of improvements to the Uckfield line, the junction at Eridge was moved almost 1 mile south to Redgate Mill in 1894.

The line was served by trains running between Tunbridge Wells and Eastbourne and, until the Second World War, a handful of these were extended to and from London Victoria. With increasing competition from road transport, the post-war years saw a rapid decline in both passenger and goods traffic, and the Cuckoo Line was listed for closure in the 1963 'Beeching Report'. As with its opening, the closure of the line came in two stages – first was the Eridge to Hailsham section which closed on 14 June 1965. A special last train, 'The Wealdsman', organized by the Locomotive Club of Great Britain, traversed the entire route on 13 June double-headed by 'U' Class 2-6-0 No. 31803 and 'N' Class 2-6-0 31411. The Polegate to Hailsham section remained open until 8 September 1968, and the track was lifted soon after.

In 1981, the Wealden District Council purchased the entire route of the railway trackbed between Heathfield and Polegate – it also owned the trackbed to the north of Heathfield as far as Mayfield but sadly this was sold off piecemeal in 1986. The Heathfield to Polegate section, along with a non-railway extension south to Hampden Park in Eastbourne became a footpath known as the Cuckoo Trail. In 1990, it was resurfaced by the cycling charity Sustrans to make it suitable for cyclists, and today it forms part of National Cycle Network Route 21. Of interest along the Trail is the street-level station booking office at Heathfield which is now a café and shop; beautifully restored Hellingly station which is now a private residence and the steel and wood sculpture mileposts erected by Sustrans. Opened in 2002, a short northerly extension to the Cuckoo Trail at Heathfield now passes through the 265-yd Heathfield Tunnel – the tunnel is lit but closes at night.

ERIDGE

ROTHERFIELD & MARK CROSS

MAYFIELD

HEATHFIELD

WALDRON & HORAM ROAD

HELLINGLY

HAILSHAM

POLEGATE

59

Three
Bridges ●—● East
Grinstead

Brighton

Worth Way

ORIGINAL LINE
6¾ miles

**LENGTH OPEN TO
WALKERS & CYCLISTS**
6 miles

ORIGINAL ROUTE OPERATOR
London & Brighton Railway

LINE OPEN TO PASSENGERS
1855–1967

OS LANDRANGER
187

NATIONAL CYCLE NETWORK
Route 21

REFRESHMENT POINTS
Rowfant, East Grinstead

CAR PARKING
East Grinstead

**NATIONAL RAIL
NETWORK STATIONS**
Three Bridges, East Grinstead

HERITAGE RAILWAY
Bluebell Railway

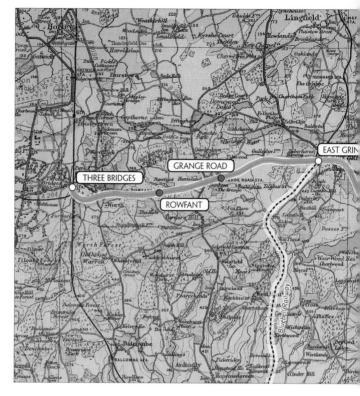

THREE BRIDGES
⇒→
EAST GRINSTEAD

The opening of the London & Brighton Railway (L&BR) in 1840 left the townsfolk and businessmen of East Grinstead 7 miles from their nearest station at Three Bridges. Concerned that the town would be permanently bypassed with a consequent loss of business, local people put pressure on two railway companies – the L&BR and the South Eastern Railway – to come up with their proposals to connect the town with Three Bridges. However, as this was in the mid-1840s at the height of the boom-and-bust period known as 'Railway Mania' nothing came of either of them. It was eventually left to the East Grinstead Railway (EGR) – a company set up in 1852 by prominent local businessmen – to put forward its own proposal. A deal was also struck with the London, Brighton & South Coast Railway (LB&SCR), successor to the L&BR, which allowed them to lease and operate the line with an option to purchase it within 10 years of opening. This time the scheme was successful, and the EGR received Parliamentary approval for its single-track line in 1853.

The railway opened to joyous celebrations, marked by a public holiday, in East Grinstead on 9 July 1855. At that time, the only intermediate station

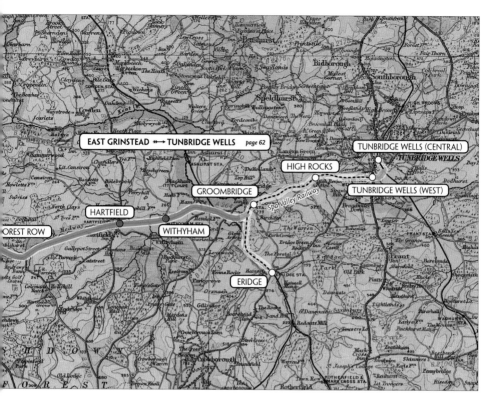

EAST GRINSTEAD ⟶ TUNBRIDGE WELLS page 62

TUNBRIDGE WELLS (CENTRAL)

HIGH ROCKS

GROOMBRIDGE

TUNBRIDGE WELLS (WEST)

HARTFIELD

FOREST ROW

WITHYHAM

ERIDGE

was at Rowfant, but another at Grange Road was opened 5 years later. Just before its 10-year option to purchase ran out, the LB&SCR bought the EGR in 1865. An eastwards extension of the railway from East Grinstead to Groombridge and Tunbridge Wells opened in 1866. East Grinstead station was rebuilt in 1882 for the opening of the Lewes & East Grinstead Railway which had its platforms at a lower level – the two lines were linked by a spur – and is today the northern terminus of the Bluebell Railway.

In a cost-saving measure, the LB&SCR introduced push-pull trains in 1905, and after the First World War through trains to and from London's Victoria and London Bridge stations. As with other branch lines around the country, the Three Bridges to Tunbridge Wells line saw rapidly declining passenger and freight traffic following the Second World War. Goods services were withdrawn in 1961 and despite the introduction of diesel-electric multiple units a year later, the line was listed for closure in the 1963 'Beeching Report'.

Local people protested but all to no avail and the line closed on 2 January 1967.

Following the purchase of much of the trackbed by West Sussex Council in 1977, the route was reopened as a footpath and bridleway, known as the Worth Way, in 1979. Twenty years later, it was resurfaced and became part of National Cycle Network Route 21. Sadly, parts of the trackbed had already been lost to developers, so there are diversions in place at the site of Grange Road station, Rowfant station and where the M23 bisects the route. Not much is left now of the railway infrastructure apart from some road overbridges and Rowfant station which is in commercial usage. At East Grinstead, the Worth Way links up with the Forest Way railway path to Groombridge (see pages 62–63).

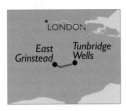

EAST GRINSTEAD
⇶
TUNBRIDGE WELLS

Forest Way

ORIGINAL LINE
13½ miles

**LENGTH OPEN TO
WALKERS & CYCLISTS**
10 miles

ORIGINAL ROUTE OPERATOR
London & Brighton Railway

LINE OPEN TO PASSENGERS
1866–1967/1985

OS LANDRANGER
187, 188

NATIONAL CYCLE NETWORK
Route 4

REFRESHMENT POINTS
East Grinstead,
Forest Row, Groombridge

CAR PARKING
East Grinstead, Forest Row

**NATIONAL RAIL
NETWORK STATIONS**
East Grinstead

HERITAGE RAILWAY
Bluebell Railway,
Spa Valley Railway

For route map see page 61

As noted on page 60, the East Grinstead Railway opened between Three Bridges and East Grinstead in 1855. It was worked from the start by the London, Brighton & South Coast Railway (LB&SCR) which went on to purchase it in 1865. Meanwhile, the East Grinstead, Groombridge & Tunbridge Wells Railway (EGG&TWR) had been authorized in 1862 to build a 13½-mile single-track line between these three places. Running powers were obtained over the Brighton, Uckfield & Tunbridge Wells Railway (BU&TWR) between Groombridge and Tunbridge Wells, which was then under construction. Serving intermediate stations at Forest Row, Hartfield, Withyham and Groombridge, the EGG&TWR opened in 1866, with the BU&TWR joining it from the south at Groombridge in 1868. In the meantime, both companies had already been absorbed by the LB&SCR in 1865. A new station had also been opened at East Grinstead in 1866 to allow through workings between Three Bridges and Tunbridge Wells.

At Tunbridge Wells, the LB&SCR station, later named Tunbridge Wells West, was linked to the South Eastern Railway station via a short tunnel

RIGHT:
*Just before the introduction of
diesel-electric multiple units a
steam operated push-pull train
departs from Groombridge
station in the 1950s.*

in 1876. East Grinstead station had to be rebuilt yet again, on two levels, when the railways from Lewes in the south and Oxted in the north were opened in 1883. Apart from commuter traffic running between London and Forest Row, passenger traffic between East Grinstead and Tunbridge Wells only warranted a push-pull service, but traffic had declined steadily after the Second World War and closure was considered by British Railways in the 1950s. This threat passed temporarily, but the introduction of modern diesel-electric multiple units failed to bring back customers and this rural line running through the tranquil Wealden landscape was listed for closure in the 1963 'Beeching Report'. Despite local objections (and its proximity to Dr Richard Beeching's home), the line between East Grinstead and Groombridge, along with the Three Bridges to East Grinstead line, closed on 2 January 1967. Served by trains to and from Eridge, the Groombridge to Tunbridge Wells West route lived on until it, too, closed on 8 July 1985.

Linking up with the Worth Way at East Grinstead, the Forest Way today follows the route of the railway as far as Groombridge. The disused railway was purchased by East Sussex County Council in 1971 and opened as a linear Country Park in 1974. Set in the High Weald Area of Outstanding Natural Beauty it is an important green corridor for wildlife, and is used by walkers, cyclists and horse riders and was resurfaced in 2002 as part of the National Cycle Network. Heading east from East Grinstead, the Forest Way reaches the site of Forest Row station where there is a large car park and a café in the former local coal merchant's office. Further east, Hartfield station has hardly changed since closure and now houses a nursery school. Following the lush Medway Valley, the Forest Way passes Withyam station – now a well-screened private residence – before ending in the village of Groombridge. The station here is served by the Spa Valley Railway which operates tourist trains between Eridge and Tunbridge Wells West.

DUNSTABLE
⇒
WELWYN GARDEN CITY

Ayot Greenway/
Lea Valley Walk

ORIGINAL LINE
16¾ miles

**LENGTH OPEN TO
WALKERS & CYCLISTS**
5½ miles

ORIGINAL ROUTE OPERATOR
Great Northern Railway

LINE OPEN TO PASSENGERS
1860–1965

OS LANDRANGER
166

NATIONAL CYCLE NETWORK
Route 57

REFRESHMENT POINTS
Luton, Wheathampstead,
Harpenden

CAR PARKING
Luton, Ayot St Peter,
Wheathampstead

**NATIONAL RAIL
NETWORK STATIONS**
Luton, Harpenden,
Welwyn Garden City

By the mid-19th century, the townsfolk and businessmen of Luton were clamouring for their own railway. With important industries such as hat making, the town was by far the largest in Bedfordshire without a railway. The neighbouring town of Dunstable, 5 miles to the west, had got its own branch line from Leighton Buzzard in 1848. To the east, the Great Northern Railway (GNR) had opened its main line from King's Cross to Doncaster in 1852 and it was from Welwyn Junction, north of Hatfield, that the Luton, Dunstable & Welwyn Junction Railway (LD&WJR) was authorized to build a 16¾-mile railway.

The first section to be built was between Dunstable and Luton, which opened in 1858. At Dunstable, there was a connection to the London & North Western Railway's branch line from Leighton Buzzard. With intermediate stations at Luton Hoo, Harpenden East, Wheathampsted and Ayot, the Luton to Welwyn Junction section opened in 1860 – the entire branch was worked from the start by the GNR. Meanwhile, in 1858, the LD&WJR had amalgamated with the Hertford & Welwyn Junction Railway to form the Hertford, Luton & Dunstable Railway which in turn was then absorbed by the GNR in 1861. In 1868, the branch lines from Dunstable and Hertford were extended to run parallel to the main line between Welwyn and Hatfield.

1868 was also the year that the Midland Railway (MR) opened its main line between London St Pancras and Bedford via Luton. Luton became a boom town and although losing much of its London-bound passenger traffic to the new MR route, the Welwyn to Dunstable line with its enormous warehouse at Luton Bute Street was kept busy with coal, agricultural and livestock traffic supplemented by trainloads of gravel from a quarry near Wheathampstead destined for London and landfill waste in the other direction. Even elephant dung from London Zoo was carried by rail to Wheathampstead to help grow lettuces. The writer George Bernard Shaw was a regular passenger on the line, cycling from his home at Ayot St Lawrence to Wheathampstead to catch a train for London.

Increasing road competition in the 1950s brought a decline in traffic, and although diesel multiple units were introduced in 1962 the line was listed for closure in the 'Beeching Report'. Closure came on 26 April 1965 although landfill waste continued to be carried to Blackbridge Sidings until 1971 and oil traffic between Luton and Dunstable until 1989.

Since closure, the section between Luton and Dunstable has been reopened as a concrete guided busway while two sections between Welwyn and Luton have been reopened as footpaths and cycleways. The 3 miles between Ayot and Wheathampstead is known as the Ayot Greenway while the 2½ miles between Harpenden East and Luton Hoo now forms part of the 50-mile Lea Valley Walk Long Distance Path which runs from Leagrave, north of Luton, to Limehouse Basin in East London. Not to miss is the secluded station site at Wheathampstead with its restored platform, name board and seats set in a wooded glade.

OPPOSITE TOP:
A disused railway bridge near
Harpenden on the footpath and
cycleway from Luton.

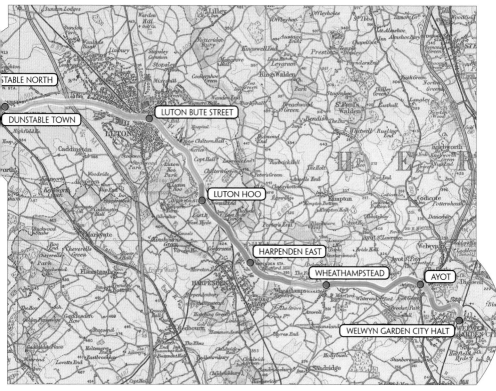

WELWYN GARDEN CITY
⟫⟫
HERTFORD

Cole Green Way

ORIGINAL LINE
6½ miles

LENGTH OPEN TO WALKERS & CYCLISTS
5½ miles

ORIGINAL ROUTE OPERATOR
Hertford & Welwyn
Junction Railway

LINE OPEN TO PASSENGERS
1858–1951

OS LANDRANGER
166

NATIONAL CYCLE NETWORK
Route 61

REFRESHMENT POINTS
Cole Green,
Hertingfordbury, Hertford

CAR PARKING
Cole Green

NATIONAL RAIL NETWORK STATIONS
Welwyn Garden City,
Hertford North,
Hertford East

The market town of Hertford was first served by a railway when the Northern & Eastern Railway opened its 7¼-mile branch line from Broxbourne in 1843. Still served by trains from Liverpool Street, the terminus of this line is at Hertford East. The second railway to reach Hertford was the Hertford & Welwyn Junction Railway (H&WJR) which opened between the Great Northern Railway's (GNR) main line at Welwyn to Cowbridge station in Hertford in 1858. Intermediate stations were provided at Cole Green and Hertingfordbury. Soon after opening, the H&WJR joined forces with the as yet unfinished Luton, Dunstable & Welwyn Junction Railway to form the Hertford, Luton & Dunstable Railway (HL&DR). The Luton to Welwyn section opened in 1860, and the following year the HL&DR was absorbed by the GNR. Cowbridge station in Hertford was linked by a short spur to the Great Eastern Railway at Hertford East and this, in theory, provided an east–west cross-country route stretching from Luton to Broxbourne. However, in reality, this potentially useful route came to an end in 1868 when both the Hertford and Luton branches were diverted to run southwards on parallel lines to Hatfield station, south of Welwyn, where any through trains had to reverse directions.

The completion of the double-track Hertford Loop by the London & North Eastern Railway in 1924 saw all passenger services from Hatfield diverted to the new Hertford North station, resulting in the closure of Cowbridge station. With the opening of the Hertford Loop, the branch line became a sleepy country byway with little passenger or freight traffic. From 1944, most trains ended or began their journeys at Welwyn Garden City. Following nationalization of the railways in 1948, many such loss-making lines around Britain came under close scrutiny from the Branch Lines Committee of the British Transport Commission with the result that many were closed. The Welwyn to Hertford line was no exception, and passenger services ceased on 18 June 1951. Despite this, goods trains continued to serve Cole Green and Hertingfordbury until 1 August 1962 when the line closed completely.

Since closure, almost all of the trackbed of the branch line from Cole Green Lane, on the eastern edge of Welwyn Garden City, to Hertford has been reopened as a footpath, cycleway and bridleway known as Cole Green Way. Its leafy green corridor is a haven of peace away from the maddening traffic. At Cole Green where parts of the platform still exist, the station site is now a car park and picnic site for users of the route – the nearby Cowper Arms dates back to 1776 and was known as the Railway Tavern in the 19th century. Further east, Hertingfordbury station is now a private residence and from here the Cole Green Way heads under the Hertford Loop viaduct to end close to the Hertford Football Club ground. Here the Lea Valley Walk can be joined – this 50-mile Long Distance Path starts near Luton and ends at Limehouse Basin in East London.

OPPOSITE TOP:
Cole Green station was in use
between 1858 and 1962.

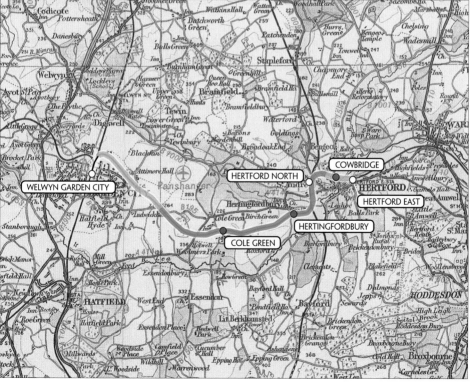

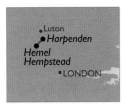

Luton
Harpenden
Hemel
Hempstead
LONDON

HARPENDEN
⤞→
HEMEL HEMPSTEAD

The Nicky Line

ORIGINAL LINE
8¾ miles

**LENGTH OPEN TO
WALKERS & CYCLISTS**
7 miles

ORIGINAL ROUTE OPERATOR
Midland Railway

LINE OPEN TO PASSENGERS
1877–1947

OS LANDRANGER
166

NATIONAL CYCLE NETWORK
Route 57

REFRESHMENT POINTS
Harpenden, Redbourn,
Hemel Hempstead

CAR PARKING
Harpenden, Redbourn,
Hemel Hempstead

**NATIONAL RAIL
NETWORK STATION**
Harpenden

The townsfolk and businessmen of Hemel Hempstead were none too pleased when the London & Birmingham Railway opened in 1837. Due to obstruction from local landowners, the route of the line took it some distance to the west of the town with a station provided at Boxmoor. Pressure for a rail link from Boxmoor to serve the town grew, but several proposals came to nothing due, again, to obstruction from local landowners. Formed in 1863, the Hemel Hempstead Railway Company spent several years fruitlessly trying to achieve their goal of building the railway. Finally, in 1866 a proposal to build the line from Boxmoor to the town and extend it northeastwards to Redbourn and Harpenden received the necessary approval and construction started. Progress was slow with the first section taking 5 years to complete, by which time the company had fallen on hard times. Eventually, the Midland Railway (MR) stepped in and completed the line in 1877.

The hoped-for through traffic failed to materialize due to restrictions placed on the connection at Boxmoor by the London & North Western Railway, and trains from Harpenden terminated at Heath Park Halt in Hemel right up until closure. Both passenger and freight traffic were always light, and to reduce operating costs the London Midland & Scottish Railway (successor to the MR) experimented briefly in 1932 with a Ro-Railer – basically a single-deck motorbus with flanged wheels. Passenger traffic was temporarily suspended in 1947 due to a national coal shortage, but it was never reinstated although coal trains continued to supply Hemel's gasworks until 1959 when the entire route fell into disuse. The final chapter came in 1968 when the line was taken over by the Hemelite Company to transport residual ash and clinker from power stations to their yard at Cupid Green for the manufacture of building blocks. This continued until 1979 when the physical connection at Harpenden was severed, and the line closed completely.

Following closure of the line, two local councils purchased the trackbed between Harpenden and the eastern outskirts of Hemel – the once little-used section between Hemel and Boxmoor had long disappeared beneath road improvements and development while the viaduct over the Gade Valley was demolished in 1960. The 7 miles of what has long been known to locals as the Nicky Line was opened as a footpath and cycleway in 1985. In Harpenden, the railway path starts just north of Harpenden station and after crossing the A1081 on the surviving Staffordshire blue-brick viaduct reaches the site of Roundwood Halt where the concrete platform and distant signal are remarkable survivors. Heading southwesterly into open countryside through a virtual tunnel of lineside trees, the Nicky Line reaches the site of Redbourn station. Here the building and platforms have long gone, but the site today has been landscaped as a picnic area. West of here, Watling Street is crossed on the 1870s-built wrought-iron bridge before the railway path burrows under the concrete monstrosity of the M1 motorway. From here, the Nicky Line heads into the outskirts of Hemel Hempstead before ending close to the Midland Hotel.

OPPOSITE TOP:
The Nicky Line footpath and cycleway crosses over Watling Street at Redbourn on this original 1870s wrought iron bridge.

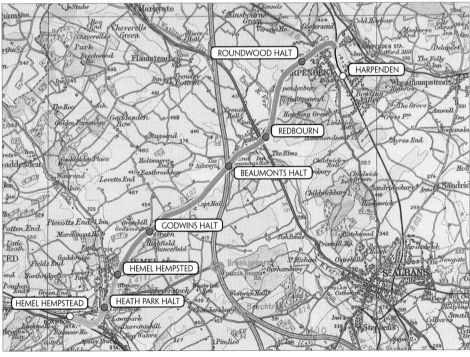

BOURNE END
➤➤➤
HIGH WYCOMBE

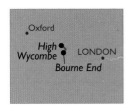

Bourne End to High Wycombe Cycle Path
(once completed)

ORIGINAL LINE
5¼ miles

LENGTH OPEN TO WALKERS & CYCLISTS
1½ miles

ORIGINAL ROUTE OPERATOR
Great Western Railway

LINE OPEN TO PASSENGERS
1854–1970

OS LANDRANGER
175

REFRESHMENT POINTS
Bourne End

CAR PARKING
Bourne End

NATIONAL RAIL NETWORK STATION
Bourne End

OPPOSITE LOWER:
Built in 1854, Brunel's original station at High Wycombe, now a listed bulding, was replaced ten years later by a through station.

Incorporated by an Act of Parliament in 1846 and engineered by Isambard Kingdom Brunel, the Wycombe Railway opened a single-line broad-gauge railway from Maidenhead, on the GWR's Paddington to Bristol main line, to High Wycombe in 1854. The company went on to extend its railway to Princes Risborough and Thame in 1862 and to Oxford in 1864. Worked from the outset by the GWR, this line allowed the latter company's trains an alternative route between Paddington and Oxford. The Wycombe Railway was absorbed by the GWR in 1867 and the entire route converted to standard gauge in 1870.

Through traffic ended when the more direct Great Western & Great Central Joint Railway opened between Northolt Junction and High Wycombe in 1906. A 2¾-mile branch line was opened by the Great Marlow Railway from Bourne End (originally named Marlow Road (Bourne End)), on the Maidenhead to High Wycombe line, in 1873. Despite losing its through traffic, the Maidenhead to High Wycombe line was kept busy with freight traffic being generated to and from the giant Soho corn and paper mill near Wooburn Green and other mills along the valley. The 1963 'Beeching Report' brought good news for rail users on the Maidenhead to High Wycombe and Bourne End to Marlow lines as they were not listed for closure, and even the building of the M40 motorway over the railway at Loudwater in the late 1960s failed to disrupt services. However, the through service between Maidenhead and Aylesbury was withdrawn on 5 May 1969, and the Bourne End to High Wycombe section itself saw a considerably reduced service. Inevitably, this was the prelude to closure which came on 4 May 1970. A closure threat to the Maidenhead-Bourne End-Marlow line in 1972 was fought off by a determined Passengers' Association.

Arriving by train at the pretty station of Bourne End, where trains to and from Marlow reverse direction, lovers of lost railways can follow the long-closed line to High Wycombe up the valley of the River Wye on foot for a distance of 1½ miles. Often muddy, the tree-lined path starts behind a modern industrial estate across the road from the Station Café at Bourne End station and skirts a housing estate and open countryside for a short distance before ending at Wooburn Green. The stations here and at Loudwater were demolished soon after closure. Beyond here, little remains of the railway route although it can be traced sandwiched between the A4094 and Flackwell Heath Golf Club where the concrete gate post of a foot crossing survives in the undergrowth. Beyond the M40, several brick arch bridges survive between Loudwater and High Wycombe where stretches of the trackbed can be walked. Brunel's original station at High Wycombe, now a Grade II-listed building, survives today as a tyre and exhaust centre. There are plans by Buckinghamshire County Council to upgrade the existing footpath between Bourne End and Wooburn Green for cyclists and disabled use and to extend it to High Wycombe.

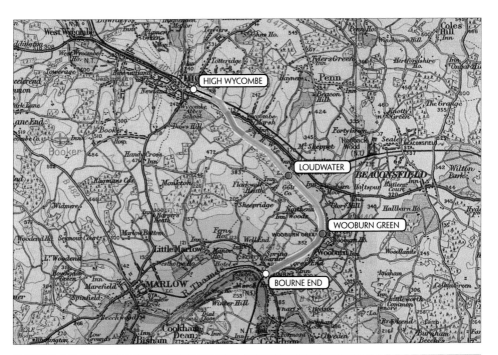

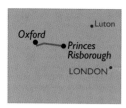

Oxford •
• Princes
  Risborough
LONDON •
• Luton

PRINCES RISBOROUGH
OXFORD

Phoenix Trail

ORIGINAL LINE
21 miles

**LENGTH OPEN TO
WALKERS & CYCLISTS**
5 miles

ORIGINAL ROUTE OPERATOR
Great Western Railway

LINE OPEN TO PASSENGERS
1862–1963

OS LANDRANGER
165

NATIONAL CYCLE NETWORK
Route 57

REFRESHMENT POINTS
Princes Risborough,
Towersey, Thame

CAR PARKING
Princes Risborough, Thame

**NATIONAL RAIL
NETWORK STATION**
Princes Risborough

HERITAGE RAILWAY
Chinnor & Princes
Risborough Railway

As we have seen on page 70, the broad-gauge Wycombe Railway opened between Maidenhead and High Wycombe in 1854. This was extended to Princes Risborough and Thame in 1862 and thence to Kennington Junction, south of Oxford, in 1864. The railway was absorbed by the Great Western Railway (GWR) in 1867 and converted to standard gauge in 1870. The 21-mile mainly single-track line between Prince Risborough and Oxford gave the GWR an alternative route for its Paddington to Oxford trains although this importance was greatly reduced after the opening of the GW & Great Central Joint Railway between High Wycombe and Northolt Junction in 1906 and the opening of the Aynho Cut-off line from Princes Risborough to Banbury, and thence to Birmingham, in 1910.

Following these developments, the Princes Risborough to Oxford line settled down to a fairly quiet existence apart from on occasional Sundays when Paddington to Birmingham expresses were diverted away from the main line during engineering work. Additional halts were opened at Iffley, Garsington Bridge and Horspath in 1908, but these had a short life, closing as a wartime economy measure in 1915. Garsington Bridge was

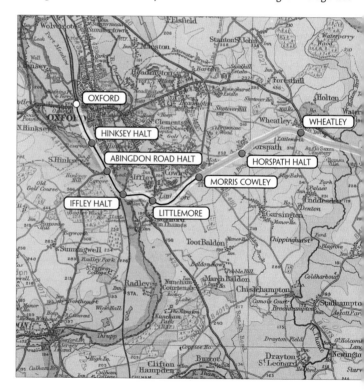

reopened in 1928 to serve the Morris Cowley factory while Horspath reopened in 1933 along with a new halt at Towersey.

The immediate years following the Second World War brought increased competition from road transport, and by the late 1950s there were only five return passenger services on weekdays. Losses were mounting, and the inevitable closure to passengers came on 7 January 1963, just before publication of the notorious 'Beeching Report'. The western section from Kennington Junction to the Morris Cowley factory remained open for freight – it is still open today serving the BMW Mini factory – while the eastern section from Princes Risborough to Thame remained open to serve an oil depot until 1991.

Since closure, the section between Thame and the western outskirts of Princes Risborough has been reopened as a footpath and cycleway by the cycling charity Sustrans. Known as the Phoenix Trail, it is also an important wildlife corridor and is noted for sightings of red kites. With seating provided at regular intervals, the trail also features 30 prizewinning sculptures built by Angus Ross and a group of local furniture students and is accessible for wheelchair users. At its eastern end, the Phoenix Trail starts near Horsenden Church, west of Princes Risborough, and soon gains the old railway trackbed for the first section to Bledlow station. Here the station building and platform have survived as has a length of track embedded in the road at the former level crossing, although further west any trace of Towersey Halt has long gone. Refreshments can be taken at the Three Horseshoes pub, a short distance from the railway overbridge at Towersey.

Continuing westward through undulating Oxfordshire farmland, the Phoenix Trail ends close to Lord Williams's School in the pretty town of Thame where, although the overall-roofed station building has sadly been demolished, the two platforms and nearby road overbridges have survived.

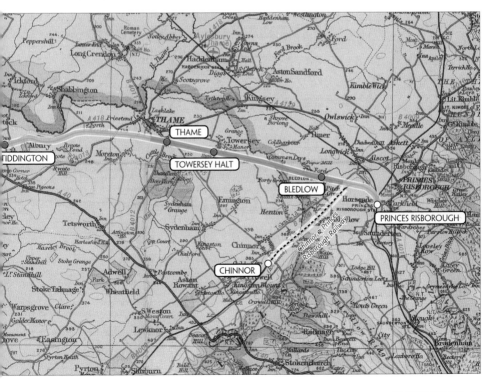

Finsbury Park to
Alexandra Palace
LONDON

FINSBURY PARK
→→→
ALEXANDRA PALACE

Parkland Walk

ORIGINAL LINE
4¼ miles

**LENGTH OPEN
TO WALKERS**
3¾ miles

ORIGINAL ROUTE OPERATOR
Great Northern Railway

LINE OPEN TO PASSENGERS
1873–1954

OS LANDRANGER
176

REFRESHMENT POINTS
Crouch Hill, Muswell Hill,
Alexandra Palace

**NATIONAL RAIL
NETWORK STATIONS**
Finsbury Park,
Alexandra Palace

**LONDON
UNDERGROUND
STATIONS**
Finsbury Park, Highgate

Despite the expanding railway network across the length and breadth of Britain, the town of Barnet and the villages of Highgate, Finchley and Edgware north of London were still without railways in the early 1860s. Enter the Edgeware [sic], Highgate & London Railway which was incorporated in 1862 to build an 8¾-mile line between the Great Northern Railway (GNR) main line at Seven Sisters (Finsbury Park), Highgate and Edgware. The scheme was financially backed by the GNR which also absorbed the company one month before the line opened on 22 August 1867.

Meanwhile, the Great Northern Palace Company had been formed in 1860 to build 'The Palace of the People' close to Muswell Hill. Construction of what was to become Alexandra Palace started in 1865, and in 1871 work started on building a branch line from Highgate station to the Palace via Muswell Hill. Although built by the Muswell Hill Railway, it was operated by the GNR from opening day on 24 May 1873 – the same day that Alexandra Palace opened. Sixteen days later, the palace burned down and the railway closed, only reopening in 1875 following rebuilding of the palace.

The coming of the railways to North London led to a massive urbanization of the area, and by the early 20th century trains were becoming increasingly congested. The extension of the London Underground's Northern Line northwards to East Finchley and Barnet was completed in 1941, but the Second World War brought the cancellation of similar treatment for the Finsbury Park to Alexandra Palace route. Steam-hauled trains continued to operate this line until closure to passengers on 5 July 1954. Freight services continued on the Alexandra Palace branch until 14 June 1956 when it was closed completely. The link from Finsbury Park to Highgate and East Finchley remained open for freight traffic until 1964 and for the transfer of London Underground stock until 1970 after which the track was lifted.

Following complete closure, almost the entire route between Finsbury Park and Alexandra Palace was reopened in 1984 as a footpath known as the Parkland Walk, and in 1990 it was declared a local nature reserve – cycling is prohibited and the route is now a green corridor popular with walkers, joggers and dog owners. From Finsbury Park, the course of the railway path takes it over embankments, through cuttings and over and under bridges, past the site of Stroud Green station and through the newly created Crouch Hill Park to Crouch End station where the two platforms survive intact. Beyond here, the Parkland Walk soon reaches the site of Highgate station and the twin single-bore tunnels that are now home to colonies of bats. As the tunnels are closed to pedestrians, a detour has to be made via Muswell Hill Road to the site of Cranley Gardens station, now a school. The trackbed of the Alexandra Palace branch can be joined here to Muswell Hill – en route taking in views of London from the 17-arch viaduct. Ally Pally and its park are but a short walk away where the station building survives as a community centre.

OPPOSITE LOWER:
A group of railway enthusiasts inspect the remains of Alexandra Palace station following closure – note the unfinished electrification on the left.

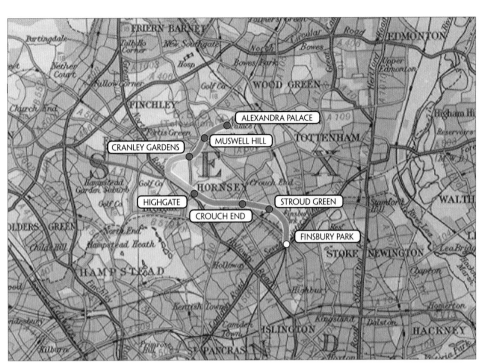

ALEXANDRA PALACE
MUSWELL HILL
CRANLEY GARDENS
HORNSEY
HIGHGATE
CROUCH END
STROUD GREEN
FINSBURY PARK

EASTERN ENGLAND

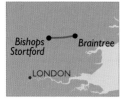

Bishops Stortford ●——● Braintree

● LONDON

Flitch Way

ORIGINAL LINE
18 miles

**LENGTH OPEN TO
WALKERS & CYCLISTS**
13 miles

ORIGINAL ROUTE OPERATOR
Great Eastern Railway

LINE OPEN TO PASSENGERS
1869–1952

OS LANDRANGER
167

NATIONAL CYCLE NETWORK
Route 16

REFRESHMENT POINTS
Takeley, Dunmow,
Rayne, Braintree

CAR PARKING
Takeley, Dunmow,
Rayne, Braintree

**NATIONAL RAIL
NETWORK STATION**
Braintree

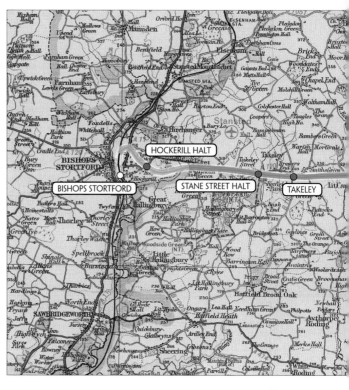

BISHOPS STORTFORD
⇻
BRAINTREE

The first railway to reach Bishop's Stortford was the Northern & Eastern Railway's line from London, which opened in 1842. It was soon leased to the Eastern Counties Railway (ECR) which went on to become a major constituent company of the newly formed Great Eastern Railway (GER) in 1862.

Meanwhile, several schemes to build a railway to the town of Dunmow had failed to materialize, and a group of local businessmen, eager to transport their produce such as malt and barley from West Essex, formed the Bishop's Stortford, Dunmow & Braintree Railway. Although receiving Parliamentary approval in 1861, the 18-mile single-track line took 8 years to complete due to the very lengthy process of land purchases. Serving intermediate stations at Takeley, Easton Lodge, Dunmow, Felsted and Rayne, the railway – which had already been taken over by the GER – finally opened on 22 February 1869. Passenger traffic was always light although the line was frequented by royalty visiting the Earl and Countess of Warwick who lived at Easton Lodge. In contrast, freight traffic consisting of agricultural produce and livestock destined for London, kept the line busy well into the 20th century.

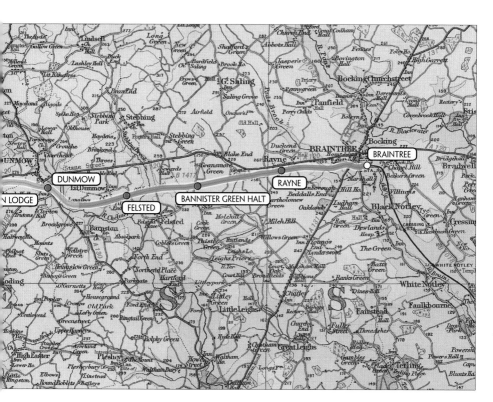

The Second World War stretched the line to capacity transporting men, materials and munitions for two nearby USAF air bases, at times making it the target for German planes. After the war, the Bishop's Stortford to Braintree line was one of many threatened with closure, losing its passenger service on 3 March 1952. Despite this, it remained open for freight which was boosted by the opening of a rail-connected Geest banana depot at Easton Lodge in 1962. Sadly, by the end of the decade much of this business had been lost to road transport and the line closed completely on 17 February 1972.

Since closure, Essex County Council has reopened much of the railway route as a footpath and cycleway known as Flitch Way. Although it starts in Bishop's Stortford, Flitch Way first joins the railway route at Tilekiln Green, to the east of the M11 and south of Stansted Airport. The route is cared for by The Friends of the Flitch Way who clear undergrowth, record wildlife, install benches and information boards. From Tilekiln Green, the Way passes the restored Stane Street Halt to reach

Takeley where the overbridge, station building and platform have all survived. Further east, the crossing keeper's cottage and wooden signal hut have survived at the site of Easton Lodge Halt. Just beyond here, the railway route has temporarily disappeared beneath the A120 Dunmow bypass, but it is rejoined to the east near Little Dunmow and heads past Felsted station (now a private residence) and Bannister Green Halt (as with Stane Street Halt it was rebuilt by the Friends of the Flitch Way) to reach Rayne station. Here the restored Grade II-listed station is a popular local café while a BR Mark II coach on a length of track acts as a visitor centre. Continuing eastwards, the Way ends in Braintree close to the town's other station which is still served by trains from Witham and Liverpool Street.

SUDBURY ⇝ LAVENHAM

ORIGINAL LINE
8¼ miles

LENGTH OPEN TO WALKERS & CYCLISTS
3 miles (cyclists)/
6½ miles (walkers)

ORIGINAL ROUTE OPERATOR
Great Eastern Railway

LINE OPEN TO PASSENGERS
1865–1961/1967

OS LANDRANGER
155

NATIONAL CYCLE NETWORK
Route 13

REFRESHMENT POINTS
Sudbury, Long Melford,
Lavenham

CAR PARKING
Sudbury, Rodbridge
Corner, Lavenham

NATIONAL RAIL NETWORK STATION
Sudbury

The market and silk-weaving town of Sudbury in Suffolk was first reached by a railway in 1849 when the Colchester, Stour Valley, Sudbury & Halstead Railway (CSVS&HR) opened its heavily engineered line from Marks Tey, the junction on the Eastern Counties Railway main line from London to Colchester. Originally leased to the ECR, the CSVS&HR was absorbed by the Great Eastern Railway (GER) in 1898.

Meanwhile, the railway was extended northwards to Long Melford and west to Clare and Haverhill in 1865. Passenger services consisted of through trains running between Haverhill or Cambridge and Colchester while freight traffic consisted mainly of livestock, grain and farm produce. This sleepy country railway came to life during the Second World War transporting fuel and bombs to several RAF bases in the area. With increasing competition from road transport, passenger and freight traffic went into decline after the war and despite the introduction of diesel multiple units in 1959 the line was listed for closure in the 'Beeching Report'. Ultimately, the Marks Tey to Sudbury section was reprieved, but the line northwards to Long Melford and Haverhill closed on 6 March 1967.

Back in 1865, the GER had opened a 16½-mile single-track line from Long Melford, on the Sudbury to Haverhill line, to Bury St Edmunds via the ancient weaving town of Lavenham. Also serving intermediate stations at Cockfield and Welnetham, this bucolic country railway led a quiet existence, only coming to life on market days until the Second World War intervened – a nearby US air force base brought increased traffic to the line, which itself was protected by numerous concrete pillboxes. As with the Haverhill line, this loss-making rural railway saw a decline in traffic after the war and despite the introduction of diesel multiple units in 1959 was closed to passengers on 10 April 1961. Freight traffic continued between Bury St Edmunds and Lavenham until complete closure on 19 April 1965.

Since closure of both lines, the 3-mile section between Sudbury and the outskirts of Long Melford has been reopened as a footpath and cycleway. From the basic modern station at Sudbury, the railway path can be accessed via the adjacent leisure centre car park. This picturesque, tree-lined route closely follows the meandering River Stour, crossing it twice on iron-girder bridges, affording glimpses of restored warehouses and water meadows en route to open country. There is a car park and picnic site at Rodbridge Corner before the path ends on the southern outskirts of Long Melford. Here walkers and cyclists must use the B1064 into the village before regaining the path on the opposite side just north of the restored station. The route continues around the eastern outskirts of the village before ending near the A134 bypass.

Walkers can access the railway path to Lavenham by following the Stour Valley Path and the St Edmund Way from the car park at Rodbridge Corner to the north of the National Trust's Melford Hall – from here, the St Edmund Way heads east to join the old railway trackbed for the last 2 miles to the outskirts of Lavenham.

OPPOSITE LOWER:
Restored warehouses can be seen from the railway path at Lavenham as it crosses the River Stour.

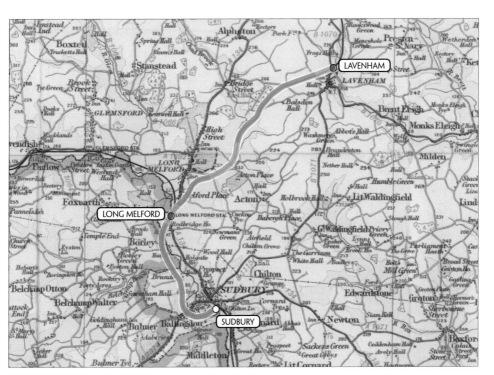

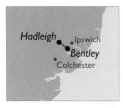

BENTLEY »→ HADLEIGH

Hadleigh Railway Walk

ORIGINAL LINE
7½ miles

**LENGTH OPEN TO
WALKERS & CYCLISTS**
2 miles

ORIGINAL ROUTE OPERATOR
Eastern Union Railway

LINE OPEN TO PASSENGERS
1847–1932

OS LANDRANGER
155

NATIONAL CYCLE NETWORK
Route 1

REFRESHMENT POINTS
Hadleigh

CAR PARKING
Hadleigh, Raydon Wood

O riginally seen as part of a cross-country route between Ipswich and the Midlands, the 7½-mile single-track branch line from a triangular junction at Bentley, on the main line between London and Ipswich, to the town of Hadleigh was incorporated in 1846. Although construction work was started by the Eastern Union & Hadleigh Junction Railway, it was soon purchased by the Eastern Union Railway which opened the line in 1847. The only major engineering feature on this level and straight line was a 50 ft embankment over a tributary of the River Brett near Hadleigh. A proposal to extend the line in a northwesterly direction up the Brett Valley to Lavenham was quietly forgotten.

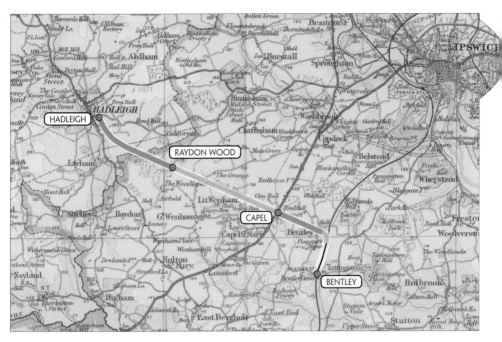

Serving intermediate stations at Capel and Raydon Wood, the line was initially served by local trains working south from Bentley to Manningtree and north from Bentley to Ipswich. However, the northern part of the triangular junction at Bentley was closed as early as 1875. For a short time, Hadleigh was also served by a through coach to and from Liverpool Street – the up coach was attached to an express at Bentley while the down working was slipped here.

Passenger traffic on the line was always light, and the introduction of a direct bus service to Ipswich in the early 1930s soon brought about the railway's demise, closing to passengers on 29 February 1932. Despite this, the flourishing local businesses of milling, malting, clothing and coconut matting in Hadleigh kept the line open for goods traffic for over another 30 years. Both Raydon Wood and Capel were kept busy during the Second World War handling fuel and armaments for a nearby American air base. The post-war years saw increasing competition from road haulage, and with dwindling freight traffic the line closed completely on 19 April 1965.

Since closure of the line, the 2-mile section from Hadleigh to Raydon Wood has been reopened as the Hadleigh Railway Walk. It is also suitable for cyclists and forms part of National Cycle Network Route 1. The walk starts at a car park close to the former railway station at Hadleigh, its building with tall ornate double chimneys and arched windows is now a well-screened private residence amidst new housing development in the old maltings. Passing a Sustrans' National Cycle Network sculpture, the tree-lined route soon enters a cutting and passes through a nature reserve before crossing the 50ft-high embankment built in 1846. Another cutting is encountered as the Walk enters Raydon Great Wood and passes under Hunters Bridge, before the route end sat a car park opposite Raydon Wood station. Here the derelict station building and platform, fenced off due to its dangerous state, shares the old goods yard with a coal depot. Beyond Raydon Wood much of the former railway is utilized as farm tracks but is now severed by the 'new and improved' A12 dual carriageway to the west of Bentley Park Hall. Bentley station, now a private residence, was closed to passengers on 7 November 1966 but still sees the passage of electric trains running between Liverpool Street and Norwich.

BRIGHTLINGSEA
⇒⇒⇒
WIVENHOE

ORIGINAL LINE
5 miles

**LENGTH OPEN TO
WALKERS & CYCLISTS**
4 miles

ORIGINAL ROUTE OPERATOR
Great Eastern Railway

LINE OPEN TO PASSENGERS
1866–1964

OS LANDRANGER
168

REFRESHMENT POINTS
Wivenhoe, Brightlingsea

CAR PARKING
Wivenhoe, Brightlingsea

**NATIONAL RAIL
NETWORK STATION**
Wivenhoe

Railways first reached the port of Wivenhoe, in the upper reaches of the Colne Estuary, in 1863 when the 2½-mile Tendring Hundred Railway (THR) opened. Connecting with the Great Eastern Railway's (GER) Hythe branch from Colchester, the line was worked by the latter company for 70 per cent of its receipts. The THR was extended to the coast at Walton-on-the-Naze in 1867, and the company was absorbed by the GER in 1883.

Meanwhile, the Wivenhoe & Brightlingsea Railway had been authorized in 1861 to build a railway connecting these two towns. With no intermediate stations, the single-track line hugged the east shore of the Colne Estuary for its entire 5 miles with a swing bridge over Alresford Creek being the only engineering feature of importance. With financial support from the GER, the line opened in 1866 and was worked by that company for 40 per cent of receipts until 1893 when GER bought it outright for £31,000.

The coming of the railway saw Brightlingsea flourish both as a seaside resort for day trippers and as a yachting centre. Its heyday was in the early 20th century when trainloads of fish, including sprats destined for the continent during the winter, and local Pyfleet oysters were dispatched to distant markets. Like many others around Britain, the branch went into decline after the Second World War due to increasing competition from road transport. During the Great Storm of January 1953, almost 3 miles of track were washed away, but although immediate closure was threatened, the line was reopened by the end of that year. In 1957, diesel multiple units were introduced as a cost-saving measure, but this was all to no avail and with passenger numbers continuing to decline the branch was listed for closure in the 'Beeching Report'. Despite strong local objections, the end came on 15 June 1964 when the line closed completely. Following closure, Brightlingsea station building survived until 1968 when it was badly damaged in a fire and then demolished.

A well-surfaced footpath now follows the top of the railway embankment from Brightlingsea station site, now a community centre, for 2¾ miles alongside the Colne Estuary as far as Alresford Creek – there is a large car park and seaside café near the beginning of the path. The embankment has been raised to aid flood defences since closure of the railway and gives windblown walkers panoramic views across the estuary to Mersea Island and the creeks and marshes along the opposite bank. Inland from the embankment are the 50 hectares of Brightlingsea Marsh, now a National Nature Reserve and home to a wide variety of interesting plants, insects and birdlife. Although the swing bridge at Alresford Creek has long been demolished, it is possible to rejoin the tracked on the opposite bank – via detour around the creek – from where a path continues along the river bank to Wivenhoe. Here, the town's station is served by Greater Anglia trains running between Liverpool Street, Colchester, Walton-on-the-Naze and Clacton-on-Sea.

OPPOSITE TOP:
The railway path at Brightlingsea runs along the top of this embankment that follows the eastern shore of the Colne Estuary.

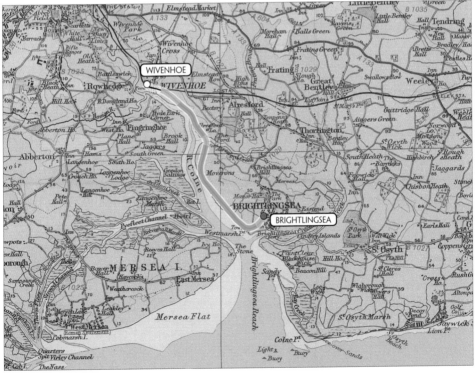

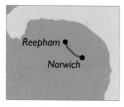

NORWICH
⇻
REEPHAM

Marriott's Way

ORIGINAL LINE
25 miles

**LENGTH OPEN TO
WALKERS & CYCLISTS**
24½ miles

ORIGINAL ROUTE OPERATOR
Lynn & Fakenham Railway/
Great Eastern Railway

LINE OPEN TO PASSENGERS
1882–1959/1880–1952

OS LANDRANGER
133

NATIONAL CYCLE NETWORK
Route 1

REFRESHMENT POINTS
Norwich, Lenwade, Whitwell,
Reepham, Aylsham

CAR PARKING
Norwich, Hellesdon, Drayton,
Attlebridge, Lenwade,
Reepham, Aylsham

**NATIONAL RAIL
NETWORK STATION**
Norwich

HERITAGE RAILWAY
Bure Valley Railway

For route map see page 88

This is the story of two railways that opened in the late 19th century but were never physically joined until 1960. First to open in 1880 was the East Norfolk Railway's (ENR) meandering rural line along the Bure Valley between Wroxham and Aylsham – with intermediate stations at Coltishall and Buxton Lamas it was operated by the Great Eastern Railway (GER). The line was extended westward to County School via Cawston, Reepham and Foulsham in 1882 by which time the ENR had been absorbed by the GER. Passenger services ceased on 15 September 1952, but the line remained open for local freight which was progressively withdrawn between 1964 and 1981. Surviving until 1983, the last trains to use the route transported concrete blocks from a factory at Lenwade via the Themelthorpe Curve (see below).

The second railway in this story was the Lynn & Fakenham Railway's line from Melton Constable to Norwich (City), which opened in 1882. A year later, the company became part of the newly formed Eastern & Midlands Railway which itself soon fell on hard times and was rescued in 1893 by the Great Northern Railway and the Midland Railway, becoming the Midland & Great Northern Joint Railway (M&GNJR). With a network of 180 route miles, this was the largest joint railway in Britain. Nicknamed the 'Muddle & Get Nowhere Railway', it fell on hard times after the Second World War, and most of it was closed to passengers on 2 March 1959. A year later, a sharp curve was laid at Themelthorpe to link the former GER route from Wroxham and Aylsham with the former M&GNJR route to Norwich City. Freight traffic continued to serve Norwich City station until 1969 – the distance between the two stations in Norwich via the Themelthorpe Curve was around 40 miles! The curve remained in use until 1983 to transport concrete blocks to build motorway bridges from a factory at Lenwade.

Since closure, almost the entire route of the two railways between Norwich and Aylsham via Themelthorpe Curve has been reopened as a level, traffic-free footpath and cycleway known as Marriott's Way – so named after the long-serving Chief Engineer and Manager of the M&GNJR, William Marriott. The well-signposted railway path starts close to the site of Norwich City station, following the River Wensum and crossing it several times on the A-framed railway bridges unique to this route. Marriott's Way is a haven for wildlife; its green corridor – much of it mixed woodland - supports a wide variety of bird, insect and plant life throughout the year. There is also much to interest lovers of old railways: Attlebridge station is now a private residence, as is the superbly restored one at Lenwade; concrete sculptures are a reminder of the line's final years; restored Whitwell & Reepham station is now home to a preservation society which operates steam trains and proposes reopening the line around Themelthorpe Curve to Reepham station; restored Reepham station is now a tea room; Cawston station is a private residence; Aylsham station is now the terminus of the 15-in-gauge Bure Valley Railway to Wroxham.

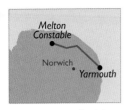

Melton Constable

Norwich

Yarmouth

Weavers' Way

ORIGINAL LINE
41½ miles

LENGTH OPEN TO WALKERS & CYCLISTS
12 miles

ORIGINAL ROUTE OPERATOR
Yarmouth & North Norfolk Railway/Eastern & Midlands Railway

LINE OPEN TO PASSENGERS
1877/1883–1959

OS LANDRANGER
133

REFRESHMENT POINTS
Aylsham, North Walsham, Stalham

CAR PARKING
Aylsham, Felmingham, North Walsham, Benngate, Briggate, East Ruston, Stalham

NATIONAL RAIL NETWORK STATION
North Walsham

HERITAGE RAILWAY
Bure Valley Railway

For route map see pages 88–89

MELTON CONSTABLE
⇉
YARMOUTH

What became a meandering cross-country route linking the Midlands to the Norfolk coast started life as a collection of local, unconnected railway companies. The first of these was the Great Yarmouth & Stalham Light Railway which had opened in stages between these two towns by 1880, in the meantime changing its name to Yarmouth & North Norfolk Light Railway. Changing its name once again to the Yarmouth & North Norfolk Railway, the company extended its line from Stalham to North Walsham in 1881 and then amalgamated with the Lynn & Fakenham Railway (L&FR) and three other companies to become the Eastern & Midlands Railway (E&MR) in 1883.

Meanwhile, to the west, the L&FR had completed its line from King's Lynn to Melton Constable in 1882. The missing link between here and North Walsham was opened by the newly formed E&MR in 1883. With a sprawling 180-mile network, most of it single track, the E&MR was soon in financial trouble and turned to the Great Northern and Midland railways for help. Thus the Midland & Great Northern Joint Railway was born in 1893, with its HQ in King's Lynn and works at Melton Constable.

The Big Four Grouping of 1923 saw the M&GNJR taken over by the newly formed London, Midland & Scottish Railway and the London & North Eastern Railway (LNER). In 1936, the LNER took over complete control and closed much of Melton Constable Works. Through-running was the lifeblood of the railway, with passenger trains from Kings Cross, the Midlands and the North to Cromer, Norwich and Yarmouth keeping it busy during the summer months along with seasonal agricultural goods traffic. This all ended with the outbreak of the Second World War.

With increasing competition from road transport, the post-war years saw a rapid decline in both local and through traffic and, apart from the Cromer to Melton Constable section which lasted another 5 years, the M&GNJR network was closed completely on 2 March 1959.

Since closure, two sections of the M&GNJR have been incorporated into the Weavers' Way Long Distance Path, linking at Aylsham with Marriott's Way from Norwich (see opposite page). The first section between Aylsham and North Walsham features dedicated car parks at each end and one at Felmingham station, now a private residence. The viaduct over the River Bure in Aylsham is also part of the Way. While the railway route south of North Walsham now forms part of the A149, it is rejoined by the Weavers' Way at Benngate, following it for the next 5 miles to Stalham, en route crossing the disued North Walsham & Dilham Canal and passing the derelict remains of Honing station where the two platforms, remains of the waiting room, signal box foundations and M&GN-style lattice fencing are hidden in the undergrowth. South of Stalham, the railway's route is now used by the realigned A149 as far as Potter Heigham where remains of the platforms and station buildings survive. An isolated section on the coast between California and Caister-on-Sea can also be followed on foot.

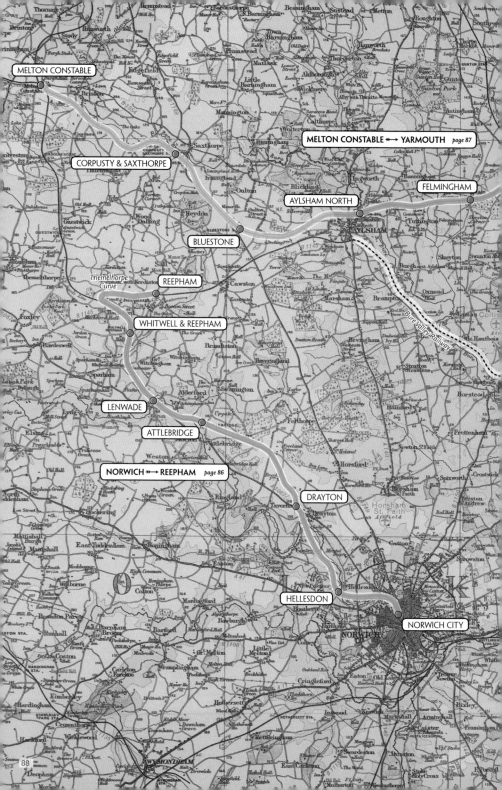

MELTON CONSTABLE

CORPUSTY & SAXTHORPE

MELTON CONSTABLE »»→ YARMOUTH *page 87*

FELMINGHAM

AYLSHAM NORTH

BLUESTONE

Themelthorpe
Curve

REEPHAM

WHITWELL & REEPHAM

Bure Valley Railway

LENWADE

ATTLEBRIDGE

NORWICH »»→ REEPHAM *page 86*

DRAYTON

HELLESDON

NORWICH CITY

RTH WALSHAM TOWN

HONING

STALHAM

SUTTON STAITHE HALT

CATFIELD

POTTER HEIGHAM

POTTER HEIGHAM BRIDGE HALT

MARTHAM for ROLLESBY

HEMSBY

CALIFORNIA HALT

LITTLE ORMESBY HALT

GREAT ORMESBY

SCRATBY HALT

CAISTER CAMP HALT

CAISTER-ON-SEA

NEWTOWN HALT

YARMOUTH BEACH

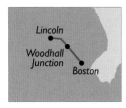

LINCOLN
⇒
BOSTON

The Water Rail Way

ORIGINAL LINE
31 miles

LENGTH OPEN TO WALKERS & CYCLISTS
17½ miles

ORIGINAL ROUTE OPERATOR
Great Northern Railway

LINE OPEN TO PASSENGERS
1848–1963/1970

OS LANDRANGER
121, 122, 131

NATIONAL CYCLE NETWORK
Route 1

REFRESHMENT POINTS
Lincoln, Bardney, Woodhall Junction, Langrick, Boston

CAR PARKING
Lincoln, Bardney, Woodhall Junction, Langrick, Boston

NATIONAL RAIL NETWORK STATIONS
Lincoln, Boston

In 1846, the Great Northern Railway was authorized by Parliament to build a main line from London to York via Grantham, Retford and Doncaster, with a loop from Peterborough to Lincoln via Spalding and Boston. Construction of the Peterborough to Lincoln loop line was rapid across a flat landscape with the section between Boston and Lincoln closely following the navigable River Witham. This opened in 1848, but it took until 1852 before the main line between London and Doncaster and thence to York with running powers over the York & North Midland Railway was completed.

The Lincolnshire Loop had a short life as a main line, and it was soon relegated to a minor status following the opening of a more direct line to Lincoln via Honington in 1867. Intermediate stations on the Loop were provided at Langrick, Dogdyke, Tattershall, Kirkstead, Stixwould, Southrey, Bardney, Five Mile House and Washingborough. In 1855, Kirkstead was renamed Woodhall Junction when the short branch line to Horncastle was opened. Bardney became a junction with the opening of the steeply graded line across the Lincolnshire Wolds to Louth in 1876. The opening of the New Line in 1913 between a junction just south of Woodhall Junction to Bellwater Junction on the Boston to Louth line provided a much shorter route for trains between Lincoln and the resort of Skegness, providing the Loop with much additional excursion traffic during summer.

Traffic went into decline following the Second World War with the Bardney to Louth line closing to passengers in 1951, and the Horncastle branch similarly in 1954. The 1963 'Beeching Report' spelt the end for most of Lincolnshire's railways and the Lincoln to Boston line was closed in two stages. First to go was the section between Woodhall Junction and Boston which closed on 17 June 1963. The northern section and the New Line to Skegness held on until 5 October 1970 when they too closed.

In recent years, much of the Lincoln Loop has been reopened by Sustrans and the Lincolnshire Waterways Partnership as a footpath and cycleway known as the Water Rail Way. Featuring 14 pieces of specially commissioned sculptures by local artists, the Way starts near Lincoln station and joins the railway trackbed at Washingborough where the station building is a private residence. There is much of railway interest along the northern section of the Way as it closely follows the River Witham: Bardney station, now a heritage centre; station buildings, platforms and signal boxes at Southrey and Stixwould; Woodhall Junction (now a private residence) with its station building, platforms and level crossing gates. South of here, the Way temporarily leaves the trackbed to follow quiet roads to Langrick, en route a short detour can be made to the station building at Tattershall which is now an art gallery. The Way rejoins the railway trackbed at Langrick where a café now stands on the site of the station, closely following the Witham through Anton's Gowt to the outskirts of Boston.

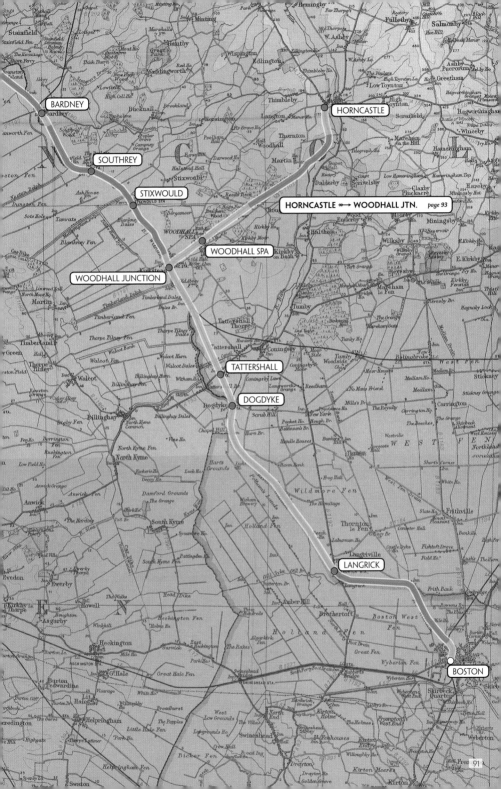

BARDNEY

SOUTHREY

STIXWOULD

HORNCASTLE

HORNCASTLE ⟷ WOODHALL JTN.   *page 93*

WOODHALL SPA

WOODHALL JUNCTION

TATTERSHALL

DOGDYKE

LANGRICK

BOSTON

91

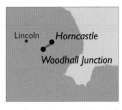

HORNCASTLE
⇥→
WOODHALL JUNCTION

The Spa Trail

ORIGINAL LINE
7 miles

LENGTH OPEN TO WALKERS & CYCLISTS
3 miles

ORIGINAL ROUTE OPERATOR
Great Northern Railway

LINE OPEN TO PASSENGERS
1855–1954

OS LANDRANGER
121, 122

REFRESHMENT POINTS
Horncastle, Woodhall Spa

CAR PARKING
Horncastle, Woodhall Spa

For route map see page 91

Companion of Captain Cook on his first great voyage around the world, the naturalist and botanist Sir Joseph Banks came to live in Horncastle, Lincolnshire in the 1790s. Leasing the Manor of Horncastle and becoming High Sheriff of the county, he was also instrumental in the building of the Horncastle Canal which linked the River Witham near Tattershall with the market town. Engineered by William Jessop, the canal opened in 1802 and despite being a financial success was overshadowed by the opening of the Great Northern Railway's (GNR) Lincoln Loop line in 1848 (see page 90). Soon Horncastle's merchants, farmers and businessmen were demanding their own railway to serve the town which then lay 7 miles from the nearest station at Kirkstead. To this end, the Horncastle Railway was formed in 1854 and with few engineering obstacles was opened between Kirkstead and Horncastle on 26 September 1854. Surprisingly the 7-mile single-track line was one of the few in Lincolnshire that was profitable, and, despite being worked from the outset by the GNR, remained independent until the 'Big Four Grouping' of 1923. The only intermediate station was at Woodhall Spa, but plans to turn the village into a major health resort failed despite the station there being rebuilt in 1896 and Kirkstead being renamed Woodhall Junction in 1922.

The Horncastle branch survived mainly on goods traffic – outgoing agricultural produce and incoming coal was its life-blood while passenger traffic was relatively light. Following the Second World War and the subsequent nationalization of Britain's railways in 1948, the newly formed British Transport Commission's Branch Lines Committee soon swung into action by putting loss-making rural lines under close scrutiny. One of its many victims was the Horncastle branch which closed to passengers on 13 September 1954. Freight services lingered on, but faced with increasing competition from road transport, these ended on 6 April 1971.

Following closure, 3 miles of the trackbed of the line between Horncastle and Woodhall Spa was purchased by Lincolnshire County Council, who reopened it as a traffic-free bridleway, footpath and cycleway known as The Spa Trail. It also forms part of the Viking Way Long Distance Path. The station building in Horncastle was demolished in the 1980s, but one of the grain warehouses once served by the railway survives as residential flats. The start of the Trail is south of the town at Thornton Lodge Farm where there is a car park, and from here it follows the defunct Horncastle Canal to the only major engineering feature on the line, Martin Bridge. After leaving the canal behind, the Trail skirts woodlands to end at a car park at Sandy Lane. A non-railway footpath continues from here for 2 miles alongside a golf course to Woodhall Spa where the station has long ago disappeared to make way for commercial development. It is but a short distance from the village to Kirkstead Bridge, the Water Rail Way (see page 90) and the restored Woodhall Junction station.

LEFT TOP:
LINCOLN TO BOSTON
Stixwould station is a stopping off point for users of the Water Rail Way.

LEFT LOWER:
Autumn leaves on the Spa Trail between Horncastle and Woodhall Spa.

CENTRAL
ENGLAND

STONEHOUSE ⇢ NAILSWORTH

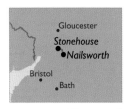

Gloucester
Stonehouse
•Nailsworth
Bristol
•
•Bath

Stroud Valley Trail

ORIGINAL LINE
5¾ miles

LENGTH OPEN TO WALKERS & CYCLISTS
4¾ miles

ORIGINAL ROUTE OPERATOR
Midland Railway

LINE OPEN TO PASSENGERS
1867–1947

OS LANDRANGER
162

NATIONAL CYCLE NETWORK
Route 45

REFRESHMENT POINTS
Dudbridge, Nailsworth

CAR PARKING
Dudbridge, Nailsworth

NATIONAL RAIL NETWORK STATION
Stroud

The Cotswold town of Stroud had been a centre for weaving and brewing since the 16th century. Transport links were much improved in 1779 when the Stroudwater Canal opened from Framilode on the River Severn, and the opening of the Thames & Severn Canal between Stroud and the River Thames at Lechlade via the 3,817-yd Sapperton Tunnel further improved the town's links with the outside world.

Railways first reached Stroud in 1845 when the broad-gauge Great Western Railway extended its line from Swindon and Kemble to Gloucester while, a few miles to the west, the Bristol & Gloucester Railway (soon to become part of the Midland Railway) had already opened its line in 1844 with a station at Stonehouse. Proposals to build a railway from here alongside the Stroudwater Canal and then up the Nailsworth Valley to link up with the GWR's branch line to Malmesbury came to nothing. Eventually the Stonehouse & Nailsworth Railway received authorization in 1863 to build a 5¾-mile single-track branch line along this route to Nailsworth. The railway opened on 4 February 1867 but by then the company was in dire financial straits – negotiations with the Midland Railway for a takeover were protracted with authorization only coming in 1878.

With the Midland in control, the company sought to extend into GWR territory by building a 1½-mile steeply-graded branch line from Dudbridge, on the Nailsworth branch, to Stroud. Featuring a 9-arch viaduct on the approach to Stroud Wallgate station, this opened for goods in 1885 and to passengers a year later. Freight was always the lifeblood of the two branches and the meagre passenger service just about survived through the Second World War before being temporarily suspended due to a national coal shortage on 16 June 1947. It was never reinstated and was officially withdrawn on 8 June 1949. Freight trains (steam-hauled until the end of 1965) continued to trundle up and down the two branches until 1 June 1966 when the lines closed completely.

Since closure, much of the trackbed of the Nailsworth branch has been reopened as a footpath and cycleway known as the Stroud Valley Trail. At its western end the Trail starts close to the Stroudwater Canal near to the site of Ryeford station which has been long-demolished to make way for improvements to the A419. Heading east, the Trail parallels the canal and the meandering River Frome to reach the site of Dudbridge station, en route passing through a linear orchard of apple and pear trees. The station is long gone but a high retaining wall survives complete with commemorative plaque. The Trail now heads south along the tranquil Nailsworth Valley and past the site of Woodchester station before diving under the A46. The last stretch to Nailsworth passes through woodland high above the restored Dunkirk Mills with the final approach skirting round the restored terminus station building and goods shed before ending in the old goods yard close to the 16th-century Egypt Mill (now a hotel), the railway warehouse and the former Railway Hotel.

OPPOSITE TOP:
The Stroud Valley Trail passes through woodland, high above the restored Dunkirk Mills at Nailsworth.

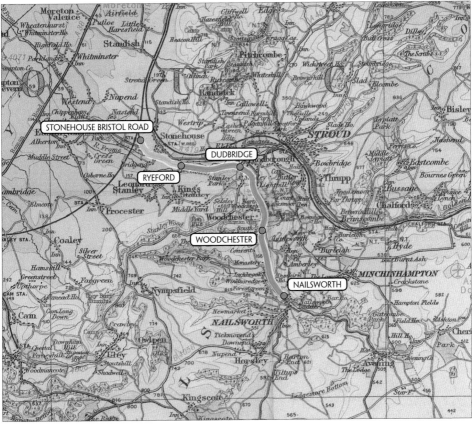

FOREST OF DEAN

Gloucester

Forest of Dean

Bristol

Forest of Dean Family Cycle Trail

ORIGINAL LINE
11 miles

LENGTH OPEN TO WALKERS & CYCLISTS
11 miles

ORIGINAL ROUTE OPERATOR
Severn & Wye Railway

LINE OPEN TO PASSENGERS
1875–1929

OS LANDRANGER
162

NATIONAL CYCLE NETWORK
42 (part)

REFRESHMENT POINTS
Parkend, Cannop, Cinderford

CAR PARKING
Parkend, Cannop, Cinderford

NATIONAL RAIL NETWORK STATION
Lydney

HERITAGE RAILWAY
Dean Forest Railway

By the early 19th century the Forest of Dean in Gloucestershire was a hive of industrial activity. For centuries the output of the many small iron ore and coal mines had been transported down to the Severn and Wye rivers on horseback for onward shipment, but the introduction of primitive horse-drawn tramways and a canal speeded up this process. The largest of the operators was the Severn & Wye Railway & Canal Company (S&WR&C), which was incorporated in 1810 and by 1813 had opened a network of 3 ft 6 in plateways and the short Lydney Canal. In 1851, the broad-gauge South Wales Railway opened along the west shore of the River Severn between Gloucester and Chepstow, but the S&WR&C took another 18 years before it converted its plateway between Lydney and Speech House Road to broad gauge and introduced steam haulage. This conversion to broad gauge was short-lived, as by 1872 the line had been relaid to standard gauge and extended to Lydbrook Junction where it met the Ross & Monmouth Railway. At the same time, the network was also extended by the opening of a mineral loop line from Drybrook Road to Whitecroft to serve a number of collieries. Passenger services were introduced in 1875, the same year that a branch from Parkend to Coleford opened.

In 1879, the S&WR&C merged with the Severn Bridge Railway to become the Severn & Wye & Severn Bridge Joint Railway, but the new company struggled financially and was eventually rescued by the Midland and Great Western railways and run as a joint railway. Passenger services were withdrawn between Lydney Town, Coleford, Cinderford and Lydbrook Junction as early as 1929, while the collision by a petrol tanker with the Severn Bridge in 1960 abruptly ended the Lydney to Sharpness service. As collieries closed, the network of mineral lines in the Forest had already shrunk by the 1950s with the last one, Northern United, closing in 1965. Stone traffic from a quarry on the Coleford branch ended in 1967, and the Forest of Dean's railways finally fell silent.

Since closure, much of the Severn & Wye network in the forest has been reopened as footpaths and cycleways, while the section from Lydney Town to Parkend has been reopened as the heritage Dean Forest Railway. Route 42 of the National Cycle Network heads north along the trackbed from Parkend to the site of Cannop Colliery, en route passing the site of Speech House Road station where a station nameboard mounted on railway sleepers marks the spot. At Cannop the Pedalabikeaway Cycle Centre hires out bikes for cyclists to explore the 11-mile circular Forest of Dean Family Cycle Trail which follows the Severn & Wye route northwards to Drybrook Road station then south along the old Mineral Loop line, past the sites of several collieries, before heading back to Cannop. There are links along former railway routes to Lydbrook and Cinderford – at the latter the Cinderford Linear Park follows the former GWR line between Bilson Green and the restored railway halt at Ruspidge.

OPPOSITE TOP:
GWR 4-4-0 No 3717 City of Truro at Parkend station on the Dean Forest Railway.

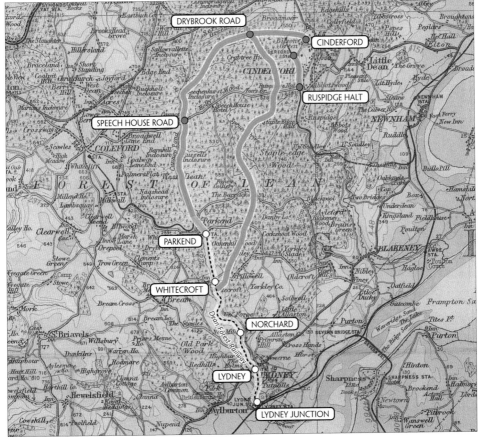

BEWDLEY ⇝ TENBURY WELLS

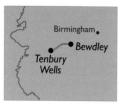

Wyre Forest
Railway Trail

ORIGINAL LINE
14 miles

**LENGTH OPEN TO
WALKERS & CYCLISTS**
2 miles

ORIGINAL ROUTE OPERATOR
Great Western Railway

LINE OPEN TO PASSENGERS
1864–1962

OS LANDRANGER
138

NATIONAL CYCLE NETWORK
Route 45

REFRESHMENT POINTS
Bewdley, Wyre Forest
Visitor Centre

CAR PARKING
Bewdley, Wyre Forest
Visitor Centre

HERITAGE RAILWAY STATION
Bewdley

HERITAGE RAILWAY
Severn Valley Railway

OPPOSITE LOWER:
Bewdley station was built for
the opening of the Severn Valley
railway in 1862. Although
closed to passenger servicies
100 years later, it's still in use
today as part of the Severn
Valley Heritage Railway.

The Tenbury & Bewdley Railway (T&BR) was incorporated in 1860 to build a 14-mile single-track branch line from Bewdley, on the Severn Valley Railway (SVR), to Tenbury Wells. Here, it was to meet the 5½-mile branch line from Woofferton, on the Hereford to Shrewsbury main line, which had opened along the route of the defunct Leominster Canal in 1861.

The T&BR opened in 1864 and together with the line from Woofferton, was worked by the GWR from the start, eventually becoming absorbed by that company in 1869. From Bewdley, it paralleled the SVR line for one mile before heading west across the River Severn on Dowles Bridge and then through the Wyre Forest. Serving intermediate stations at Wyre Forest, Cleobury Mortimer, Neen Sollars and Newnham Bridge, this rural railway led a fairly leisurely existence although the eastern section became busier when the 12¾-mile Cleobury Mortimer & Ditton Priors Light Railway opened in 1908. This branch line initially served quarries at Clee Hill and later an Admiralty munitions depot at Ditton Priors. Absorbed by the GWR in 1922, it lost its passenger service in 1938 and was taken over by the Admiralty in 1957.

In 1961, the Woofferton–Tenbury Wells–Bewdley passenger service was threatened with closure, and by this time the few passengers remaining were easily accommodated in pre-war diesel railcars. At the eleventh hour the Tenbury Wells to Bewdley service was reprieved, but the line to Woofferton closed completely on 31 July 1961. A sparse weekday service continued to operate on the rest of the line for another year, but the end came on 1 August 1962 when all passenger services ceased and the line west of Cleobury Mortimer closed completely. East of here, it remained open for freight trains from the Admiralty depot at Ditton Priors until 16 April 1965.

Following closure of the railway, most of the attractive station buildings along the line have been converted into private residences, but west of Wyre Forest station the railway's route along the Rea and Teme Valleys to Tenbury Wells is only recognizable in the form of embankments, cuttings and bridges as none of this has so far been reopened as a footpath. The exception is the 2-mile wooded section north of Bewdley, on the west bank of the Severn, and through the Wyre Forest which is now a footpath and cycleway. Owned by the Forestry Commission, the 6,500-acre forest is designated a National Nature Reserve while many of the trails and paths that criss-cross it can be accessed from a visitor centre on the A417 3 miles west of Bewdley. The railway path starts at a car park at Dry Mill Lane 1 mile northeast of Bewdley – to reach it follow the NCN Route 45 signs from the town centre. To the east lies the River Severn where the gaunt brick and stone piers of Dowles Bridge can be clearly seen by passengers on the heritage Severn Valley Railway. The remains of the bridge can also be reached on foot along both banks of the river from Bewdley.

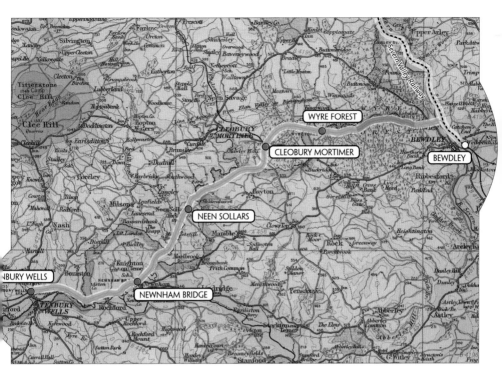

WYRE FOREST

CLEOBURY MORTIMER

BEWDLEY

BEWDLEY

NEEN SOLLARS

NBURY WELLS

NEWNHAM BRIDGE

STRATFORD-UPON-AVON ⇥ HONEYBOURNE

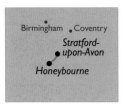

Birmingham • Coventry
Stratford-
• upon-Avon
Honeybourne

Stratford Greenway

ORIGINAL LINE
9 miles

LENGTH OPEN TO WALKERS & CYCLISTS
5 miles

ORIGINAL ROUTE OPERATOR
Oxford, Worcester & Wolverhampton Railway

LINE OPEN TO PASSENGERS
1859–1969

OS LANDRANGER
150, 151

NATIONAL CYCLE NETWORK
Route 5

REFRESHMENT POINTS
Stratford-upon-Avon, Milcote

CAR PARKING
Stratford-upon-Avon, Milcote

NATIONAL RAIL NETWORK STATION
Stratford-upon-Avon

The first railway to reach the town of Stratford-upon-Avon was a branch line from Honeybourne which was opened by the Oxford, Worcester & Wolverhampton Railway (OW&WR) in 1859. Known for good reasons as the 'Old Worse & Worse', the OW&WR morphed into the West Midlands Railway in 1860 and finally became part of an enlarged Great Western Railway (GWR) in 1863. The next railway to reach Stratford was the Stratford-upon-Avon Railway which opened its branch line from Hatton in 1860. Initially both railways had separate termini in Stratford, but these were replaced by a single joint station in 1861.

Until 1908, Stratford was at the end of two connected branch lines, but in that year it became an important stop on the GWR's new main line between Birmingham and Cheltenham. This was achieved by the opening of the new North Warwickshire Line from Tyseley to Bearley where it joined the existing Stratford-upon-Avon Railway to Stratford, thence along the former OW&W route to Honeybourne and southwards from here on a new main line to Cheltenham Malvern Road. The new GWR line was an important north–south corridor for trains between the Midlands and the Southwest via Bristol, and South Wales via Gloucester. An innovative express service on the latter route of streamlined diesel railcars introduced in the 1930s was highly successful, continuing with diesel multiple units into the 1960s. Summer holiday traffic was also heavy between the Midlands and holiday resorts in Devon and Cornwall, continuing until 1965 – steam-hauled to the end. Local traffic was less important, and the stopping train service between Stratford and Cheltenham had ceased in 1960 along with the closure of intermediate stations, no doubt to clear a path for the heavy iron-ore trains that were introduced that year from Northamptonshire to South Wales via Stratford. Passenger trains continued until 1969 when the Worcester– Honeybourne–Stratford service was withdrawn, and from that date the route was only used by through freight trains and the occasional diverted passenger train. A derailment of a freight train north of Cheltenham in 1976 closed the line as a through route for good although the section from Cheltenham Racecourse to Broadway has since reopened as the heritage Gloucestershire–Warwickshire Railway.

Since closure the 5-mile section of the line between the Seven Meadows Roundabout at Stratford and Long Marston has been reopened as a footpath and cycleway known as the Stratford Greenway. There is car parking at the Stratford end where several old BR coaches are now home to a café and cycle hire shop. About 1 mile southwest of here the Greenway passes Stratford racecourse and crosses the River Avon on Stannals Bridge, a substantial girder structure, before reaching the site of Milcote station where the platforms survive and an old BR coach is home to another café. From this halfway point the Greenway continues southward to reach Long Marston where it links up with the Heart of England Way Long Distance Path. The track from here to Honeybourne serves a former MOD depot which is used to store surplus locomotives and rolling stock.

OPPOSITE LOWER:
The Greenway south of Stratford-upon-Avon crosses the River Avon on Stennals Bridge.

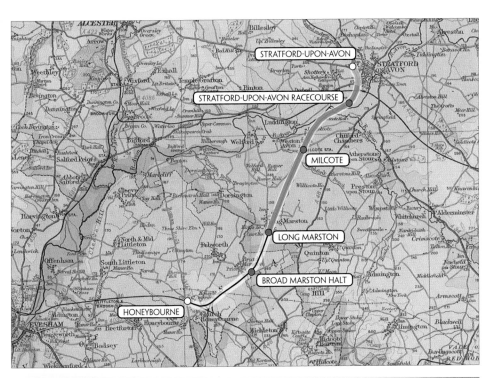

STRATFORD-UPON-AVON

STRATFORD-UPON-AVON RACECOURSE

MILCOTE

LONG MARSTON

BROAD MARSTON HALT

HONEYBOURNE

STAFFORD ⤞ WELLINGTON

Derby •
Stafford •
Wellington •
Birmingham •

Newport to Stafford Greenway

**ORIGINAL LINE
(TO WELLINGTON)**
18¾ miles

**LENGTH OPEN TO
WALKERS & CYCLISTS**
12 miles

ORIGINAL ROUTE OPERATOR
London &
North Western Railway

LINE OPEN TO PASSENGERS
1849–1964

OS LANDRANGER
127

NATIONAL CYCLE NETWORK
Route 55

REFRESHMENT POINTS
Stafford, Derrington,
Haughton, Gnossal

CAR PARKING
Stafford, Derrington,
Haughton, Gnossal

**NATIONAL RAIL
NETWORK STATION**
Stafford

The coming of the railways in the early 19th century soon saw Britain's canal network in decline. However, several canal companies in the West Midlands had the foresight to join forces in 1846 and form the Shropshire Union Railways & Canal Company (SUR&CC) with the aim of building railways along existing canals. In reality the company only built one railway and had a joint share in another. The former was the double-track railway between Stafford and Wellington, in Shropshire, while the latter was the main line between Wellington and Shrewsbury which it shared with the Shrewsbury & Birmingham Railway.

All this was not lost on the London & North Western Railway (LNWR), and in 1847 it leased the SUR&CC's canals and its planned railways. With no major engineering features, the Stafford to Wellington line opened in 1849 and was worked by the LNWR and, with the completion of the Shrewsbury to Wellington line in the same year, gave the company direct access to Shropshire. The LNWR absorbed the SUR&CC in 1922. With intermediate stations at Haughton, Gnosall, Newport, Donnington, Trench Crossing and Hadley, the line was served by through stopping trains running to and from Shrewsbury. Although local freight traffic was light, consisting mainly of coal and munitions from Donnington, the route was heavily used by through freight trains. Listed for closure in the

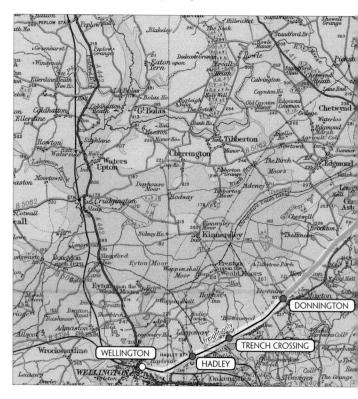

'Beeching Report', the line lost its passenger service on 7 September 1964 although through freight traffic continued until complete closure east of Donnington in July 1967. The 3¾-mile stub at the western end remained open to serve a colliery at Donnington until 1979, but the track remained intact and today serves the Telford International Freight Park.

Since closure the 12 miles of the Stafford to Newport section has been reopened as a footpath and cycleway known as the Newport to Stafford Greenway. The route provides a habitat for plants and wildlife and is one of the best areas in the county for butterflies because of the abundance of plants and wildflowers. In 1999 the Greenway was incorporated into the 41-mile Way for the Millennium which mainly follows canal towpaths from Burton-upon-Trent before joining the old railway route at Stafford.

While none of the stations along this route have survived, all the bridges are intact. Westwards from Stafford the Greenway passes under the M6 motorway to the village of Derrington and the nearby Red Lion pub. To the west of the village lies Smallbrook Hall, which dates from the 14th century, and a railway crossing keeper's cottage where remains of the level crossing gates can still be seen. Continuing westward the route passes through the site of Haughton station where the waiting room and ticket office were once under the impressive road overbridge. The Greenway continues westwards, passing through a long cutting before arriving at the village of Gnosall. Here it passes over the Shropshire Union Canal with its leisure cruisers, locks and the waterside Navigation Inn. Beyond Gnosall the Greenway heads through open countryside before ending at Outwoods, 2 miles east of Newport.

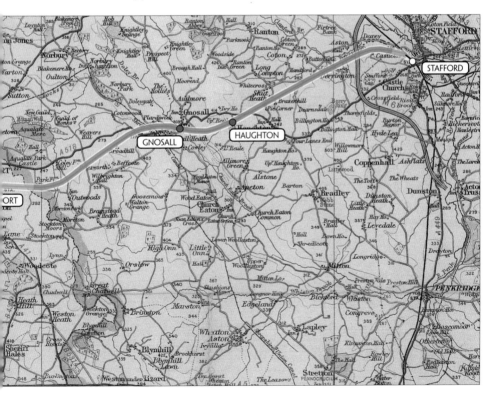

Market
Harborough

Coventry | Kettering

Northampton

Brampton
Valley Way

ORIGINAL LINE
18 miles

**LENGTH OPEN TO
WALKERS & CYCLISTS**
14 miles

ORIGINAL ROUTE OPERATOR
London &
North Western Railway

LINE OPEN TO PASSENGERS
1859–1960

OS LANDRANGER
141, 152

NATIONAL CYCLE NETWORK
Route 6

REFRESHMENT POINTS
Market Harborough,
Brixworth, Brampton,
Boughton, Northampton

CAR PARKING
Market Harborough,
Kelmarsh, Draughton
Crossing, Brampton,
Boughton, Northampton

**NATIONAL RAIL
NETWORK STATIONS**
Market Harborough,
Northampton

HERITAGE RAILWAY
Northampton &
Lamport Railway

MARKET HARBOROUGH
⇶
NORTHAMPTON

Built to serve the burgeoning Northamptonshire iron-ore industry, the 18-mile, single-track line between Market Harborough and Northampton was opened by the London & North Western Railway in 1859. The major engineering works were the tunnels at Kelmarsh and Oxendon. On opening there were intermediate stations at Kelmarsh, Lamport, Brixford and Pitsford & Brampton – the latter built to serve the 5th Earl of Spencer of Althorp Hall. Stations at Clipston & Oxendon and Spratton were opened in 1863 and 1864 respectively, at about the same time that the line was doubled and provided with extra single-bore tunnels at Kelmarsh and Oxendon.

Passenger traffic was of secondary importance on this primarily freight-carrying line and mainly consisted of a stopping service which by 1948 included three trains starting or finishing their journey at Nottingham. The 64¾ miles between Northampton and Nottingham could take up to 3 hours. With dwindling numbers of passengers using the line, this local service was withdrawn on 4 January 1960, but through freight trains continued for many more years. While the intermediate stations had closed, through passenger trains were re-introduced in 1969 but withdrawn again in 1972 – freight trains continued until 15 August 1981.

In 1987 13 miles of the trackbed was purchased by Northamptonshire County Council and 1 mile at the northern end by Leicestershire County Council. It was reopened as a linear park known as the Brampton Valley Way in 1993, and today it also forms part of the Midshires Way Long Distance Path. Never far from the parallel A508, the footpath and cycleway starts close to a car park at the Bell Inn, Northampton Road in Market Harborough and soon enters open country. Near Great Oxendon, one of the two single-bore tunnels is now used by the Brampton Valley Way – the 462-yd tunnel is unlit so torches or cycle lights are recommended. Further south the Way reaches the site of Kelmarsh station where there is a car park and picnic site. South of here the Way passes over one of the original road overbridges before reaching the single-bore 322-yd Kelmarsh Tunnel. Travelling through this unlit tunnel on foot or by bike is an eerie experience.

Beyond Kelmarsh Tunnel the Way dives under the A14 dual carriageway before reaching the car park and picnic site at Draughton Crossing. Continuing southwards through open country, the tree-lined Way crosses the A508 at the site of Lamport station before heading on to Brixworth. South of Brixworth the Way soon meets up with the Northampton & Lamport Railway, a heritage railway that opened to the public in 1996 and is planning to extend northwards over the River Nene to Brixworth. The Way shares the trackbed for 2 miles through the railway's headquarters at Pitsford & Brampton station to a new southern terminus at Boughton where there is car parking and a pub. South of Boughton the Way continues along the railway trackbed to the site of the junction with the Northampton Loop Line before ending its journey through the streets of Northampton to the town's station.

MARKET HARBOROUGH

CLIPSTON & OXENDON

KELMARSH

LAMPORT

BRIXWORTH

SPRATTON

Northampton & Lamport Railway

PITSFORD & BRAMPTON

NORTHAMPTON

MARPLE »→ MACCLESFIELD

Manchester
Marple
Sheffield
Macclesfield

Middlewood Trail

ORIGINAL LINE
10½ miles

**LENGTH OPEN TO
WALKERS & CYCLISTS**
10 miles

ORIGINAL ROUTE OPERATOR
North Staffordshire Railway
and Manchester, Sheffield &
Lincolnshire Railway

LINE OPEN TO PASSENGERS
1869–1970

OS LANDRANGER
109, 118

NATIONAL CYCLE NETWORK
Route 55

REFRESHMENT POINTS
Marple, Poynton, Wood Lanes,
Bollington, Macclesfield

CAR PARKING
Marple, Poynton, Wood Lanes,
Bollington, Macclesfield

**NATIONAL RAIL
NETWORK STATIONS**
Marple Rose Hill,
Middlewood, Macclesfield

Born out of a desire by Macclesfield businessmen for a direct railway to Manchester, the Macclesfield, Bollington & Marple Railway (MB&MR) was incorporated in 1864 to be built and operated jointly by the North Staffordshire Railway and the Manchester, Sheffield & Lincolnshire Railway. The railway was built to accommodate double track and the only engineering feature of note was a 23-arch viaduct at Bollington. With intermediate stations at Marple Rose Hill, High Lane, Poynton and Bollington, the 10½-mile railway opened for passengers in 1869. A higher-level interchange station with the London & North Western Railway's Stockport to Buxton line at Middlewood was opened in 1879, and a curve was also added here that joined these two lines in 1885.

The 1920s and 1930s saw the line kept busy with workman's trains to and from Manchester and an intensive shuttle service between Macclesfield and Bollington. However, the post-war years saw increased competition from road transport, and the introduction of diesel multiple units in 1957 failed to stem the dwindling traffic south of Rose Hill. The loss-making line was listed for closure in the 1963 'Beeching Report' and, despite strong local objections, the section from Rose Hill to Macclesfield closed on 5 January 1970.

Following closure, the trackbed was reopened in 1985 as a 10-mile footpath and cycleway known as the Middlewood Trail. The Trail starts at Marple Rose Hill station, served by trains from Manchester, where there is a car park and the adjacent Railway Inn. From here it heads south out into open countryside, passing over the western entrance to Disley Tunnel – still open for business on the Manchester to Sheffield main line – to the site of High Lane station. Here the Trail passes through a narrow tunnel under the A6 before reaching Middlewood station. Once an interchange station, the lower station at Middlewood is still served by trains running between Manchester and Buxton, while the iron railway bridge above it now carries the Middlewood Trail. The low-level station at Middlewood is one of the very few in Britain that have no road access and is reached along woodland paths or from the Middlewood Trail.

South of Middlewood the Trail passes under several road overbridges, first passing the site of Jackson's Brickworks before entering Poynton station. Located close to the Macclesfield Canal where there is car parking, the Nelson Pit Visitor Centre and a café, the station site at Poynton has been landscaped with a picnic site set between the two platforms. A mile south of Poynton the canal and railway route rub shoulders at Wood Lanes where there is parking, a picnic site and café.

Keeping close company with the canal the Trail continues southward to Bollington. Here a low 23-arch viaduct carries it above the town, which can be accessed via a steep flight of steps that lead to a convenient car park. Continuing over the viaduct the Trail soon parts company with the canal and heads alongside the A523 dual carriageway into Macclesfield where it ends near the railway station.

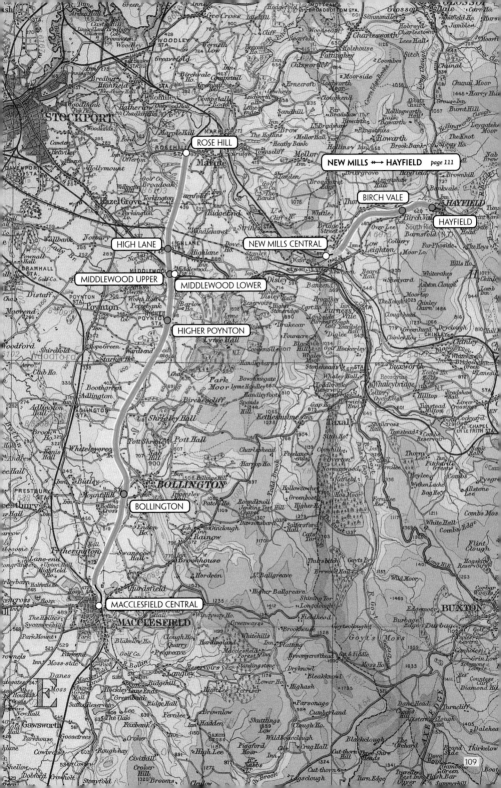

ROSE HILL

NEW MILLS ⟶ HAYFIELD   page 111

BIRCH VALE

HAYFIELD

HIGH LANE

NEW MILLS CENTRAL

MIDDLEWOOD UPPER

MIDDLEWOOD LOWER

HIGHER POYNTON

BOLLINGTON

MACCLESFIELD CENTRAL

NEW MILLS ⇾ HAYFIELD

Manchester • Hayfield
New Mills •• Sheffield

Sett Valley Trail

ORIGINAL LINE
3 miles

LENGTH OPEN TO WALKERS & CYCLISTS
2½ miles

ORIGINAL ROUTE OPERATOR
Manchester, Sheffield & Lincolnshire Railway

LINE OPEN TO PASSENGERS
1868–1970

OS LANDRANGER
110

REFRESHMENT POINTS
Hayfield, Birch Vale, New Mills

CAR PARKING
Hayfield, New Mills

NATIONAL RAIL NETWORK STATION
New Mills Central

For route map see page 109

I n its quest to reach Manchester, the Midland Railway opened a line from Millers Dale to New Mills via Dove Holes Tunnel in 1867. A year later the Manchester, Sheffield & Lincolnshire Railway (MS&LR) extended its Manchester to Hyde branch line, which had opened in 1858, to New Mills. The section of line between New Mills and Hyde Junction was vested jointly as the Sheffield & Midland Railway Companies' Committee in 1869.

In addition to extending its line from Hyde to New Mills, the MS&LR continued on up the Sett Valley to the cotton milling town of Hayfield. With an intermediate station at Birch Vale this 3-mile single-track branch line also opened in 1868. For the rest of its 102-year life the Hayfield branch was well-served by through trains to and from Manchester – here, both Central and London Road stations were served by trains to and from Hayfield until Central's closure in 1969. The branch line was very popular with walkers during the 1920s and 1930s when up to 5,000 people each weekend would travel from Manchester to trespass on the wild moorlands around Kinder Scout.

At the end of the 19th century Stockport Corporation decided to build a new reservoir at the head of the Kinder Valley, 2 miles east of Hayfield. Hundreds of navvies were housed in the town and the railway was extended up the valley to the construction site. Carrying men and materials, the railway was a familiar scene in the streets of the town until the reservoir was completed in 1912.

Although listed for closure in the 1963 'Beeching Report', the Hayfield branch hung on to life until 5 January 1970 when it closed.

Although Hayfield station was demolished in 1975, 2½ miles of the railway route from here to New Mills has since been reopened as a footpath and cycleway known as the Sett Valley Trail. The site of Hayfield station is now a car park, information centre and bus station. Much of the route of the reservoir railway from Hayfield can also be walked today.

From Hayfield the tree-lined Trail heads down the Sett Valley for a mile to the site of the long-demolished Birch Vale station. On the roadside here is a small café which has become popular with Trail users. The next 1½ miles threads down the valley before ending at New Mills. The short tunnel that was once used by the railway is now blocked up but a short walk through the town that once boasted nine cotton mills and three weaving mills ends at New Mills Central station, once the junction for the Hayfield line and still served by trains running between Manchester (via Romiley) and Sheffield via the Hope Valley. Set high on a ledge above the River Goyt, and approached down a very narrow lane, Central station has no car parking or turning space but is still worth a visit to see the refurbished MR signal box (semaphore signals were replaced by colour light signals in 2007) and the original station buildings.

LEFT TOP:
MARPLE TO MACCLESFIELD
Complete with platforms, the site of Higher Poynton station is a landscaped picnic site on the Middlewood Trail.

LEFT LOWER:
Completed in 1924, the restored Midland Railway-style at New Mills Central controlled the junction for the Hayfield branch.

ASHBOURNE ⇢ PARSLEY HAY

Manchester · Sheffield

Parsley Hay

Ashbourne · Derby

Tissington Trail

ORIGINAL LINE
13¼ miles

LENGTH OPEN TO WALKERS & CYCLISTS
13 miles

ORIGINAL ROUTE OPERATOR
London & North Western Railway

LINE OPEN TO PASSENGERS
1899–1954

OS LANDRANGER
119

NATIONAL CYCLE NETWORK
Route 68

REFRESHMENT POINTS
Ashbourne, Tissington, Parsley Hay

CAR PARKING
Ashbourne, Thorpe, Tissington, Alsop–en–le–Dale, Ruby Wood, Hartington Station, Parsley Hay

As noted on page 119, the London & North Western Railway (LNWR) purchased the Cromford & High Peak Railway in 1887, following which they rebuilt and rerouted the northern section so that it ran between Buxton and Parsley Hay, thus avoiding four steep inclines in the Goyt Valley. From a new junction at Parsley Hay, the LNWR built a line to Ashbourne that opened in 1899. The town of Ashbourne had been rail-served since 1852 when the North Staffordshire Railway opened from Rocester, but with the coming of the LNWR a new joint station was opened. The new route gave the LNWR access to the large limestone quarrying industry to the south of Buxton which provided lucrative traffic for the company. Passenger traffic in this sparsely populated part of Derbyshire was never heavy, and an experiment to operate through coaches from London Euston to Buxton via Ashbourne ended at the beginning of the First World War. Along with the all-important stone traffic, the railway also transported milk, collected from the intermediate stations in churns and despatched overnight to London.

Along with those on the former NSR line from Rocester, timetabled passenger trains were withdrawn on 1 November 1954, but the line continued to be used until 1963 by summer excursion trains for ramblers and Well Dressing ceremonies. During heavy snowfall it also provided the only link with the outside world. Freight traffic ceased between Rocester, Ashbourne and Hartington on 7 October 1963 but continued between Hartington, Parsley Hay and Hindlow until 1967. North of Hindlow the line remains open today for limestone traffic from the Lafarge quarries at Dowlow.

Following closure, the trackbed from Parsley Hay to Ashbourne was purchased by Derbyshire County Council and the Peak District National Park in 1968 and reopened in 1971 as a footpath and cycleway (one of the first in Britain) known as the Tissington Trail. At its southern end, the Trail now uses the recently reopened railway tunnel at Ashbourne, which features a gradient of 1 in 59. North of here at the cycle hire centre at Mapleton Lane, the Trail briefly dips down and up where a viaduct once stood. Continuing northwards on a slightly rising gradient, the site of Thorpe Cloud station is reached – this is at the entrance to Dovedale and was a popular destination up until closure of the line. The next station site is at Tissington where, as with others along this route, there is a car park and picnic site. Continuing northwards through the site of Alsop-en-le-Dale station, the Trail passes through Coldeaton Cutting – 60-ft-deep, ¾-mile-long – on a 4¾-mile stretch to Hartington station. Some 2 miles from the village it once served, the station site features the preserved LNWR signal box which is now used as a visitor centre. Along the final stretch, the Trail crosses Hand Dale Viaduct before entering Heathcote Cutting on the approach to Parsley Hay. Here, at the junction with the High Peak Trail (see page 119), there is a car park, cycle hire shop and café.

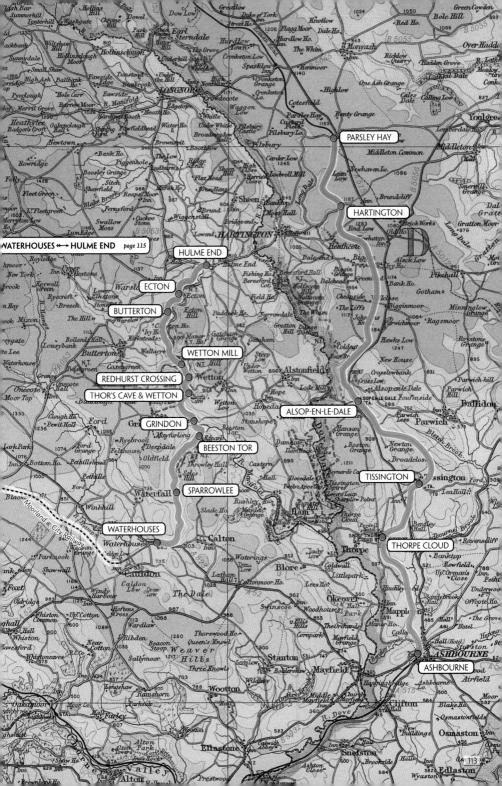

WATERHOUSES ⟶ HULME END   *page 115*

PARSLEY HAY

HARTINGTON

HULME END

ECTON

BUTTERTON

WETTON MILL

REDHURST CROSSING

THOR'S CAVE & WETTON

GRINDON

BEESTON TOR

ALSOP-EN-LE-DALE

SPARROWLEE

TISSINGTON

WATERHOUSES

THORPE CLOUD

ASHBOURNE

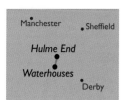

Manchester • Sheffield

Hulme End
•

Waterhouses •
• Derby

Manifold Way

ORIGINAL LINE
8 miles

**LENGTH OPEN TO
WALKERS & CYCLISTS**
8 miles

ORIGINAL ROUTE OPERATOR
North Staffordshire Railway

LINE OPEN TO PASSENGERS
1904–1934

OS LANDRANGER
119

NATIONAL CYCLE NETWORK
Route 54

REFRESHMENT POINTS
Waterhouses, Wetton Mill,
Hulme End

CAR PARKING
Waterhouses, Grindon,
Wetton Mill, Hulme End

For route map see page 113

LEFT TOP:
ASHBOURNE TO PARSLEY HAY
*The restored LNWR signalbox
at Hartington is now a café
and information centre.*

LEFT LOWER:
*The Manifold Way passes
Wetton Mill, where there is a
café, on its scenic route between
Waterhouses and Hulme End.*

WATERHOUSES
⇛
HULME END

The secluded Manifold Valley on the border of Derbyshire and Staffordshire had been a centre of copper and lead ore mining since the 16th century, but by the early 19th century the workings had become exhausted. The coming of the railways to the Peak District in the mid-19th century soon brought droves of Victorians eager to explore the region's scenery but the Manifold Valley remained virtually untouched by tourism, depending mainly on dairy farming now that mining had ceased. To open up the valley, a proposal for two railways was put forward: a 9½-mile standard-gauge line linking Leek with Waterhouses; an 8-mile narrow-gauge line linking Waterhouses with Hulme End. Both railways were to be owned and operated by the North Staffordshire Railway (NSR). Known as the Leek & Manifold Valley Light Railway, the 2-ft 6-in-gauge line featured minimal engineering structures and minimal station facilities – the only major feature was the 150-yd Swainsley Tunnel, which was built so that the view from a nearby mansion was not despoiled.

The Leek & Manifold opened in 1904 and the standard-gauge line from Leek a year later, but traffic never lived up to expectations and the little line only came to life on summer weekends when hordes of day trippers arrived from the Potteries. The only steady source of income was carrying milk which was collected in churns from the seven wayside halts along the valley. Traffic was boosted when a creamery was opened at Ecton in 1920, but within a few years the NSR had been absorbed by the newly formed London Midland & Scottish Railway (LMS) and road transport had begun to make inroads. The milk traffic was lost to road haulage in 1932 and the line closed in 1934.

Fortunately the trackbed of the railway between Waterhouses and Hulme End was given to Staffordshire County Council who opened it as a footpath in 1937. A 1½-mile section through Swainsley Tunnel to Wetton Mill has been shared with motorists since the 1950s. Known as the Manifold Way, the path starts at the site of Waterhouses station where the former NSR goods shed is a café and cycle hire centre. From here it crosses the A52, before following the meandering River Hamps, crossing it on fourteen former railway bridges before reaching the site of Beeston Tor station. Threading through the towering limestone hills the path soon enters the Manifold Valley to reach a car park at the site of Grindon station. This is the most scenic part of the route and is overlooked by the famous Thor's Cave, once inhabited by Stone Age man, set 250 ft above the valley floor. North of here the path joins company with the road through Wetton Mill where a café provides refreshments for passersby. After passing through Swainsley Tunnel, the path parts company with the road, passing the site of Ecton station and its creamery, before ending at the former terminus station of Hulme End. Here the former station building has been restored and the ticket office is home to a visitor centre.

Monsal Trail

ORIGINAL LINE
20 miles

**LENGTH OPEN TO
WALKERS & CYCLISTS**
8½ miles

ORIGINAL ROUTE OPERATOR
Midland Railway

LINE OPEN TO PASSENGERS
1849/1863–1968

OS LANDRANGER
119

NATIONAL CYCLE NETWORK
Route 680

REFRESHMENT POINTS
Bakewell, Hassop, Monsal
Dale, Miller's Dale

CAR PARKING
Bakewell, Hassop,
Monsal Head, Tideswell Dale,
Miller's Dale

**NATIONAL RAIL
NETWORK STATION**
Matlock

HERITAGE RAILWAY
Peak Rail

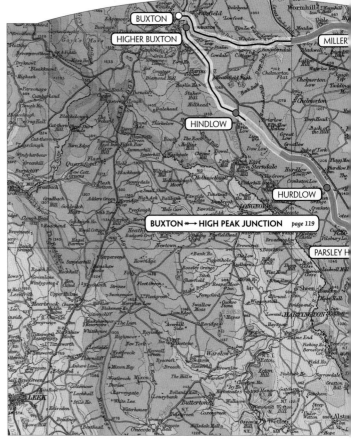

BUXTON ⤏ HIGH PEAK JUNCTION   page 119

BUXTON ⤏ MATLOCK

Railways first reached the spa town of Matlock in the Derbyshire Peak District in 1849 when the Manchester, Buxton, Matlock & Midlands Junction Railway opened from Ambergate to Rowsley. The 11¼-mile branch line was leased jointly by the Midland (MR) and London & North Western (LNWR) railways, but the former had ambitious plans to reach the spa town of Buxton and Manchester and extended the line through the Wye Valley from Rowsley to Miller's Dale and Buxton. Heavily engineered with numerous viaducts and tunnels, the highly scenic line opened in 1863. Manchester was finally reached by the MR in 1867 via a new line from Miller's Dale to Chinley through Dove Holes Tunnel and thence along Manchester, Sheffield & Lincolnshire Railway tracks.

Although difficult to work, the new through route was a great success with the MR calling it 'Little Switzerland' in their publicity. The new railway was initially heavily criticized by landowners and Victorian conservationists, but it soon found favour with the Duke of Rutland and the Duke of Devonshire through whose land the railway passed. Both had private waiting rooms at their local stations despite the former insisting that the line should be hidden in a tunnel across his Haddon Hall estate. Used by

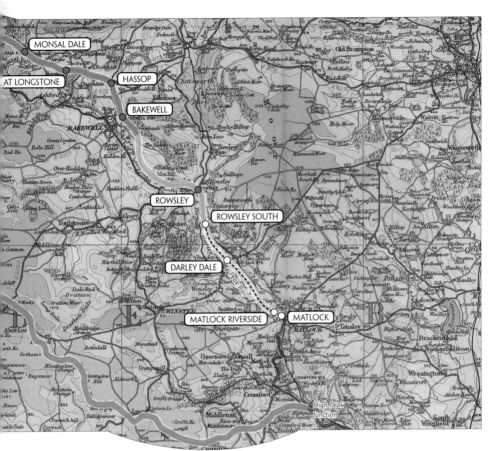

through trains between London St Pancras and Manchester Central, in its latter years this highly scenic line was used by the diesel 'Blue Pullman' services between the two cities until they were withdrawn in 1967. Despite not being listed for closure in the 'Beeching Report', the route was sacrificed in favour of the more northerly line along the Hope Valley which had been due to close. Local passenger trains between Matlock and Chinley and along the Buxton branch from Miller's Dale ceased on 6 March 1967 and remaining through services on 1 July 1968.

Today a local passenger service operates between Derby, Ambergate and Matlock, and the section from Buxton to Chinley via Topley Pike and Dove Holes Tunnel is used by aggregate traffic from quarries at Hindlow. Opened as a heritage railway in 1992, the 3¼-mile stretch between Matlock and Rowsley South is operated by Peak Rail.

The remaining trackbed along the Wye Valley with its lofty viaducts and numerous tunnels was taken over by the Peak District National Park in 1980 and reopened a year later as a footpath known as the Monsal Trail. For years the four tunnels remained closed, but in 2011 they were reopened making the Trail a level route accessible for cyclists and wheelchair users. Starting at Topley Pike, east of Buxton, and finishing at Coombs Road Viaduct just beyond Bakewell, this must be one of the most scenic railway paths in England, and it has much to interest lovers of lost railways. Station buildings and platforms survive at Miller's Dale, Great Longstone, Hassop and Bakewell, while the magnificent 5-arch Headstone Viaduct gives stunning views of the unspoilt Wye Valley. An extension through Haddon tunnel to Rowsley then alongside Peak Rail to Darley Dale has been proposed by Derbyshire County Council.

BUXTON
➔➔ HIGH PEAK JUNCTION

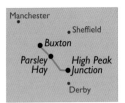

High Peak Trail

ORIGINAL LINE
33 miles

LENGTH OPEN TO WALKERS & CYCLISTS
17 miles

ORIGINAL ROUTE OPERATOR
Cromford & High Peak Railway/London & North Western Railway

LINE OPEN TO PASSENGERS
1856–1877/1894–1954

OS LANDRANGER
119

NATIONAL CYCLE NETWORK
Routes 54 and 68

REFRESHMENT POINTS
High Peak Junction, Black Rocks, Parsley Hay

CAR PARKING
High Peak Junction, Black Rocks, Middleton Top, Minninglow, Friden, Parsley Hay, Hurdlow

HERITAGE RAILWAY
Steeple Grange Light Railway (located a few miles south of High Peak Junction)

For route map see pages 116–117

LEFT TOP:
BUXTON TO MATLOCK
Although opened in 1981 the Monsal Trail between Topley Pike and Coombs Road viaduct was only completed by the reopening of four tunnels in May 2011.

LEFT LOWER:
A view of the High Peak Trail in the Peak District National Park on a sunny day.

Built to link two canals on either side of the Derbyshire Peak District, the Cromford & High Peak Railway was one of the earliest railways in Britain when it opened in 1831. The 33-mile route between the Peak Forest Canal at Whaley Bridge and the Cromford Canal at Cromford Wharf featured eight inclines – rope-worked by stationary steam engines - and reached a height of over 1,200 ft at Ladmanlow. The level sections between the inclines were initially worked by horses but these were progressively replaced by steam locomotives. Progress for mineral goods wagons was of necessity slow, and passengers were only carried from 1855 to 1877 when a fatal accident brought this to an end. The C&HPR was leased by the London & North Western Railway (LNWR) in 1862, absorbing it in 1887, which then set about building a new line between Buxton and Harpur Hill, bypassing three of the steepest inclines in the Goyt Valley. From a new junction at Parsley Hay, the LNWR opened a line to Ashbourne in 1899 where it connected with the North Staffordshire Railway. Regular passenger services on the Ashbourne to Buxton route ended on 1 November 1954, but it continued to be used by excursion trains until the summer of 1963 with freight services ending on 7 October of that year.

With its four inclines – three worked by stationary steam engines – the former C&HPR line between Cromford and Parsley Hay continued to serve numerous limestone quarries along its route. Gradients ranged from the 1-in-8 of Sheep Pasture Incline to the 1-in-14 of Hopton Incline; the latter was the steepest in Britain to be worked by adhesion steam locomotives, while the 55-yd radius curve at Gotham was also the sharpest standard-gauge curve. By the 1960s quarries were closing and mineral traffic dwindling – the first section to close, in 1963, was the rope-worked 1-in-8½ Middleton Incline. Steam-worked to the end by Class J94 0-6-0Ts, the rest of the line soldiered on until closure in the spring of 1967.

Following complete closure, the trackbed of the C&HPR between Dowlow (south of Buxton) and Cromford was purchased by Derbyshire County Council in 1971. Since then it has been reopened as a footpath, cycleway and bridleway known as the High Peak Trail. Well provided with car parks, picnic sites and other facilities along its length, the 17-mile Trail is traffic-free and level (apart from the inclines), affording fine elevated views from its impressive dry-stone embankments of the surrounding countryside. At its eastern end the original C&HPR buildings are in the Derwent Valley World Heritage Site while, at Steeple House Junction, the 18-in-gauge Steeple Grange Light Railway operates trains along the former branch line to Middleton Quarry. At Middleton Top, the 1829-built stationary steam engine at the top of incline has been restored to working order and is occasionally open to the public. With its excellent visitor facilities, the site of the railway junction at Parsley Hay is today the junction for the Tissington Trail to Ashbourne (see page 112).

NORTH RODE ⇢→ UTTOXETER

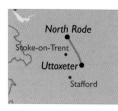

North Rode
Stoke-on-Trent
Uttoxeter
Stafford

Churnet Valley

ORIGINAL LINE
27¾ miles

**LENGTH OPEN TO
WALKERS & CYCLISTS**
9½ miles

ORIGINAL ROUTE OPERATOR
North Staffordshire Railway

LINE OPEN TO PASSENGERS
1849–1960/1965

OS LANDRANGER
118/128

REFRESHMENT POINTS
Rushton Spencer, Rudyard,
Leek, Oakamoor, Alton,
Denstone

CAR PARKING
Rushton Spencer, Rudyard,
Leek, Oakamoor, Alton,
Denstone

HERITAGE RAILWAY
Churnet Valley Railway/
Rudyard Lake Railway

Formed in 1845, the North Staffordshire Railway (NSR) mainly served the industrialized region known as The Potteries and by 1913 had a route network of 216 miles. With its headquarters in Stoke-on-Trent, the company opened its own carriage and wagon works here in 1849 and also built locomotives between 1868 and 1923. The company's crest featured the Staffordshire knot which led to it being nicknamed 'The Knotty' by local people. Transporting coal and minerals was the railway's lifeblood, but it also was responsible for carrying the enormous output of china and pottery goods that were manufactured in the area. The company also went on to own the Trent & Mersey Canal, the 18th-century Rudyard Lake reservoir and the narrow-gauge Leek & Manifold Valley Light Railway (see page 115).

Despite its industrial core, the railway also went to great lengths to publicize a few of its routes that were famed for their scenic beauty. One of these was the 27¾-mile double-track line along the Churnet Valley between North Rode and Uttoxeter which was opened in 1849 and which the NSR heavily promoted for its tourist potential. Closely following the Churnet Valley between Leek and Uttoxeter, the railway also ran along the shore of Rudyard Lake where the company built a hotel and golf course – dubbed 'Staffordshire's Little Switzerland', the route featured heavily in the company's 150-page guide book 'Picturesque Staffordshire'. Also serving as a useful diversionary route for freight trains avoiding Stoke-on-Trent, the line was kept busy transporting agricultural and livestock traffic to and from the twice-weekly market at Leek and excursion traffic to Rudyard Lake and Uttoxeter Racecourse.

Becoming part of the London Midland & Scottish Railway in 1923, the NSR's scenic routes such as the Churnet Valley line were soon facing competition from road transport. While the narrow-gauge line in the Manifold Valley closed in 1934, the Churnet Valley struggled through into nationalization, but by the late 1950s its future looked grim. Closure to passengers for the Macclesfield to Uttoxeter service came on 7 November 1960, although a minimal service of workmen's trains continued to run between Leek and Uttoxeter until 4 January 1965. Freight services to Oakamoor Sand Sidings ceased in 1988.

Since closure, two separate sections of the Churnet Valley Line have each been reopened as a footpath and cycleway – separating them is the Churnet Valley Railway which operates heritage trains between Leekbrook Junction and Kingsley & Froghall. At its northern end, a 5-mile railway path from Rushton Spencer to the outskirts of Leek runs alongside Rudyard Lake, a delightful spot enhanced by the 1½-mile 10¼-in-gauge Rudyard Lake Miniature Railway.

At the southern end of the line, the 4½-mile section from Oakamoor to Denstone can also be walked and cycled along the wooded Churnet Valley. En route the Grade II-listed Italianate-style station at Alton Towers – once used by the Earl of Shrewsbury who lived on his estate nearby – and the stationmaster's house have been restored by the Landmark Trust into holiday accommodation.

NORTH RODE

BOSLEY

RUSHTON

Rudyard Lake Railway

RUDYARD LAKE

RUDYARD

LEEK

LEEK BROOK HALT

CHEDDLETON

Churnet Valley Railway

CONSALL

KINGSLEY & FROGHALL

OAKAMOOR

ALTON TOWERS

DENSTONE

ROCESTER

UTTOXETER

121

HOOTON →→ WEST KIRBY

West Kirby • Liverpool
• • Hooton

Wirral Way/ Wirral Country Park

ORIGINAL LINE
12 miles

**LENGTH OPEN TO
WALKERS & CYCLISTS**
11½ miles

ORIGINAL ROUTE OPERATOR
Great Western & London &
North Western Joint Railway

LINE OPEN TO PASSENGERS
1866/1886–1956

OS LANDRANGER
108, 117

NATIONAL CYCLE NETWORK
Route 56/Regional Route 89

REFRESHMENT POINTS
Willaston, Neston,
Heswall, West Kirby

CAR PARKING
Willaston, Neston,
Heswall, West Kirby

**NATIONAL RAIL
NETWORK STATIONS**
West Kirby, Neston, Hooton

OPPOSITE TOP:
*With its signalbox and length
of track, beautifully preserved
Hadlow Road station, near
Willaston, is the highlight of the
Wirral Way.*

The 12-mile single-track line between Hooton, on the Chester to Birkenhead main line, and the west Wirral town of West Kirby was opened in two stages by the GWR & LNWR Joint Railway (GW&LNWJR). The main line had been opened in 1840 by the Chester & Birkenhead Railway which then went on to merge with the Birkenhead, Lancashire & Cheshire Railway in 1859 to become the Birkenhead Railway. It was taken over by the GW&LNWJR in 1860.

On 1 October 1866 the joint company first opened a 4¾-mile branch from Hooton to Parkgate. Intermediate stations were provided at Hadlow Road and Neston, where a moribund colliery was reopened. The branch was later extended 7¼ miles up the Wirral coastline from Parkgate to West Kirby in 1886 – the latter station had already been served by Wirral Railway trains from Birkenhead since 1878. The new extension served intermediate stations at Heswall, Thurstaston, Caldy and Kirby Park and the whole route was well-served by a frequent number of passenger trains up until the outbreak of the Second World War. Although Neston Colliery closed in 1927, passenger traffic peaked on the line in the 1930s with up to 20 return services on weekdays.

Passenger traffic went into decline in the post-war years with many customers being wooed away by bus operators. Train services were reduced and the only bright spot was schoolchildren who still travelled by train on weekdays during term time to and from West Kirby. Sadly even this wasn't enough to save the line, which closed to passengers on 17 September 1956. Goods traffic and diesel multiple unit learner drivers continued to use the route until its complete closure on 7 May 1962.

Since closure almost the entire route from Willaston, near Hooton, and along the coast of the Dee Estuary to West Kirby has been reopened as the Wirral Way footpath and cycleway through a linear park known as the Wirral Country Park. The first of its kind in Britain, the park was opened in 1973 and today supports numerous species of butterflies and birds, especially along the coastal stretch between West Kirby and Parkgate. Popular with ramblers and cyclists alike, it has useful connections with the national rail network at West Kirby and Neston, while Hooton station is a short walk away from its eastern end. There are two visitor centres along this old railway path with the one at Hadlow Road station near Willaston (just west of Hooton) being of great interest to lovers of lost railways. Here the 1866-built station building (the only survivor along this route) and platform have been beautifully restored to reflect the 1950s period, complete with signal box, signal and a length of track. The other visitor centre is at Thurstaston station, south of West Kirby, where the two platforms have survived – located close to the coast, the station here closed to passengers in 1954, 2 years before others on this route. A proposal to reopen 4 miles between Hooton and Neston as a heritage railway seems to have been quietly forgotten.

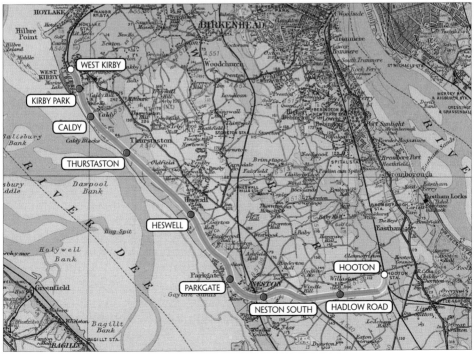

WALES

HOLYWELL JUNCTION
→→→
HOLYWELL

Taking its name from the holy well of St Winefride – a place of pilgrimage since the saint's martyrdom in the 7th century – the market town of Holywell in Flintshire had become an important centre for lead mining, limestone quarrying, copper smelting and cotton milling by the 18th century. Mountain streams powered the numerous mills and factories in the Greenfield Valley. By the early 19th century, a horse-drawn tramway was also operating down the valley carrying limestone to a small harbour at Greenfield. In the opposite direction copper ore from the giant Parys Mountain mine on Anglesey was taken up the valley to smelters. In 1848 a station (later named Holywell Junction) serving the town was opened 1½ miles to the north on Robert Stephenson's new Chester & Holyhead Railway. The tramway was rebuilt by the Holywell Railway and reopened using steam haulage in 1867, but the decline in the cotton milling, copper smelting and limestone industries led to its abandonment in the 1870s.

The overgrown line lay dormant until 1891 when it was bought by the London & North Western Railway (LNWR) which initially planned to reopen it as an electric tramway – this never transpired, but the LNWR started operating a motor bus service from the main line station to the town in 1905. So successful was this that the company eventually reopened the branch line with an intermediate station at St Winefride's (for pilgrims to the holy well) in 1912. Connecting with main line trains at Holywell Junction the steeply graded branch line – the 1-in-27 gradient was one of the steepest adhesion-worked lines operated by steam in Britain – was well served by a regular passenger service until it closed in 1954, an early victim of increasing competition from road transport. Part of the line remained open to serve textile mills until 1957.

Apart from a short section near the site of Holywell Junction, the entire route of the Holywell Railway up the Greenfield Valley can be explored on foot today. Although closed to passengers in 1966, the grand station at Holywell Junction, now a private residence, still sees the passage of trains along the North Wales Coast Line – the vintage upper quadrant semaphore signalling here is due to be replaced by modern colour light signals in the near future.

Set in the 70-acre Greenfield Valley Heritage Park, the route of the Holywell Railway can be accessed from a car park adjacent to the ruined Basingwerk Abbey from the 12th century which is located north of the A548 at Greenfield/Maes-Glas. Various sites of industrial archaeology from the 18th and 19th centuries can also be visited along the route. This includes the Battery Factory which once made pots and pans from sheet brass; Meadow Mill which produced rolled copper sheets; Lower Cotton Mill and the ruins of the Abbey Wire Mill. A reconstructed farm and visitor centre is located near Basingwerk Abbey. The 1½-mile railway trail ends under the attractive stone arched bridge in Holywell Town where the former station site has now been landscaped. Car parking is available nearby.

OPPOSITE LOWER:
Built for Robert Stephenson's Chester & Holyhead Railway in 1848, Holywell Junction station closed in 1954 and is now a private residence.

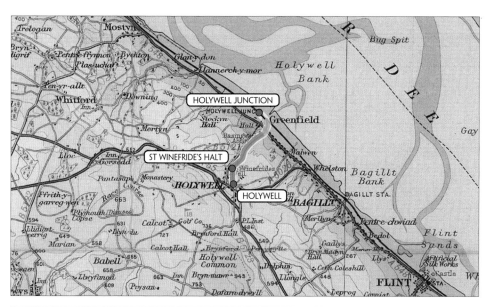

HOLYWELL JUNCTION

ST WINEFRIDE'S HALT

HOLYWELL

PRESTATYN ⟫⟶ DYSERTH

Prestatyn Liverpool

Dyserth

Prestatyn–Dyserth Way

ORIGINAL LINE
3¼ miles

LENGTH OPEN TO WALKERS & CYCLISTS
3 miles

ORIGINAL ROUTE OPERATOR
London & North Western Railway

LINE OPEN TO PASSENGERS
1905–1930

OS LANDRANGER
116

REFRESHMENT POINTS
Prestatyn, Dyserth

CAR PARKING
Prestatyn, Dyserth

NATIONAL RAIL NETWORK STATION
Prestatyn

The opening of the Chester & Holyhead Railway along the North Wales coast in 1848 and the Vale of Clwyd Railway in 1858 soon led to proposals for a 4½-mile tramway to be built from Prestatyn, on the coastal railway, to serve the mines and quarries around Dyserth - lead and copper ore and haematite had been mined here for centuries. A proposal put forward in 1864 was seen as too ambitious and would have been abandoned if the London & North Western Railway (LNWR) hadn't stepped in with their own plans. The LNWR's scheme was for a 3¼-mile single-track branch line from Prestatyn to Dyserth, terminating at quarries north of the village. Authorization was received in 1866 and the steeply-graded line opened for freight traffic in 1869.

The scenic charms of the Dyserth Valley and its tourist potential eventually led to a steam railmotor service being introduced in 1905. Short platforms for this service were opened at Prestatyn main station, Rhuddlan Road, Meliden and Dyserth. The passenger service was an immediate success and further halts were opened at Chapel Street (Prestatyn) in 1906, St Melyd Golf Links in 1923 and Allt-y-Craig in 1928. Apart from Prestatyn, the only station to have a ticket office was at Dyserth – passengers joining at the halts were issued tickets by an early version of the modern conductor/guard.

The line became so busy with daytrippers that a push-pull train was introduced in 1920 – on summer weekends the train virtually ran non-stop up and down the line carrying thousands of visitors eager to see the ruins of Dyserth Castle and local waterfalls. The economic depression of the late 1920s along with competition from buses saw passenger numbers in decline and the service was withdrawn on 22 September 1930. However, limestone for the steel works at Shotton and other stone traffic from the quarries continued to be transported by rail until this, too, was hit by road transport, continuing until 8 September 1973 when the line closed completely.

Since closure almost the entire route of the Dyserth branch from Prestatyn has been reopened as a footpath and cycleway. The well-surfaced three-mile Prestatyn-Dyserth Way starts close to Prestatyn station which is served by trains running between Chester and Holyhead. Before long the path passes under several road bridges to pass the site of Rhuddlan Road station and heads southwards up the Dyserth valley and into open countryside. After two miles the path enters the site of Meliden station where the goods shed and a loading gauge are remarkable survivors.

Continuing south from Meliden, the path skirts the steep slopes of Greig Fawr to the east, its 500 ft summit offering superb views of the tree-lined railway route down the valley to Prestatyn and the Irish Sea beyond. The path continues around the base of Greig Fawr before ending its journey under a three-arched bridge in a car park at the site of Dyserth goods yard – here an old crane has been restored as a reminder of the railway's importance to the local industries.

OPPOSITE LOWER:
An LNWR steam rail motor departs from Meliden in the early 20th century.

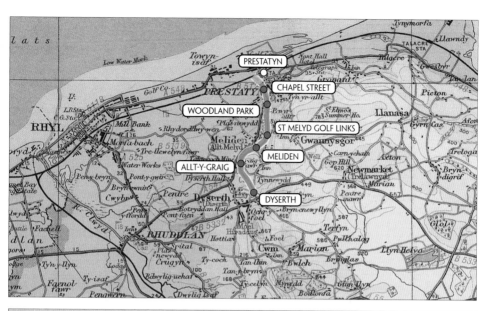

PRESTATYN

CHAPEL STREET

WOODLAND PARK

ST MELYD GOLF LINKS

MELIDEN

ALLT-Y-GRAIG

DYSERTH

THE STATION, MELIDEN

PORT PENRHYN ⇢ BETHESDA

Lon Las Ogwen

ORIGINAL LINE
6 miles/4½ miles

LENGTH OPEN TO WALKERS & CYCLISTS
4 miles

ORIGINAL ROUTE OPERATOR
Penrhyn Railway/London & North Western Railway

LINE OPEN TO PASSENGERS
1884–1951

OS LANDRANGER
115

NATIONAL CYCLE NETWORK
Route 5/Route 82

REFRESHMENT POINTS
Port Penrhyn, Tregarth

CAR PARKING
Port Penrhyn, Tregarth

NATIONAL RAIL NETWORK STATION
Bangor

This is the story of three railways. The earliest dates back to 1798 when the horse-drawn 2-ft 0½-in-gauge Llandegai Tramway opened between a flint mill at Llandegai in North Wales and the coast at Port Penrhyn. Three years later the Penrhyn Railway extended the tramway to slate quarries in Bethesda – the 6-mile line had three rope-worked inclines with the four sections between them being worked by horses. The flint mill at Llandegai closed in 1831, but transporting slate down to the coast from the Penrhyn Quarry continued, and in the late 1870s it was rebuilt as the Penrhyn Quarry Railway to a gauge of 1 ft 10¾ in with deviations to avoid the inclines. Diminutive steam locomotives were also introduced at this time. A fairly ramshackle affair for much of its life, the railway only carried slate plus a few quarrymen hitching lifts to and from work on the wagons.

With standard-gauge railways spreading to nearly every corner of Britain, the people of Bethesda were soon clamouring for their own passenger-carrying railway. Eventually, in 1880, authorization was given for the London & North Western Railway (LNWR) to build a 4½-mile single-track branch line from a junction to the west of Bangor (on the North Wales Coast main line) to Bethesda. Featuring two viaducts and a tunnel and with intermediate stations at Felin Hen and Tregarth, the steeply graded line opened to local rejoicing on 1 July 1884. In many places it paralleled and crossed over the narrow-gauge Penrhyn Quarry Railway. Steam railmotors were introduced in 1906 by the LNWR and a fairly intensive service was initially provided but, by the 1930s, both freight and passenger traffic had fallen into decline with the latter being restricted during the Second World War, never to recover. Closure to passengers on this loss-making line came on 3 December 1951 although freight traffic continued until 7 October 1963.

Following years of decline for the North Wales' slate industry, the Penrhyn Quarry Railway closed on 24 July 1962, the track was lifted and donated to the resurgent Ffestiniog Railway at Porthmadog along with two of the Hunslet steam locomotives dating from 1893, *Blanche and Linda*.

Since closure, the trackbed of the narrow-gauge line up from Port Penrhyn as far as the A5 road and from here to Tregarth along the standard-gauge trackbed have been reopened as a footpath and cycleway known as Lon Las Ogwen. There is still much to interest lovers of lost railways including the harbour, wharves and short tunnel at Port Penrhyn and the 7-arch standard-gauge viaduct over the Afon Cegin at Glasinfryn. Much of the route is through broad-leaved woodlands along the Cegin Valley and glimpses of the narrow-gauge line and its bridges can be seen along the upper stretch. Between Tregarth and Bethesda the 5-arch standard-gauge viaduct over the Afon Ogwen, and the 279-yd Bethesda Tunnel await reopening as part of Lon Las Ogwen

A half-mile section of the Penrhyn Quarry Railway was reinstated at Felin Fawr, Bethesda, in 2012 and there are currently plans to extend this museum line further.

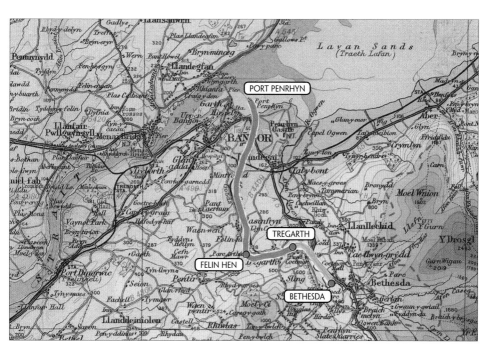

CAERNARFON ⇢→ AFON WEN

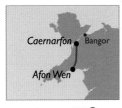

Lon Eifion

ORIGINAL LINE
18¾ miles

**LENGTH OPEN TO
WALKERS & CYCLISTS**
12 miles

ORIGINAL ROUTE OPERATOR
Carnarvonshire Railway

LINE OPEN TO PASSENGERS
1867–1964

OS LANDRANGER
115, 123

NATIONAL CYCLE NETWORK
Route 8

REFRESHMENT POINTS
Caernarfon, Dinas, Groeslon,
Penygroes

CAR PARKING
Caernarfon, Dinas, Groeslon,
Penygroes, Bryncir

HERITAGE RAILWAY
Welsh Highland Railway

**HERITAGE RAILWAY
STATIONS**
Caernarfon, Bontnewydd,
Dinas

This is the story of the four railways to reach Caernarfon, one of which is a recent newcomer to the North Wales scene. Built by Robert Stephenson, the first of these was the 9-mile, 3-ft 6-in-gauge Nantlle Railway which opened from slate quarries in the Nantlle Valley to Caernarfon Harbour via Penygroes in 1828. Although known to carry passengers, it was in reality a horse-drawn tramway built to carry slate for onward shipment from the harbour. The first standard-gauge line was opened between Menai Bridge station and Caernarfon by the Bangor & Carnarvon Railway (B&CR) in 1852. In 1865, the Nantlle Railway was taken over by the newly formed Carnarvonshire Railway (CR) which had been authorized in 1862 to build a standard-gauge line from Caernarfon to Porthmadog – the narrow-gauge line was rebuilt as a single-track standard-gauge line between Caernarfon and Penygroes in 1866, and the extension southwards to the Cambrian line at Afon Wen opened the following year. By 1870 the London & North Western Railway had taken over both the B&CR and the CR (including what was left of the Nantlle Railway) and had opened a branch line from Caernarfon to Llanberis.

A latecomer to North Wales was the 1-ft 11½-in-gauge North Wales Narrow Gauge Railway which opened between Dinas Junction, south of Caernarfon, and Bryngwyn in 1877. It later became the Welsh Highland Railway and was finally completed to Porthmadog via Beddgelert in 1923. It closed in 1937 following a period when it was leased by the Ffestiniog Railway.

The Caernarfon to Afon Wen line was injected with new life in 1947 when the Butlins Holiday Camp at Penychain, near Afon Wen, opened for business. During the summer season through trains from as far afield as London Euston – of which 'The Welshman' was the premier service – would operate via the North Wales Coast Line to Bangor and then along the route via Caernarfon. Recommended for closure in the 'Beeching Report', the Caernarfon to Afon Wen section closed completely on 7 December 1964, although the section from Menai Bridge to Caernarfon lasted until 5 January 1970.

Since closure, 12 miles of the trackbed between Caernarfon and Bryncir has reopened as a footpath and cycleway known as Lon Eifion. It was joined between Caernarfon and Dinas in 2000 by the reborn Welsh Highland Railway which, since 2011, operates tourist narrow-gauge trains to Porthmadog along the reopened and highly scenic line via Beddgelert. Lon Eifion and the railway are separated by a fence as far as Dinas, and served by a halt at Bontnewydd at the midway point. At Dinas, Lon Eifion parts company with the railway and continues southward to reach the site of Groeslon station where there is a café and the Inigo Jones Slate Works. Further south the well-surfaced path continues through Penygroes and Pant Glas (where the brick-built railway shelter still stands) to end at Bryncir where there is a car park alongside the surviving platforms and a water tank.

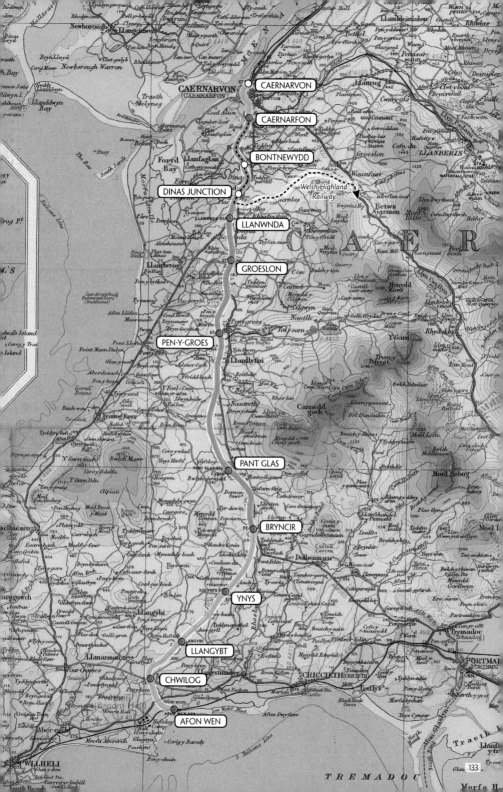

CAERNARVON

CAERNARFON

BONTNEWYDD

DINAS JUNCTION

Welsh Highland Railway

LLANWNDA

GROESLON

PEN-Y-GROES

PANT GLAS

BRYNCIR

YNYS

LLANGYBT

CHWILOG

AFON WEN

133

BARMOUTH ⤞ DOLGELLAU

Dolgellau
Barmouth

Aberystwyth

Mawddach Trail

ORIGINAL LINE
9¼ miles

**LENGTH OPEN TO
WALKERS & CYCLISTS**
9 miles

ORIGINAL ROUTE OPERATOR
Cambrian Railways/Great
Western Railway

LINE OPEN TO PASSENGERS
1865/1870–1965

OS LANDRANGER
124

NATIONAL CYCLE NETWORK
Route 8

REFRESHMENT POINTS
Barmouth, Penmaenpool,
Dolgellau

CAR PARKING
Barmouth, Morfa Mawddach,
Penmaenpool, Dolgellau

**NATIONAL RAIL
NETWORK STATIONS**
Barmouth, Morfa Mawddach

PAGES 124–125:
*An early 20th century view of
Barmouth Bridge and Cader
Idris – opened in 1867, the
764-yd-long structure carries
the railway and a footpath
across the Mawddach estuary to
Morfa Mawddach (for the
Mawddach Trail).*

OPPOSITE LOWER:
*A more recent image of the
Barmouth Bridge.*

What became the Great Western Railway's (GWR) 54½-mile single-track route from Ruabon to Barmouth was built by five different companies in six stages between 1862 and 1870. In order of opening they were: Vale of Llangollen Railway (Ruabon to Llangollen, 1862); Llangollen & Corwen Railway (Llangollen to Corwen, 1865); Aberystwyth & Welsh Coast Railway (Barmouth Junction to Penmaenpool, 1865); Corwen & Bala Railway (Corwen to Bala, 1868); Bala & Dolgelly Railway (Bala to Dolgellau, 1868); Bala & Dolgelly Railway (Dolgellau to Penmaenpool, 1870). All the railways involved were not only financially backed by the GWR but were also later absorbed by it.

The route gave the GWR access to the developing seaside resorts of the West Wales coastline and also connections with two other routes: the London & North Western Railway's rural line northwards from Corwen Denbigh and Rhyl (completed 1865), and its own line to Blaenau Ffestiniog (completed 1883). Until the outbreak of the Second World War the line was kept very busy during the summer months carrying holidaymakers to Barmouth and Pwllheli in through restaurant car trains from London Paddington, Birmingham, Birkenhead and Manchester. Sadly, decline set in after the war with passenger services ceasing on the connecting lines to Rhyl in 1953 and to Blaenau Ffestiniog in 1960. The route also lost out to the Cambrian main line between Shrewsbury, Aberystwyth and Pwllheli when it was recommended for closure in the 1963 'Beeching Report'. By then through freight services had already been withdrawn and the remaining passenger service restricted to stopping trains. Closure was scheduled for 18 January 1965, but severe floods on 12 December 1964 hastened the end as they cut the line in several places. All that remained until the official closure date were spartan steam-hauled trains between Ruabon and Llangollen and between Barmouth Junction and Bala.

Since closure three sections of the Ruabon to Barmouth line have been reborn. In the east the Llangollen Railway now operates heritage trains for 10 miles along the Dee Valley between Llangollen and Corwen, while the 2ft-gauge Bala Lake Railway operates trains for 4½ miles alongside Lake Bala between Bala and Llanuwchllyn. For walkers, cyclists and bird watchers, the 9-mile Mawddach Trail follows the trackbed of the railway alongside the stunningly beautiful Mawddach Estuary between Dolgellau and Morfa Mawddach station (still served by trains) – from here it continues across the estuary along the side of Barmouth railway bridge via a toll path to reach Barmouth. Providing stunning views across the estuary towards Snowdonia, this is undoubtedly the most scenic traffic-free railway path in Wales and rates as one of the best in Britain. Not forgetting Barmouth Bridge, of interest to railway lovers are the surviving curving platforms at Morfa Mawddach (formerly Barmouth Junction) and the signal box at Penmaenpool which is now used as a bird hide. This idyllic spot alongside the river also features a wooden toll bridge from the 19th century and the George III hotel where refreshments can be taken. From here the Trail heads east to finish in the town of Dolgellau.

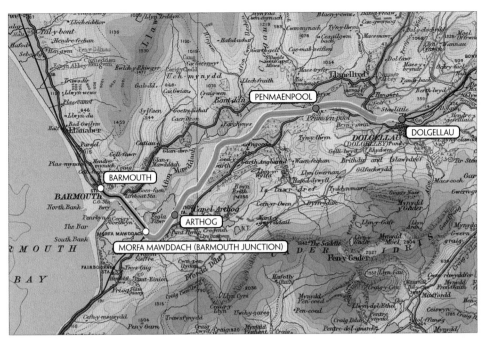

BARMOUTH

PENMAENPOOL

DOLGELLAU

ARTHOG

MORFA MAWDDACH (BARMOUTH JUNCTION)

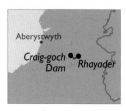

RHAYADER
⇶→
CRAIG-GOCH DAM

Elan Valley Trail

ORIGINAL LINE
9 miles

LENGTH OPEN TO WALKERS & CYCLISTS
8 miles

ORIGINAL ROUTE OPERATOR
Birmingham Corporation Water Department

LINE OPEN TO PASSENGERS
1896–1916

OS LANDRANGER
147

NATIONAL CYCLE NETWORK
Route 81

REFRESHMENT POINTS
Rhayader, Caban Coch

CAR PARKING
Rhayader, Caban–Coch, Craig–Goch

Railways first reached the small town of Rhayader in mid-Wales in 1864 when the Mid-Wales Railway opened its single-track line from Llanidloes to Tallylyn Junction, east of Brecon. Several decades later the Birmingham Waterworks Committee was looking for a suitable site where they could build reservoirs to supply drinking water to their city – with an average rainfall of 70 inches per year the sparsely populated Elan Valley west of Rhayader was a perfect location for such a scheme.

Authorized by Parliament in 1892, the project involved the purchase of many square miles of land, the construction of six reservoirs and their dams, the building of a model village for construction workers and a 73-mile aqueduct to carry the water to Birmingham. To service this massive building project, the Birmingham Corporation Water Department built a standard-gauge railway which opened in 1896 from exchange sidings at a junction with the Mid-Wales line at Neuadd south of Rhayader Tunnel. The 'main line', with gradients as steep as 1-in-33, extended for 9 miles up the Elan Valley to the site of the furthest dam at Craig-Goch. En route it also served the new model village, construction sites for dams at Caban-Coch, Careg-Ddu and Pen-y-Gareg which, together with a branch line to Dol-y-Mynach Dam and numerous sidings and head shunts, totalled 33 miles of track.

The as-yet-unfinished project was visited by King Edward VII and Queen Alexandra in 1904 but it took another 2 years before it was completed and the reservoirs had filled up, submerging farms, chapels and the former home of the romantic poet, Percy Shelley. Having served its purpose, the railway had closed completely by 1916.

Despite the long passage of time since closure, much of the route of the Elan Valley Railway can be followed today. Known as the Elan Valley Trail, an 8-mile well-surfaced traffic-free footpath and cycleway from the southern outskirts of Rhayader to Craig-Goch dam, follows the route of the old railway line around four of the Elan Valley reservoirs and their dams. The Trail starts at the dedicated car park near the site of the former Cambrian Railways station in Rhayader, and from here it heads uphill to join the trackbed of the Cambrian Railways Mid-Wales line. A detour over the top of the bricked up Rhayader Tunnel is followed by a downhill stretch following the valley of the Afon Elan to the Elan Valley Visitor Centre.

The visitor centre has been converted from the old railway workshops, and the adjacent car park was once the site of the locomotive shed and sidings. The Trail continues northwards from here, keeping company with the road along the east shore of Carreg-Ddu Reservoir before it heads uphill away from the road to reach the 123-ft-high Pen-y-Gareg Dam. The Trail continues around the wooded shoreline of Pen-y-Gareg Reservoir before ending at Craig-Goch Dam. Here there is a small car parking space and toilets reached by a narrow road across the top of the dam. A great walk or ride away from the madding crowd!

OPPOSITE LOWER:
Craig-Goch Dam is the westernmost limit of the Elan Valley Trail from Rhayader.

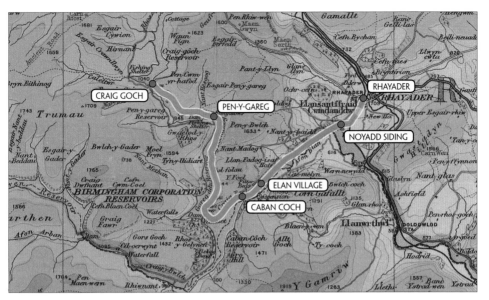

CRAIG GOCH

PEN-Y-GAREG

RHAYADER

NOYADD SIDING

ELAN VILLAGE

CABAN COCH

BIRMINGHAM CORPORATION RESERVOIRS

DOWLAIS ⇢ BRECON

Taff Trail
(part)

ORIGINAL LINE
24 miles

**LENGTH OPEN TO
WALKERS & CYCLISTS**
7 miles

ORIGINAL ROUTE OPERATOR
Brecon & Merthyr Tydfil
Junction Railway

LINE OPEN TO PASSENGERS
1868–1962

OS LANDRANGER
160/161

NATIONAL CYCLE NETWORK
Route 8

REFRESHMENT POINTS
Pant, Talybont–on–Usk

CAR PARKING
Pant, Torpantau,
Talybont-on-Usk

HERITAGE RAILWAY
Brecon Mountain Railway

Authorized in 1859, the Brecon & Merthyr Tydfil Junction Railway (B&MTJR) opened 6¾ miles of single-track line between Brecon and Talybont-on-Usk in 1863. Further authorization had been received in 1860 for a 17¼-mile extension southwards from Talybont-on-Usk to Merthyr Tydfil. This opened across remote countryside in 1868 and involved the building of Beacon Tunnel at Torpantau. The curving 667-yd tunnel, at 1,313 ft above sea level the highest railway tunnel in Britain, was approached from the north by a 6½-mile-long 1-in-38 gradient. Despite being near-bankrupt, the B&MTJR had already purchased the Rumney Railway in 1863 giving it access to the port of Newport.

While the lower half of the enlarged B&MTJR was intensively worked carrying coal down the valleys and iron ore up them, the northern half across the remote Brecon Beacons led a fairly quiet existence. Becoming part of the Great Western Railway in 1922, the entire Brecon to Newport route was in serious trouble by the 1950s – dwindling coal traffic in the valleys and competition from road transport had placed the entire route at risk. The end came for this loss-making line at the end of 1962 when all the steam-hauled train services to Brecon – from Neath, Moat Lane Junction, Hereford and Newport – were withdrawn. Goods traffic continued to reach Brecon from Newport until 1964 when the line closed completely.

Since closure, 5 miles of the southern section between Pant and Torpantau has been reopened by the 1-ft 11¾-in-gauge Brecon Mountain Railway. At Pant are the company's workshops where powerful American and German-built steam locomotives are restored and maintained while, 80 ft below the car park, lies the former London & North Western Railway's Morlais Tunnel, its course marked by three brick ventilation shafts. At Torpantau, little remains of one of the remotest stations in Britain – only the platform edges and brick bases of some of the buildings can still be discerned in this lonely spot.

Beyond Torpantau, a flooded cutting leads to the southern portal of Beacon Tunnel although access is blocked by vegetation and fencing. The northern (east facing) portal of the curving tunnel is easy to access by walking down a forest track from a parking area north of Torpantau station. Eastwards from the tunnel the forest track follows the old railway route down through the Talybont Forest for nearly 7 miles to Talybont-on-Usk. This section forms part of the Taff Trail Long Distance Path and The Beacons Way, en route passing the site of lonely Pentir Rhiw station before descending alongside Talybont Reservoir where, at the northern end, there is a seasonal tea room and road access. The railway path ends at the pretty village of Talybont-on-Usk where the inaccessible railway bridge girders cross the restored Monmouthshire & Brecon Canal close to the popular White Hart Inn.

While the former station at Talybont-on-Usk survives as a private residence, the railway route beyond here to Talyllyn Junction and Brecon is difficult to follow and, apart from a few cuttings and the odd road overbridge, has disappeared into the landscape.

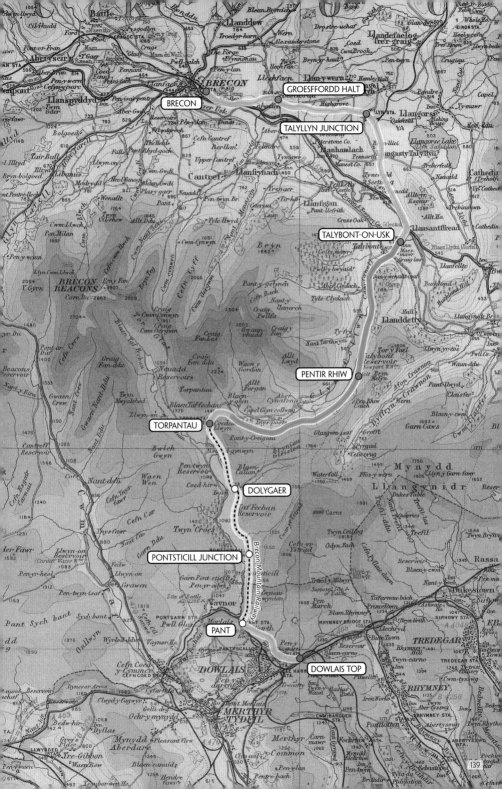

BRECON

GROESFFORDD HALT

TALYLLYN JUNCTION

TALYBONT-ON-USK

PENTIR RHIW

TORPANTAU

DOLYGAER

PONTSTICILL JUNCTION

PANT

DOWLAIS TOP

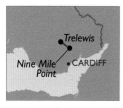

NINE MILE POINT
→→
TRELEWIS

Celtic Trail

ORIGINAL LINE
10 miles

**LENGTH OPEN TO
WALKERS & CYCLISTS**
8½ miles

ORIGINAL ROUTE OPERATOR
Sirhowy Tramroad/London &
North Western Railway/Great
Western Railway

LINE OPEN TO PASSENGERS
1865–1960

OS LANDRANGER
171

NATIONAL CYCLE NETWORK
Route 47

REFRESHMENT POINTS
Ynysddu, Hengoed, Trelewis

CAR PARKING
Half Moon Nine Mile Point,
Wyllie, Hengoed, Trelewis

**NATIONAL RAIL
NETWORK STATION**
Hengoed

OPPOSITE LOWER:
*In memory of 'King Coal',
this circle of colliery dram
wagons – Wheel o' Drams – is
located at he eastern end of
Hengoed Viaduct.*

One of the earliest railways to be sanctioned by an Act of Parliament, the 4-ft 2-in-gauge Sirhowy Tramroad opened in 1805 between Tredegar Ironworks and Nine Mile Point, where it met the Monmouthshire Canal. The canal was later rebuilt as a standard-gauge railway between Newport and Pontypool and a new connection was built from Risca to Nine Mile Point where it met the Sirhowy Tramroad. The latter was rebuilt to standard gauge in 1863, renamed the Sirhowy Railway, and steam-hauled passenger services were introduced in 1865. The London & North Western Railway (LNWR) took over operations in 1876, having already reached the head of the Sirhowy Valley by leasing the uncompleted Merthyr, Tredegar & Abergavenny Railway in 1862.

With running powers between Nine Mile Point and Newport, the LNWR operated passenger services from Nantybwch, on the Heads of the Valleys Line north of Tredegar, down the Sirhowy Valley and into GWR territory at Newport. Coal traffic was its lifeblood and during the First World War long coal trains, known as 'Jellicoe Specials', would head northwards via Abergavenny to the far north of Scotland to supply the Royal Navy's fleet at Scapa Flow.

The LNWR routes in South Wales became part of the newly formed LMS in 1923, but the depression of the 1930s led to a gradual decline in both freight and passenger traffic, and by the 1950s the outlook was grim for the line. Passenger services between Newport and Nantybwch ceased on 13 June 1960 although coal traffic continued between Tredegar and Risca until closure on 4 May 1970.

Today, 6 miles of the Sirhowy Railway between Nine Mile Point and Wyllie forms part of a footpath and cycleway known as the Celtic Trail. The railway path starts at the Sirhowy Valley Country Park at Half Moon, near Risca, where there is a visitor centre and a car park. The route to the car park at Nine Mile Point has been resurfaced and is open to visitors' cars during the daytime. From here the Trail heads up the Sirhowy Valley past the site of Pont Lawrence Halt to Ynysddu station where there are remains of the old platform. The tree-lined route continues northwards up the valley to the site of Wyllie Halt and ends ½-mile north of here close to the A472.

While the former route of the Sirhowy Railway continues northwards up the Sirhowy Valley, the Trail heads west alongside the A472 for just over a mile before reaching the magnificent Hengoed Viaduct. Spanning the Rhymney Valley, the curving 16-arch, 130ft-high Hengoed Viaduct was completed in 1854 and, until closure on 15 June 1964, was used by trains running on the former GWR line between Pontypool Road and Neath. It was reopened as part of the Celtic Trail in 2000 and features, at its eastern end, the eye-catching 'Wheel o' Drams' sculpture. The Trail continues westwards from the viaduct through Hengoed before it joins company with the Ystrad Mynach to Cwm Bargoed freight-only line, paralleling it through Nelson & Llancaiach to Trelewis.

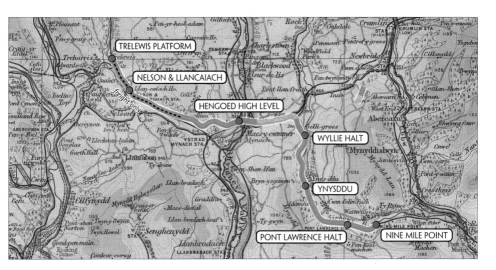

TRELEWIS PLATFORM

NELSON & LLANCAIACH

HENGOED HIGH LEVEL

WYLLIE HALT

YNYSDDU

PONT LAWRENCE HALT

NINE MILE POINT

freight only

MONMOUTH ⤳ CHEPSTOW

Wye Valley Walk

ORIGINAL LINE
15½ miles

**LENGTH OPEN TO
WALKERS & CYCLISTS**
8 miles

ORIGINAL ROUTE OPERATOR
Great Western Railway

LINE OPEN TO PASSENGERS
1876–1959

OS LANDRANGER
162

REFRESHMENT POINTS
Tintern, Redbrook

CAR PARKING
Tintern, Redbrook

**NATIONAL RAIL
NETWORK STATION**
Chepstow

Apart from a 3-ft 6-in-gauge horse-drawn plateway, that opened between iron-ore mines in the Forest of Dean and the River Wye in 1817, the first standard-gauge railway to reach Monmouth was the Coleford, Monmouth, Usk & Pontypool Railway which opened between Pontypool and Monmouth (Troy) in 1857. It was extended across the Wye on a viaduct in 1861 and was leased to the West Midland Railway (absorbed by the Great Western Railway (GWR) in 1863). Coleford itself was only reached in 1883. The Ross & Monmouth Railway then opened along the meandering Wye Valley between Ross-on-Wye and Monmouth (May Hill) in 1873. Operated from the start by the GWR, it was extended to Troy station in 1874.

Finally, the Wye Valley Railway reached Monmouth from Chepstow in 1876. This scenic single-track line followed the picturesque River Wye, crossing it several times and passing through two tunnels at its southern end. Serving the tourist attraction of Tintern Abbey along with limestone quarries and paper mills, the railway was operated from the start by the GWR but was never a financial success and was absorbed by its operator in 1905.

Closure of the four railways serving Monmouth started in 1917 when the short-lived line to Coleford closed, although Whitecliff Quarry continued to be served from Lydney until 1967. The other three lines radiating out from Monmouth survived through the Second World War, but all were losing money and the first to close was the line from Pontypool Road in 1955. The two picturesque Wye Valley lines both closed on 5 January 1959, although goods traffic continued between Monmouth and Chepstow until 1964. After that date only the southern section between Chepstow and quarries at Tintern and Tidenham remained open with the former closing in 1981 and the latter in the early 1990s.

Since closure, several sections of the Wye Valley Railway and the Ross & Monmouth railway have reopened as footpaths as part of the Wye Valley Walk Long Distance Path. At its southern end the mothballed track from Wye Valley Junction near Chepstow to Tidenham Tunnel has survived and is awaiting a Sustrans proposal to reopen it as a footpath and cycleway through Tidenham and Tintern tunnels. The trackbed between the boarded-up tunnels is now a woodland footpath which can be accessed via a bridge over the Wye from Tintern. From here a footpath leads to the restored Tintern station; the station building is now a café, the signal box sells arts and crafts and several old railway coaches house gift shops. Further up the valley, the trackbed is a footpath between Llandogo and Redbrook, where it crosses the Wye close to the Boat Inn. At Monmouth the stone viaduct over the Wye has survived although its iron central section has been removed, while the girder bridge that once carried the railway northwards to Ross-on-Wye is intact and now forms part of National Cycle Network Route 423. Much of the Ross & Monmouth Railway route is now used by the Wye Valley Walk as far as Symonds Yat.

MONMOUTH TROY

REDBROOK

ST BRIAVELS & LLANDOGO

TINTERN

TIDENHAM

CHEPSTOW

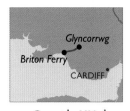

BRITON FERRY
⇒
GLYNCORRWG

South Wales Mineral Railway

ORIGINAL LINE
12 miles

LENGTH OPEN TO WALKERS & CYCLISTS
7 miles

ORIGINAL ROUTE OPERATOR
South Wales Mineral Railway

LINE OPEN TO PASSENGERS
1918–1930 (Cymmer to Glyncorrwg)

OS LANDRANGER
170

NATIONAL CYCLE NETWORK
Route 887 (part)

REFRESHMENT POINTS
Briton Ferry, Cymmer, Glyncorrwg

CAR PARKING
Briton Ferry, Cymmer, Glyncorrwg

A uthorized in 1853 and engineered by Isambard Kingdom Brunel, the 7-ft 0¼-in-gauge South Wales Mineral Railway (SWMR) was costly to build and featured a 1½-mile, 1-in-10 rope-worked incline at Briton Ferry, the 1,109-yd Gyfylchi Tunnel and gradients along the upper Afan Valley as steep as 1-in-22. The railway was leased by the Glyncorrwg Coal Company and the first section was opened between Briton Ferry and collieries at Tonmawr in 1861, although completion to Glyncorrwg via the Afan and Corrwg valleys took another 2 years because of the delay in building the tunnel.

The SWMR was converted to standard gauge in 1872 but the Glyncorrwg Coal Company was never a great success and consequently the railway suffered too, being placed in the hands of an official receiver (OR) in 1878. In the same year a substantial viaduct was built over the River Afan at Cymmer to connect the Glycorrwg collieries with the GWR's Llynfi Valley line. The OR eventually managed to rid himself of the SWMR in 1908 when it was sold to the Port Talbot Railway (PTR), which, itself, was being worked by the Great Western Railway (GWR). As a result, the Briton Ferry incline was closed and traffic from the SWMR was diverted onto the PTR's Tonmawr branch.

The only timetabled passenger service to operate on the SWMR was a short-lived affair that ran between Cymmer and Glyncorrwg from 1918 until 1930, although workmen's trains continued to operate up the Corrwg valley to Glyncorrwg until the late 1950s. In 1947 the section of the SWMR between Cymmer and Tonmawr via Gyfylchi Tunnel was closed following a landslip, and coal traffic from Glyncorrwg was then diverted along the GWR route down the Llynfi Valley. The closure of the remaining pit at Glyncorrwg in 1970 finally spelled the end for the final section of the SWMR up the valley from Cymmer.

Much of the route of the South Wales Mineral Railway can be followed on foot or mountain bike today. From Briton Ferry Cemetery a steep footpath follows the route of the incline, passing under several of Brunel's bridges along its 1½-mile length. At Tonmawr the trackbed of the mineral railway can also be followed on foot, but further progress west to the Afan Valley is blocked by the bricked-up Gyfylchi Tunnel. Over in the Afan Valley the eastern portal of the tunnel can be reached on foot or mountain bike from the visitor centre at the Afan Forest Country Park at Cynonville (see page 146). From the eastern portal of the tunnel, the route up the Afan Valley is now a wide forest track suitable for walkers or mountain bikers. The disused viaduct at Cymmer is passed en route while refreshments can be taken at the former Rhondda & Swansea Bay Railway station which is now a restaurant and bar. Route 887 of the National Cycle Network from Port Talbot is joined here for the final section up the Corrwg Valley to Glyncorrwg, en route passing the Glyncorrwg Ponds Visitor Centre with its café, bike hire facilities, and three world-class mountain bike trails.

OPPOSITE TOP:
Built in 1878 and last used in 1970, the remains of the freight-only viaduct that connected the GWR line from Maesteg with the South Wales Mineral Railway at Cymmer.

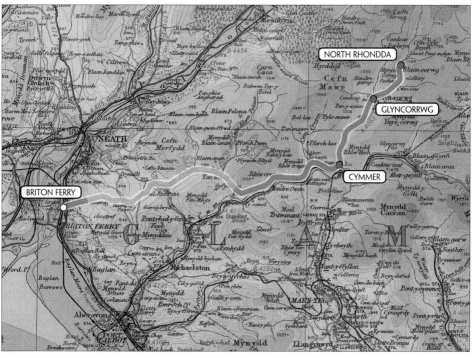

ABERAVON ⇻ TREHERBERT

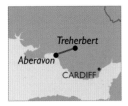

Treherbert
Aberavon
CARDIFF

Rhondda & Swansea Bay Railway

ORIGINAL LINE
14¾ miles

LENGTH OPEN TO WALKERS & CYCLISTS
11 miles

ORIGINAL ROUTE OPERATOR
Rhondda & Swansea Bay Railway

LINE OPEN TO PASSENGERS
1885/1890–1962/1968

OS LANDRANGER
170

NATIONAL CYCLE NETWORK
887 (part)

REFRESHMENT POINTS
Aberavon, Port Talbot, Cwmafan, Afan Forest Visitor Centre (Cynonville), Cymmer, Blaengwynfi

CAR PARKING
Aberavon, Port Talbot, Cwmafan, Pontrhydyfen, Afan Forest Visitor Centre (Cynonville), Cymmer, Blaengwynfi

NATIONAL RAIL NETWORK STATION
Port Talbot

The Rhondda & Swansea Bay Railway (R&SBR) was authorized in 1882 to link the coalfields of the Rhondda Valley with the port of Swansea. The first stage of the steeply graded railway was opened up the Afan Valley from Aberavon to Cymmer in 1885, but it took until 1890 before the single-track 3,443-yd Rhondda Tunnel (the longest in Wales) was completed. The railway was extended westwards from Aberavon to Neath and Danygraig in 1895, when through passenger services between Swansea Riverside and Treherbert commenced.

Working heavy coal trains from the Rhondda to Aberavon was no mean feat as there was a rising gradient through the Rhondda Tunnel and, once through, they were faced with descending the Afan Valley to Aberavon, a tricky business with loaded loose-coupled wagons. With its long sandy beach Aberavon became a popular destination on summer weekends for day trippers from Swansea and the Rhondda Valley. The R&SBR was effectively taken over by the Great Western Railway (GWR) in 1906. Swansea Riverside closed in 1933, and trains were diverted to Swansea East Dock until 1936 when they were diverted into the GWR's High Street terminus.

In June 1960, 1½ miles of the R&SBR's line between Cymmer and Blaengwynfi was closed to save the cost of repairing a viaduct and a tunnel. From then on, R&SBR trains were diverted onto the parallel Llynfi Valley line along this section. With declining traffic, the line closed to passengers between Briton Ferry and Cymmer on 3 December 1962. The section from Cymmer to Blaengwynfi and Treherbert continued to be served by trains from Bridgend until 26 February 1968 when the Rhondda Tunnel was closed due to its poor state of repair. From then trains from Bridgend terminated at Cymmer until the Llynfi Valley line closed on 22 June 1970.

Since closure, the 11-mile section from Aberavon Seafront up the Afan Valley to Cymmer and Blaengwynfi has been reopened as a footpath and cycleway. Heading northwards from Aberavon and Port Talbot the path closely follows the River Afan through Cwmafan, where there is an art installation featuring local celebrities Richard Burton, Rob Brydon and Dick Wagstaff, and up the narrowing wooded valley to Pontrhydyfen where the valley is spanned by an aqueduct and a railway viaduct.

Continuing up the wooded valley, the path crosses the Afan on a modern bridge supported on 19th century stone piers. With the fast-flowing river far below, it reaches the well-preserved Cynonville Halt under a stone overbridge. The Afan Forest Visitor Centre, with its car park, cycle hire centre, picnic sites, campsite and mining museum, is a short climb to the south of here via a tunnel under the A4107.

From Cynonville Halt the path continues eastwards past the site of Duffryn Rhondda Halt and up the wooded valley to Cymmer before ending at Blaengwynfi. At Cymmer, the iron viaduct across the valley was built by the Llynfi & Ogmore Railway in 1878 to link the railway with the SWMR and the collieries at Glyncorrwg, but today it is closed to walkers and cyclists.

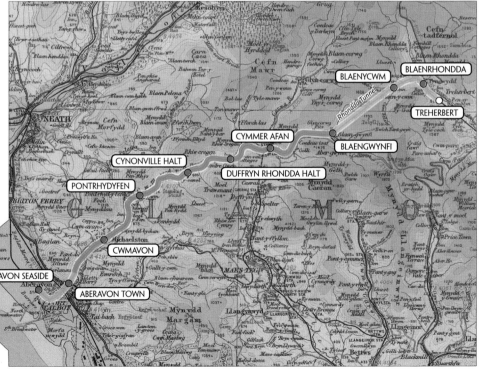

CHIRK »→ HENDRE QUARRY

Glyn Valley Tramway

ORIGINAL LINE
9½ miles

**LENGTH OPEN TO
WALKERS & CYCLISTS**
4 miles
(excluding roadside verge)

ORIGINAL ROUTE OPERATOR
Glyn Valley Tramway

LINE OPEN TO PASSENGERS
1891–1933

OS LANDRANGER
125/126

REFRESHMENT POINTS
Chirk, Pontfadog, Glyn Ceiriog

CAR PARKING
Chirk, Glyn Ceiriog

**NATIONAL RAIL
NETWORK STATION**
Chirk

I n the first half of 19th century, transporting slate by packhorse from quarries in the Ceiriog Valley to the Ellesmere Canal in the border town of Chirk was a slow process. With some foresight, a new turnpike road that was opened along this route in 1863 came with a wide verge to one side that could in the future be used by a tramway. Specifically designed to transport slate between Glyn Ceiriog and the canal, the Glyn Valley Tramway was incorporated in 1870 as a 2-ft 4¼-in-gauge horse-drawn roadside tramway. The line opened in 1873 and everything went well until a new granite quarry opened at Hendre, 3 miles south of Glyn Ceiriog – the increased traffic of granite setts, carried by packhorse to the railhead, soon put the tramway under great strain.

To cope with this increased traffic, the tramway was rebuilt in 1888 and steam tram locomotives were introduced. The line from Pontfaen to the Ellesmere Canal wharf was closed and replaced by a new route from Pontfaen that finished next to the Great Western Railway's station at Chirk and alongside the canal. At the same time a 3-mile extension was opened between Glyn Ceiriog and Hendre Quarry. Passenger services were introduced in 1891 with stations at Chirk and Glyn Ceiriog, while roadside waiting rooms were provided at Dolywern and Pontfadog. The railway prospered into the 20th century and was particularly busy carrying day trippers on Bank Holidays, but after the First World War increased competition from road transport and a decline in demand for granite and slate eventually led to its closure. First to go were passenger services which ended on 6 April 1933 followed by freight services on 6 July 1935, when the tramway was abandoned.

Despite over 80 years since closure, much of the route of the Glyn Valley Tramway can be followed on foot today. At Chirk the course of the railway can be followed from the Blackpark Canal Basin on the Shropshire Union Canal, through woodland alongside the Wrexham-Shrewsbury main line where the Glyn Valley Tramway Trust is slowly clearing the trackbed in preparation for track laying. The course of the tramway alongside the B4500 road between Pontfaen and Glynceiriog can be clearly seen along the wide roadside verge on the left, while the waiting room at Pontfadog has been restored by the Glyn Valley Tramway Group and is open to the public. Further along, an old girder bridge that carried the tramway over the River Ceiriog and the Dolywern waiting room can be seen in the grounds of a Leonard Cheshire Home – ask permission to visit first! At Glyn Ceiriog the old engine shed has been restored by the New Glyn Valley Tramway & Industrial Heritage Trust, while a photographic display of the railway can be seen in the nearby Glyn Valley Hotel.

OPPOSITE LOWER:
The transshipment sidings at Chirk was where slate from Hendre Quarry was loaded from Glyn Valley Tramway wagons onto GWR wagons

South of Glyn Ceiriog the trackbed of the tramway between Coed-y-Glyn and Hendre Quarry is now a pleasant footpath running through National Trust-owned land, featuring en route a girder bridge over the River Ceiriog and ruined quarry buildings at Hendre.

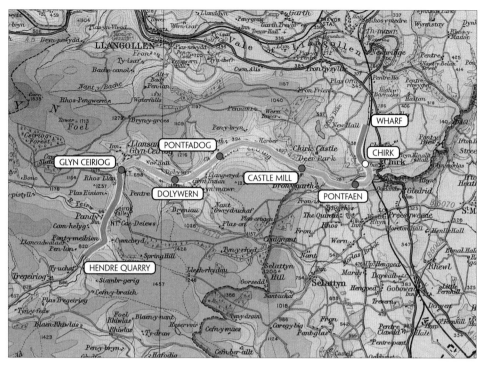

10456. - ROBIN HOOD BAY

NORTHERN ENGLAND

MORECAMBE »→ WENNINTON

Wennington
Morecambe
Blackpool.

Lancaster– Morecambe Greenway/ River Lune Millennium Path

ORIGINAL LINE
14 miles

LENGTH OPEN TO WALKERS & CYCLISTS
8 miles

ORIGINAL ROUTE OPERATOR
North Western Railway

LINE OPEN TO PASSENGERS
1848/1849–1966

OS LANDRANGER
97

NATIONAL CYCLE NETWORK
Route 69/Regional Route 90

REFRESHMENT POINTS
Morecambe, Lancaster, Halton, Caton

CAR PARKING
Morecambe, Lancaster, Halton, Caton

NATIONAL RAIL NETWORK STATIONS
Morecambe, Lancaster

Railways first reached the historic city of Lancaster in 1840 when the Lancaster & Preston Junction Railway opened – 6 years later this railway became part of the West Coast Main Line when the Lancaster & Carlisle Railway was completed. To the west of Lancaster lies Morecambe Bay, and it was at the small resort village of Poulton-le-Sands that the newly-incorporated Morecambe Bay Harbour & Railway Company (MBH&R) planned to build a harbour with a railway linking it to Lancaster. The 3½-mile railway opened in 1848 by which time the MBH&R had amalgamated with the North Western Railway (NWR).

With its eyes set on a route to Scotland, the NWR had, by 1850, opened its line from Skipton to Ingleton via Clapham and from Clapham to Lancaster via Wennington – the company's dream of an Anglo-Scottish route via Ingleton came to naught. The Midland Railway (MR) took over NWR operations in 1852, leased it in 1859 and purchased it in 1871. Served by trains from Leeds and further afield, the growing resort of Poulton-le-Sands soon expanded into a popular seaside resort becoming officially known as Morecambe in 1889. The MR completed Morecambe Harbour in 1905, and 2 years later opened a grand terminus close to the seafront. In 1908 the line between Heysham, Morecambe, and Lancaster

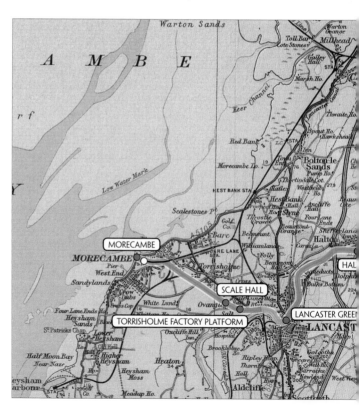

was electrified with the electric multiple units collecting their current from overhead lines supplied with electricity generated by the MR's power station at Heysham. This early electric railway continued to operate successfully until 1951 when steam trains temporarily took over, reopening as a test-bed for high voltage equipment 2 years later.

By the 1960s Morecambe's popularity as a holiday destination was fading, and the Wennington-Lancaster (Green Ayre)–Morecambe route was recommended for closure in the 'Beeching Report'. Passenger services ceased on 3 January 1966 although goods trains still used the Lancaster to Wennington section until complete closure on 8 January 1968. Morecambe (and Heysham to the south) continues to be rail-served by trains from Leeds and Skipton via Carnforth and from Lancaster.

Since closure, the former electrified route between Morecambe and Lancaster has been reopened as a footpath and cycleway known as the Lancaster–Morecambe Greenway. The MR terminus at Morecambe was closed in 1994 and a new terminus station built to the east – the restored original building now houses a pub, restaurant, arts centre and tourist information office. At Lancaster the Greenway links up with the railway path to Caton via the eye-catching Millennium Bridge over the River Lune. Known as the River Lune Millennium Path it makes use of the railway trackbed for 5 miles along the Lune Valley from the site of Green Ayre station (now a supermarket) to Halton and Caton. En route the path passes under the Lancaster Canal aqueduct to Halton where the restored station building and platform are now used by a rowing club. East of Halton the path crosses a loop of the meandering River Lune on Grade II-listed arched bridges before finishing at Caton. Beyond here, another half-mile stretch of the railway path has been reopened alongside the A683 to finish on the south bank of the river.

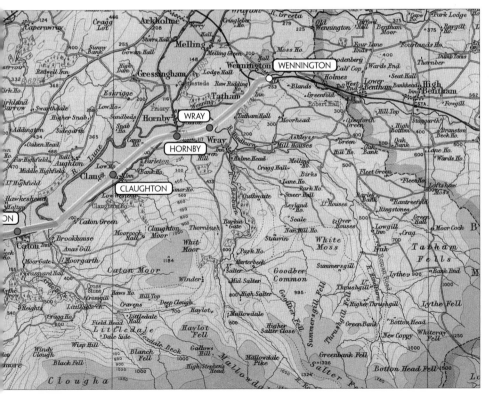

Carlisle

Cockermouth

Penrith

Keswick Railway Footpath

ORIGINAL LINE
31¼ miles

LENGTH OPEN TO WALKERS & CYCLISTS
4 miles

ORIGINAL ROUTE OPERATOR
London & North Western Railway

LINE OPEN TO PASSENGERS
1865–1972

OS LANDRANGER
89/90

NATIONAL CYCLE NETWORK
Route 71

REFRESHMENT POINTS
Keswick, Threlkeld

CAR PARKING
Keswick, Threlkeld

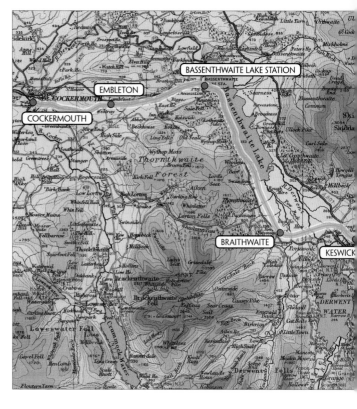

PENRITH ⇥ COCKERMOUTH

Authorized in 1861, the Cockermouth, Keswick & Penrith Railway was the only railway to be built across the Lake District. It was designed not only to tap into lucrative tourist traffic, but also to carry mineral traffic to ironworks at Workington. At its eastern end it connected with the London & North Western Railway (LNWR) at Penrith while to the west it connected with the Cockermouth & Workington Railway (C&WR) that had opened in 1847. The steeply graded line opened to freight traffic in 1864 and to passengers the following year and was worked, apart from mineral traffic, by the LNWR. Mineral trains were worked by the North Eastern Railway via the Stainmore route over the Pennines and a spur at Red Hills Junction south of Penrith. Both the CK&PR and the C&WR were taken over by the LNWR in 1866.

The opening of the railway through some of England's finest scenery certainly had its detractors, but Victorian tourists flocked to Keswick by train where a large railway hotel was built next to the station. Passenger numbers continued to increase with the founding of the Keswick Convention in 1875 – this large annual gathering of Evangelical Christians is still held in the town during the summer months. Seasonal passenger traffic was so heavy that parts of the line were doubled, but

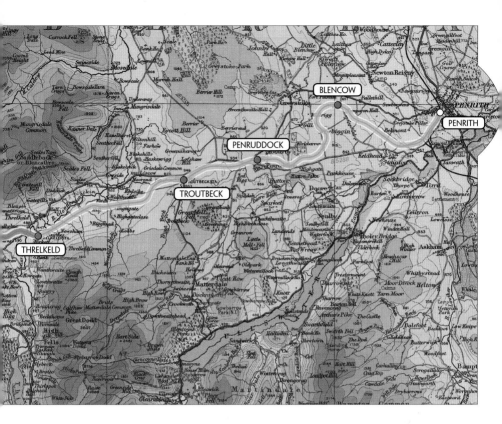

journey times in trains hauled by veteran LNWR locomotives continued to be very slow. While mineral traffic went into terminal decline following the end of the First World War other freight traffic such as locally quarried stone, livestock and timber held up well into the 1950s. However, by then, competition from road transport was having a serious negative effect on passenger numbers, and despite the introduction of diesel multiple units in 1955 they never recovered. The through summer passenger trains from London Euston, Manchester and Newcastle were withdrawn and the entire route between Penrith and Workington recommended for closure in the 1963 'Beeching Report'. The line west of Keswick closed completely on 18 April 1966 although the Penrith to Keswick section struggled on until it, too, succumbed on 6 March 1972. At the eastern end freight trains serving the limestone quarries at Flusco and Blencow ceased in June 1973.

Since closure, much of the Cockermouth to Keswick section of the line has been obliterated by the realigned A66 road – this includes the highly scenic part along the shore of Bassenthwaite Lake west of Keswick. However a 4-mile section of the trackbed along the wooded Greta Valley between Keswick and Threlkeld was purchased by the Lake District National Park and reopened as a traffic-free footpath and cycleway known as the Keswick Railway Path. This highly scenic route includes a short tunnel and crosses the River Greta no fewer than eight times on the original bowstring bridges. At Keswick the restored station building and platform are now incorporated into the former railway hotel – this impressive building is marketed as the Keswick Country House Hotel. A proposal to reopen the railway between Penrith and Keswick is under consideration.

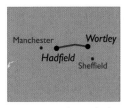

Manchester • Wortley •
Hadfield • Sheffield •

MANCHESTER ⤻ SHEFFIELD VIA WOODHEAD TUNNEL

Longdendale Trail/ Trans–Pennine Trail

ORIGINAL LINE
41½ miles

LENGTH OPEN TO WALKERS & CYCLISTS
Hadfield to Woodhead 6½ miles/Dunford Bridge to Wortley 10½ miles

ORIGINAL ROUTE OPERATOR
Sheffield, Ashton–under–Lyne & Manchester Railway

LINE OPEN TO PASSENGERS
1845–1970/1983

OS LANDRANGER
110

NATIONAL CYCLE NETWORK
Routes 62 and 627

REFRESHMENT POINTS
Hadfield, Penistone, Wortley

CAR PARKING
Hadfield, Crowden, Torside, Dunford Bridge, Penistone, Cote Green (Wortley)

NATIONAL RAIL NETWORK STATIONS
Hadfield, Penistone

OPPOSITE TOP:
The entrances to the three 3-mile long Woodhead tunnels at Woodhead are now well and truly barred by their owners, the National Grid.

PAGE 158–159:
The original single–bore tunnels at Woodhead can clearly be seen on the left of this photo taken from an electric train about to enter the new twin track tunnel in the late 1950s.

Authorized in 1837 and one of the earliest main railway trunk routes to be built in Britain, the Sheffield, Ashton-under-Lyne & Manchester Railway (SA&MR) was an amazing feat of early Victorian engineering. Linking the two major industrial centres of Manchester and Sheffield on either side of the rugged Pennine Hills, the 41½-mile double-track line featured long viaducts at Dinting and Etherow and the 3-mile 13-yd single-bore Woodhead Tunnel, at the time of its opening one of the longest in the world. The tunnel took 8 years to complete and cost the lives of 26 navvies. Engineered by Charles Vignoles and Joseph Locke, the railway opened for business via Penistone in 1845. Before long it became obvious that the single-bore Woodhead Tunnel had become a bottleneck on this busy line. A second parallel bore was opened in 1852, but its construction cost the lives of 28 navvies who died from an outbreak of cholera. Despite this improvement to traffic flows, the tunnels were always appalling places for drivers and firemen of steam locomotives who were often nearly asphyxiated by the smoke.

In the meantime, the S&MR had merged with two other companies in 1847 to become the Manchester, Sheffield & Lincolnshire Railway (MS&LR). For all its life, coal was the lifeblood of the railway, linking as it did the coalfields of South Yorkshire with the ports of Manchester and Liverpool. Heavy coal trains always needed rear-end banking assistance while passenger expresses were normally double-headed. The MS&LR changed its name to the Great Central Railway (GCR) in 1897 in anticipation of the opening of its London Extension to Marylebone, which was completed in 1899. Under its general manager, Sir Sam Fay, this go-ahead railway went on to open the giant Wath Marshalling Yard near Sheffield in 1907 and vast coal-handling docks at Immingham in 1912.

The problems in operating heavy coal trains over the Woodhead route eventually led to proposals to electrify the line after the First World War. Finally, in 1936, the London & North Eastern Railway (LNER), successor to the GCR, started work on installing an overhead 1.5kV DC system, but progress on this was halted by the outbreak of the Second World War in 1939. Work restarted on the electrification in 1945, a new double-track tunnel at Woodhead was constructed and new EM1 and more powerful EM2 electric locomotives were built at Gorton Works. Work on the line was completed on 14 June 1954, and the new electric locomotives were universally welcomed by drivers of the heavy coal trains through the tunnel. Sadly, any euphoria was short-lived as, within 15 years, the coalfields of South Yorkshire had gone into terminal decline and technological advances had made the 1.5kV DC system obsolete.

The writing was on the wall for the Woodhead line, and all passenger services between Manchester and Sheffield were withdrawn in January 1970 – all that remained were electric suburban trains between Manchester, Glossop and Hadfield (these still operate today) and a local

diesel multiple unit service between Huddersfield and Sheffield that used the route between Penistone and Sheffield. Coal traffic continued to be electrically-hauled, but this ended on 17 July 1981 leaving just the local dmu service between Penistone and Sheffield until May 1983 when it was diverted via Barnsley. The mothballed main line and its electrification masts were finally ripped up in the mid-1980s, ending any hope that it might reopen. Hailed by the British Railways Board in 1955 as 'Britain's First All-Electric Main Line', the modernized Woodhead line only had a working life of 17 years – what a waste!

Since closure, two distinct sections of this railway have been incorporated into the Trans-Pennine Trail, a 207-mile long distance footpath and cycleway stretching across northern England from Southport in Lancashire to Hornsea in East Yorkshire. The old railway route southeast of Penistone forms part of the 70-mile branch of the Trail that runs between Leeds to Chesterfield. The section from Hadfield to the eastern portals of the Woodhead Tunnels is also known as the Longdendale Trail. One of the two original single-bore Woodhead Tunnels has been used since 1963 by the National Grid to carry the trans-Pennine 400kV electricity cables under the Peak District National Park. Despite much controversy, the cables have been relocated to the newer double-track tunnel, thus preventing any reopening in the future.

Opened in 1992, the 6½-mile traffic-free Longdendale Trail starts close to Hadfield station and heads up the valley alongside three enormous reservoirs that were completed in 1884 by Manchester Corporation. Despite the traffic on the A628 on the opposite side of the valley and the striding line of pylons, this is a highly scenic route which ends at the western portals of the Woodhead Tunnels. Above the portal of the modern tunnel, a stone commemorates its opening by British Railways in 1954 while, nearby, the platforms of Woodhead station are remarkable survivors. While the Longdendale Trail ends here, the Trans-Pennine Trail takes to side roads across moorland above the 3-mile tunnel, rejoining the old railway route at Dunford Bridge.

From the car park at Dunford Bridge, this 10½-mile section of the Trans-Pennine Trail heads east through the Wogden Foot Nature Reserve, an amazing grassland rich with over 86 plant species which has been developed on former railway sidings. Continuing eastward, the Trail passes the site of Hazlehead station and the Bullhouse Minewater Project before reaching Penistone where the railway station is served by trains on the scenic Penistone Line between Huddersfield and Barnsley. The Trail now heads southeasterly to Oxspring where the main Pennine Trail (NCN 62) branches off to the east – the railway trackbed from here is used by the 70-mile branch of the Pennine Trail (NCN Route 627) that runs between Leeds to Chesterfield. En route to the end of the railway path at Wortley, the Trail passes through the 1948 single-bore of the 308-yd curving Thurgoland Tunnel which is lit up between 6am and midnight. The railway path ends at Wortley where the station has survived despite closure in 1955 – the nearest car park here is at Cote Green.

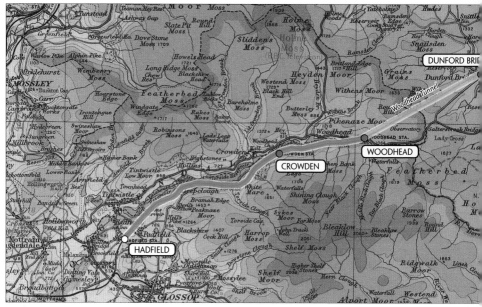

DUNFORD BRIDGE

WOODHEAD

CROWDEN

HADFIELD

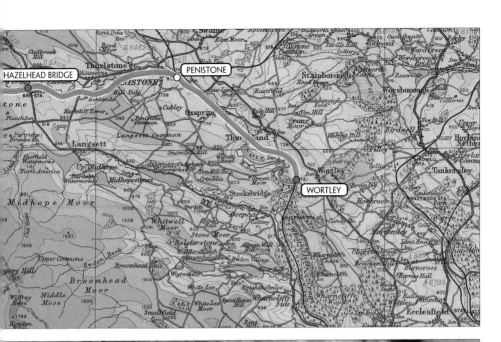

LOW MOOR ⇢→ DEWSBURY

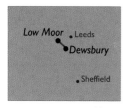

Low Moor • Leeds
• Dewsbury

• Sheffield

Spen Valley Greenway

ORIGINAL LINE
9¾ miles

LENGTH OPEN TO WALKERS & CYCLISTS
7 miles

ORIGINAL ROUTE OPERATOR
Lancashire & Yorkshire Railway

LINE OPEN TO PASSENGERS
1848/1869–1962/1965

OS LANDRANGER
104

NATIONAL CYCLE NETWORK
Route 66

REFRESHMENT POINTS
Cleckheaton, Heckmondwike, Ravensthorpe

CAR PARKING
Cleckheaton, Heckmondwike, Ravensthorpe

NATIONAL RAIL NETWORK STATION
Low Moor

OPPOSITE TOP:
Scrap metal sheep's head at Liversedge is one of several striking sculptures to be found beside the Spen Valley Greenway.

Originally proposed by the West Riding Union Railway, the Lancashire & Yorkshire Railway (L&YR) first reached the 'wool capital' of Bradford from the south along the Spen Valley from Mirfield in 1848 and, until its heavily engineered line up the Hebble Valley from Halifax was completed in 1852, this was the only rail approach from the south to the city. With intermediate stations at Heckmondwike, Liversedge, Cleckheaton and Low Moor, the line initially terminated at a terminus at Adolphus Street in Bradford. This soon proved inadequate, so a new terminus, Bradford Exchange, was opened in 1867.

The last part of the Spen Valley route from Heckmondwike to Thornhill (Dewsbury) with an intermediate station at Ravensthorpe was opened by the L&YR in 1869 and involved the construction of a 12-arch viaduct over the Calder & Hebble Navigation.

Serving this centre of the 'shoddy' industry, the Spen Valley line was kept busy for a century, but with increased competition from road transport after the Second World War the Heckmondwike to Thornhill section was living on borrowed time. With only six trains in each direction on weekdays, closure to passengers came on 1 January 1962. Diesel multiple units were introduced for the Bradford to Huddersfield via Heckmondwike and Mirfield service in 1959, but these cost-saving measures were not enough to save the line and it was recommended for closure in the 'Beeching Report'. Passenger services ceased on 14 June 1965 when the section from Mirfield to Heckmondwike was closed completely. The Spen Valley continued to be served by freight trains between Low Moor and Heckmondwike until 1981 while the southern section from Thornhill Junction to Liversedge Spen was kept open for freight traffic until 1990.

Following complete closure, the entire route between Low Moor and the Calder-Hebble Navigation at Thornhill was reopened in 2001 as a 7-mile footpath and cycleway known as the Spen Valley Greenway. Featuring a collection of striking sculptures, the Greenway starts close to the recently reopened station at Low Moor before heading south past Oakenshaw and into open country. First crossing the A58 on a high bridge, the Greenway crosses the M62 on a steel girder bridge that was built in the early 1970s when the line was still open for goods traffic. One mile south of the motorway crossing, the Greenway passes through the town of Cleckheaton where the station site is now occupied by a supermarket. Another mile further on is Liversedge followed by an urban landscape to Heckmondwike where one of the station platforms has surprisingly survived.

Continuing south along the Spen Valley, the Greenway reaches the site of Ravensthorpe station where the old stone goods shed is a remarkable survivor. The railway path then crosses the A644 Huddersfield Road at Scout Hill on a new purpose-built arched bridge opened in 2009. Immediately south of this it crosses the Calder & Hebble Navigation on the original 12-arch stone viaduct built in 1867 before diving under the Leeds to Manchester Trans-Pennine main line and ending alongside the Calder & Hebble Navigation.

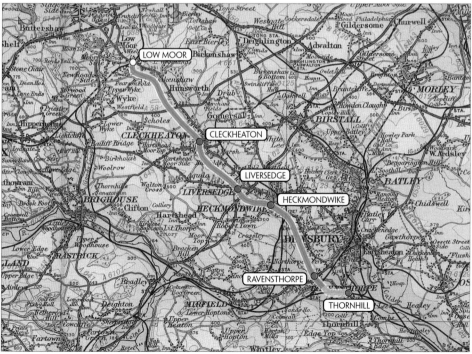

MIDDLETON–IN–TEESDALE
⟶⟶
BARNARD CASTLE

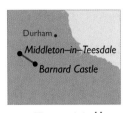

Durham •
• Middleton–in–Teesdale
• Barnard Castle

Tees Valley
Railway Walk

ORIGINAL LINE
8¾ miles

**LENGTH OPEN TO
WALKERS & CYCLISTS**
6 miles

ORIGINAL ROUTE OPERATOR
North Eastern Railway

LINE OPEN TO PASSENGERS
1868–1964

OS LANDRANGER
92

REFRESHMENT POINTS
Middleton–in–Teesdale,
Mickleton, Romaldkirk,
Cotherstone

CAR PARKING
Middleton–in–Teesdale,
Mickleton, Romaldkirk,
Cotherstone

Railways first reached the market town of Barnard Castle in Teesdale, County Durham, in 1856 when the Stockton & Darlington Railway's (S&DR) route from Darlington opened. Within 6 years the S&DR had absorbed two newer railways that linked Bishop Auckland and Barnard Castle with Tebay and Penrith via Stainmore Summit. The S&DR was absorbed by the North Eastern Railway (NER) in 1863.

The final railway to serve Barnard Castle was the Tees Valley Railway, which was incorporated in 1865 to build a single-track line from the town up the Tees Valley to serve stone quarries at Middleton-in-Teesdale. A proposed extension across the hills to the town of Alston failed to materialize. Featuring two viaducts, and with intermediate stations at Cotherstone, Romaldkirk and Mickleton, the line opened on 12 May 1868 – it was worked from the outset by the NER but remained independent until 1882. Stone quarries at Greengates, Crossthwaite, Park End and Middleton were all served by their own sidings and a narrow-gauge line was opened in the early 20th century to aid the construction of large reservoirs at Grassholme and Selset.

While passenger traffic was of secondary importance, the scenic branch line was once used by day trippers visiting the famous High Force waterfall – charabancs carried them from Middleton-in-Teesdale station to this beauty spot in the summer. Following the end of the Second World War much of the stone traffic was lost to road transport and, with passenger numbers also in decline, British Railways introduced diesel multiple units in 1957. It was all to no avail as the line was recommended for closure in the 'Beeching Report'. Even before this was published, Barnard Castle had lost its railway across the Pennines via Stainmore Summit in January 1962. Passenger services from Darlington to Barnard Castle and Middleton-in-Teesdale ceased on 30 November 1964, and freight services ended on 5 April 1965.

Since closure, 6 miles of this scenic branch line has been reopened as the Tees Valley Railway Walk. While the station at Middleton-in-Teesdale has been restored to its former glory as part of a caravan park, the railway path starts ½-mile east of here, reached along the river bank via Lonton. Heading southeast, the path soon crosses the River Lune on a 5-arch viaduct, completed in 1868, before reaching the site of Mickleton station with its car park and picnic site. The traffic-free path is a superb way of leisurely exploring glorious Teesdale, offering far-reaching views from what is now a green corridor rich in plant, butterfly and bird life. Two miles further on, the path reaches Romaldkirk where the old station building is a private residence presided over by a NER signal. After a short detour through the village, the path heads south to cross the River Balder on a tall 9-arched viaduct before reaching Cotherstone where the station building is also a private residence. After a short detour around the station, the path continues to Lartington where it ends. To reach Barnard Castle, walkers can continue their journey on the Teesdale Way Long Distance Path from Cotherstone.

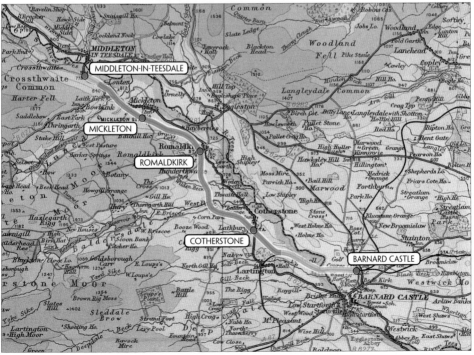

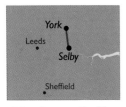

York to Selby Railway Path

ORIGINAL LINE
13 miles

**LENGTH OPEN TO
WALKERS & CYCLISTS**
15 miles
(11 miles are traffic-free)

ORIGINAL ROUTE OPERATOR
North Eastern Railway

LINE OPEN TO PASSENGERS
1871–1983

OS LANDRANGER
105

NATIONAL CYCLE NETWORK
Route 65

REFRESHMENT POINTS
York, Naburn, Selby

CAR PARKING
York, Escrick, Riccall, Selby

**NATIONAL RAIL
NETWORK STATIONS**
York, Selby

*OPPOSITE TOP:
The centre of York station was
used as a zero point for the
distance measurement for much
of the early rail network in the
northeast of England.*

YORK ⇥ SELBY

The route of the East Coast Main Line (ECML) as we know it today took nearly 150 years to evolve. First to arrive on the scene was the York & North Midland Railway which opened from Leeds to York in 1839. The company was part of the railway empire of the 'Railway King', George Hudson, who, ten years later, fell from power a disgraced man. Engineered by George Stephenson, the Y&NMR linked up with the North Midland Railway at Normanton in 1840 and via connections with the Birmingham & Derby Junction Railway, the Midland Counties Railway and the London & Birmingham Railway offered for the first time a through passenger service (taking 14 hours) between London and York. All this changed in 1850 when the Great Northern Railway started running through trains from the capital to York via Doncaster, Knottingly and Burton Salmon. In the same year, the route north from York to Edinburgh via Newcastle was completed and the ECML was open for business.

Journey times on the ECML were considerably improved in 1871 when the North Eastern Railway opened a shorter route between Doncaster and York – it ran from Shaftholme Junction, north of Doncaster, to Chaloner's Whin Junction, south of York, via Selby, crossing the River Ouse on swing bridges at Naburn and Selby. Six years later, the original dead-end station at York was replaced by the current through station, cutting journey times further. The ECML then remained unchanged until 1983, when the route through Selby was closed and replaced by a new cut-off between Temple Hirst Junction, south of Selby, to Colton Junction on the York to Leeds main line. This new line not only avoided the speed restrictions in place over the Ouse swing bridges, but also the new Selby coalfield which was then coming into full production.

Following closure of the line between Selby and York, the fledgling sustainable cycling charity Sustrans purchased the trackbed for £1. The second former railway route to be taken over by the charity, it reopened in 1987 as a footpath and cycleway and today also forms part of the 207-mile Trans-Pennine Trail.

The York to Selby Railway Path is 15 miles long, of which 11 miles is traffic-free. The waymarked route starts at York railway station and heads past the new secure cycle-hub station before following the River Ouse past Rowntree Park, under the new Millennium Bridge and then alongside York Racecourse. It joins the former railway trackbed near Bishopthorpe, and here walkers and cyclists are greeted by a scale model of the Sun, the start of a scale model of the Solar System that ends at Riccall with Pluto. En route, the old steam-powered swing bridge at Naburn features the Fisher of Dreams sculpture. The station beyond here is now a café and hostel while at Escrick there is a small grass maze and car park. The railway section ends at Riccall and, with a few diversions, the path then parallels the A19 road (built along the trackbed) to end in Selby.

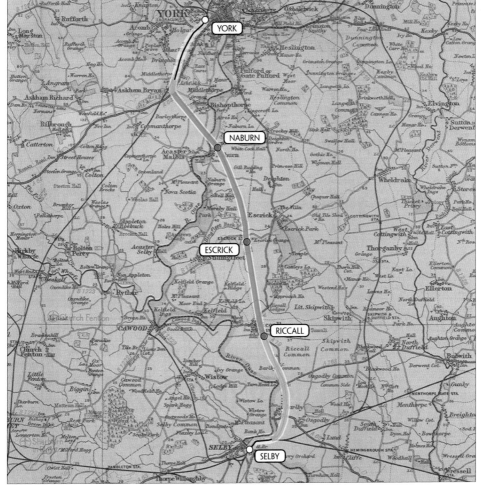

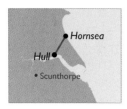

Hornsea Rail Trail

ORIGINAL LINE
15½ miles

**LENGTH OPEN TO
WALKERS & CYCLISTS**
13 miles

ORIGINAL ROUTE OPERATOR
North Eastern Railway

LINE OPEN TO PASSENGERS
1864–1964

OS LANDRANGER
107

NATIONAL CYCLE NETWORK
Route 65

REFRESHMENT POINTS
Hull, Sutton–on–Hull,
New Ellerby, Hornsea

CAR PARKING
Hull, Skirlaugh,
New Ellerby, Hornsea

**NATIONAL RAIL
NETWORK STATION**
Hull

For route map see page 168

*ABOVE RIGHT:
Converted into private
residences, the superbly restored
station at Hornsea is also the
eastern terminus of the
Trans-Pennine Trail
from Southport.*

HULL »→ HORNSEA

B uilt across the sparsely-populated flat Holderness countryside, the single-track Hull & Hornsea Railway opened in 1864 and was worked from the outset by the North Eastern Railway (NER). Intermediate stations were provided at Wilmington, Sutton-on-Hull, Swine, Skirlaugh, Ellerby (closed 1902), Burton Constable (renamed Ellerby in 1922), Whitedale, Hatfield (later renamed Sigglesthorne), Goxhill and Hornsea Bridge. Goxhill station, renamed Wassand in 1904, was only open on market days.

The railway was absorbed by the NER in 1866, and the track was doubled in the early 20th century. The coming of the railway to Hornsea brought vast numbers of daytrippers from Hull on summer weekends, and within ten years the population of the town had doubled. By the 20th century, Hornsea had become a popular seaside resort, commuter traffic to Hull provided year-round revenue and intermediate stations shipped out agricultural produce from local farms.

By the 1950s, increasing competition from road transport saw passenger numbers declining, but the introduction of diesel multiple units in 1957 failed to stem the tide. Stations became unstaffed in 1960 with tickets being issued on the train, but the line was recommended for closure in the 'Beeching Report', Despite strong local protests, passenger services

ceased on 19 October 1964. Goods trains continued to serve Hornsea Bridge until 3 May 1965.

Since closure, almost the entire route of the branch line from Wilmington in Hull to Hornsea has been reopened as a traffic-free footpath and cycleway known as the Hornsea Rail Trail which, today, also forms part of the 207-mile Trans-Pennine Trail.

Signposted through the streets of Hull as the Trans-Pennine Trail, the off-road section starts about 1 mile northeast of Hull Paragon station. For the first 2½ miles it heads northwards through the city's suburbs, en route passing the site of Sutton-on-Hull station which has been landscaped as a children's play area. The Trail soon reaches open countryside and heads off in a northeasterly direction to cross Holderness Drain on a bridge before striking off across the flat landscape for 1½ miles to reach the site of Swine station (now a private residence). A similar distance on from Swine, the Trail crosses the A165

to the site of Skirlaugh station where there is a car park and picnic site in a woodland setting.

Beyond Skirlaugh, the Trail passes the site of the original Ellerby station before reaching the village of New Ellerby where there is a large car park on the station site – refreshments can be taken at the adjacent Railway Inn. Next comes the restored station building and platform at Whitedale followed by Sigglesthorne station where the staggered platforms and station building (also a private residence) survive on either side of the road. From Sigglesthorne the Trail continues past the 'market days only' station of Wassand, now a private residence, before heading northeastwards to end in style at the superbly restored red brick Hornsea Town station where there is a paved area with modern sculpture celebrating the end (or start) of the Trans-Pennine Trail from Southport.

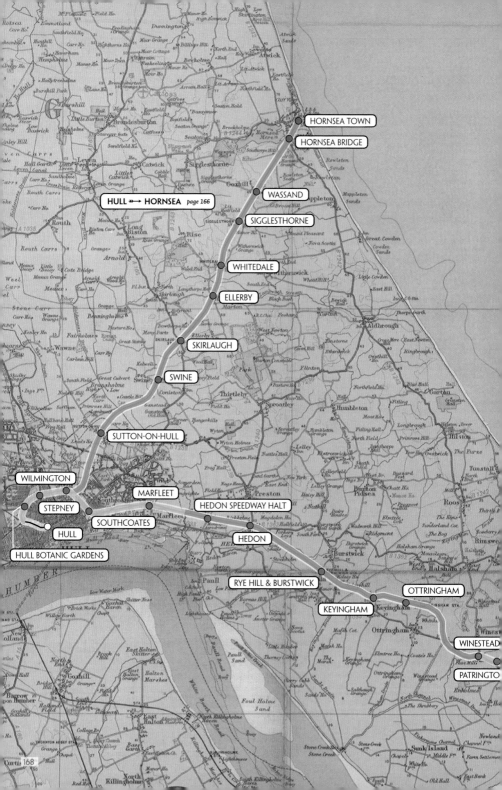

HORNSEA TOWN

HORNSEA BRIDGE

WASSAND

HULL → HORNSEA *page 166*

SIGGLESTHORNE

WHITEDALE

ELLERBY

SKIRLAUGH

SWINE

SUTTON-ON-HULL

WILMINGTON

STEPNEY

MARFLEET

HEDON SPEEDWAY HALT

SOUTHCOATES

HULL

HEDON

HULL BOTANIC GARDENS

RYE HILL & BURSTWICK

OTTRINGHAM

KEYINGHAM

WINESTEAD

PATRINGTO

HULL ⟫→ WITHERNSEA

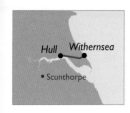

Hull Withernsea

• Scunthorpe

ORIGINAL LINE
17½ miles

**LENGTH OPEN TO
WALKERS & CYCLISTS**
11¼ miles
(cyclists: 5½ miles)

ORIGINAL ROUTE OPERATOR
Hull & Holderness Railway

LINE OPEN TO PASSENGERS
1854–1964

OS LANDRANGER
107

NATIONAL CYCLE NETWORK
Route 66 (part)

REFRESHMENT POINTS
Hedon, Burstwick,
Keyingham, Withernsea

CAR PARKING
Hedon, Withernsea

**NATIONAL RAIL
NETWORK STATION**
Hull

The Hull & Holderness Railway opened across the flat landscape between Hull (Victoria Dock) and Withernsea in 1854. Intermediate stations were provided at Marfleet, Hedon, Rye Hill & Burstwick, Keyingham, Ottringham, Winestead (closed 1904), Partington and Hollym Gate (closed 1953). From 1860, the railway was worked by the North Eastern Railway which took it over 2 years later. Trains began to use Hull Paragon terminus in 1864, and increasing traffic along the line led to three sections being doubled in the early 20th century. Before the coming of the railway, the village of Withernsea had a population of around 100, but within ten years this had dramatically increased, and by the end of the 19th century hotels, guest houses, a promenade and pier had been built for Victorian holidaymakers.

With increasing competition from road transport and the changing habits of holidaymakers, the post-Second World War years brought a decline in passenger numbers while agricultural produce from the South Holderness farms was lost to lorries. Introducing diesel multiple units in 1957 and issuing tickets on the trains in 1960 failed to halt the losses, and passenger services were withdrawn on 19 October 1964. Goods traffic continued to Withernsea until 3 May 1965 after which the line was cut back to Hedon – this last section closed in 1968.

Today the trackbed of the Withernsea branch from Marfleet (on the eastern outskirts of Hull) to Winestead is a footpath with the first 5-or-so miles as far as Burstwick doubling up as a cycle path.

East of Marfleet station (now a private residence), the path passes through a depressing industrial landscape and is not particularly inspiring, so a good starting point is at Hedon where there is a car park and where the station building, platform and goods shed have all survived. From here it heads southeasterly around the outskirts of the village and into flat South Holderness countryside to reach Rye Hill & Burstwick station (now a private residence) and currently the end of the cycle path. The footpath resumes its eastward journey to reach the site of a level crossing over an unclassified road south of Burstwick village where short lengths of rails are still embedded in the verge. Further east is Keyingham station (now a private residence), followed by Ottringham station where there is plenty to interest lovers of lost railways with a short length of rail, a concrete level crossing post and a rotting gate hanging on its rusty iron hinge. Across the road lies the station building (now a private residence), platforms, goods shed and small red brick goods office.

From Ottringham the path heads off south, crossing the A1033, before ending near Winestead station, now a private residence – on the opposite side of the road a pair of rotting wooden level crossing gates still hang precariously from their concrete posts.

The last 3 miles of the trackbed from north of Partington to Withernsea is now a farm track, but at journey's end there is no trace of the terminus station and its platform canopy as they were demolished in the 1990s.

WITHERNSEA

OLLYM GATE

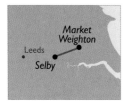

Bubwith Rail Trail

ORIGINAL LINE
17½ miles

LENGTH OPEN TO WALKERS & CYCLISTS
13 miles

ORIGINAL ROUTE OPERATOR
York & North Midland Railway

LINE OPEN TO PASSENGERS
1848–1965

OS LANDRANGER
106/107

REFRESHMENT POINTS
Bubwith, Foggathorpe, Holme

CAR PARKING
Everingham
(Roadside parking at Bubwith, Foggathorpe, and Holme)

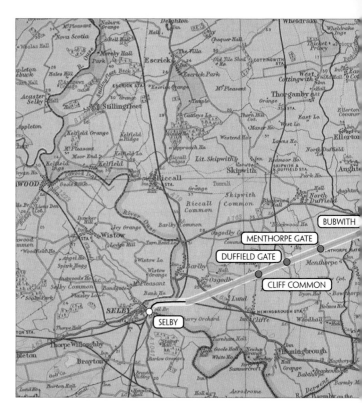

SELBY ⇒ MARKET WEIGHTON

With no major engineering features, the fairly level railway between Selby and Market Weighton was opened by the York & North Midland Railway (Y&NMR) in 1848. Intermediate stations were provided at Cliff Common, Menthorpe Gate, Bubwith, High Field, Foggathorpe, Holme Moor and Everingham.

At Market Weighton the railway met the Y&NMR's line from York, which had opened in 1847. This was extended by the North Eastern Railway to Beverley in 1865 (see page 172). Market Weighton became a railway crossroads in 1890 when the Scarborough, Bridlington & West Riding Junction Railway opened its 13¼-mile route to Driffield, allowing through trains to run between the West Yorkshire conurbations to the resorts of Bridlington, Filey and Scarborough via Selby and Market Weighton.

In 1913, Cliff Common station became a junction for the newly opened Derwent Valley Light Railway to Layerthorpe in York. This delightful agricultural and privately owned line was closed in stages between 1965 and 1981.

Serving only small villages and farming communities, the Selby to Market Weighton route generated little local traffic but was useful as part of a

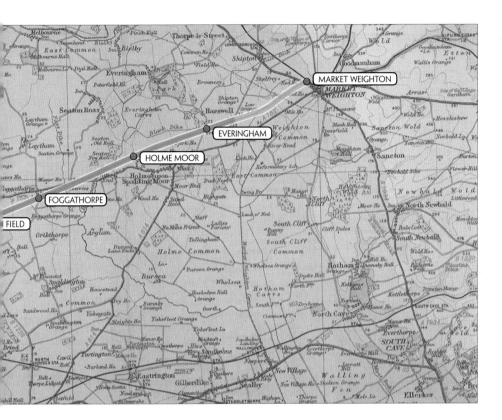

cross-country corridor between West and East Yorkshire – local services were provided by steam railmotors from the 1920s until the Second World War. However, the line came to life on Summer Saturdays with holiday trains from Lancashire, Yorkshire and Derbyshire heading for Bridlington, Scarborough and Butlins Holiday Camp at Filey. Together with the return traffic, the signalmen and crossing keepers at the 22 level crossings on the line were kept very busy from early morning to early evening. While Menthorpe Gate station closed in 1953 and the remaining intermediate stations closed on 20 September 1954, the line was kept open for through trains during the summer months until closure on 14 June 1965. The Market Weighton to Driffield line also closed on that day.

Since closure, the 13-mile section of the railway from Bubwith to the outskirts of Market Weighton has been reopened as a footpath known as the Bubwith Rail Trail. The Trail starts on the east bank

of the River Derwent at the village of Bubwith where there is still much evidence of this long lost railway – the stationmaster's house and ticket office are now a private residence while the overgrown platforms and fencing can be discerned in the undergrowth alongside the Trail. From here it heads eastwards, straight as a die to the outskirts of Market Weighton, passing sleepy villages on its level route through the countryside. Nearly all the attractive stationmasters' houses have survived with those at High Field, Holme Moor and Everingham (Grade II-listed) all now private residences. Surrounded by high fences, the latter has been beautifully restored and extended. There is also a small car park for Trail users at Everingham and lost railway sleuths will find the cast iron base of a crane that has survived the ravages of time. All the station platforms along the line also survive but are gradually being overtaken by nature. The Trail ends 2 miles short of Market Weighton at a layby on the A614.

MARKET WEIGHTON ⤳ BEVERLEY

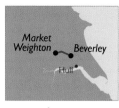

Market Weighton, Beverley, Hull

Hudson Way Rail Trail

ORIGINAL LINE
11½ miles

LENGTH OPEN TO WALKERS & CYCLISTS
11 miles

ORIGINAL ROUTE OPERATOR
North Eastern Railway

LINE OPEN TO PASSENGERS
1865–1965

OS LANDRANGER
106/107

REFRESHMENT POINTS
Market Weighton, Cherry Burton, Beverley

CAR PARKING
Market Weighton, Kiplingcotes, Beverley

NATIONAL RAIL NETWORK STATION
Beverley

OPPOSITE LOWER:
Kiplingcotes Station was built for the use of Lord Beaumont Hotham of nearby Dalton Hall – today the well preserved station, goods shed and signal box is a useful starting point for users of the Hudson Way Rail Trail.

The railway between Market Weighton and Beverley began life as a proposal by George Hudson's York & North Midland Railway for a railway linking York and Hull. The 20½-mile line between Bootham Junction and Market Weighton opened in 1847 and the company's single-line railway from Selby to Market Weighton opened in 1848 (see page 170).

Easterly progress beyond Market Weighton came to an abrupt halt due to Hudson's disgrace and resignation in 1849 following a financial scandal. The Y&NMR became part of the North Eastern Railway (NER) in 1854, but building the single-line extension from Market Weighton to Beverley was delayed by several years due to disputes with local MP and landowner, Lord Beaumont Hotham. This was resolved when Hotham was given his own station at Kiplingcotes to serve the family seat at nearby Dalton Hall.

With intermediate stations at Kiplingcotes and Cherry Burton, the NER opened the 11½-mile line in 1865 and immediately started running through trains along the entire route between York and Hull. The line was doubled in 1889, and the former town became a railway crossroads in 1890 when the 13¼-mile line to Driffield was opened.

The route between York and Hull had a healthy service of passenger trains into the 1960s when diesel multiple units were introduced. In 1961, the route was earmarked for modernization, but this was cancelled at the beginning of 1962 – a year later the four railways converging on Market Weighton were recommended for closure in the 'Beeching Report'. With an alternative route between York and Hull via Selby, the line closed on 29 November 1965.

Following closure, the trackbed between Market Weighton and Beverley was purchased in 1971 by the East Riding County Council and has since been reopened as a footpath and cycleway known as the Hudson Way Rail Trail. The Trail starts at the site of Market Weighton station which was demolished in 1979 – the nearly 5-acre site is leased by Market Weighton Town Council and managed as an open space known as the Monkey Run. Heading east, the Trail passes the former junction of the railway to Driffield before passing under a brick overbridge where a footpath leads to St Helen's Well. Two miles along the Trail lies the Kiplingcotes Chalk Pit nature reserve, which is administered by the Yorkshire Wildlife Trust and is a favourite haunt for bird watchers.

Heading through the gently undulating Yorkshire Wolds, the Trail passes over a graceful arched bridge before entering remote Kiplingcotes station, where there is a car park. The station building, platforms and goods shed have all survived while the signal box is now an information centre run by the Yorkshire Wolds Heritage Trust.

Continuing eastwards for another 4 miles, the Trail alternately runs along the top of embankments and through cuttings spanned by road overbridges before reaching Cherry Burton station (now a private residence). From here it runs in a straight line for another 3 miles to the outskirts of Beverley where there is a car park for Trail users off the A1035 town bypass.

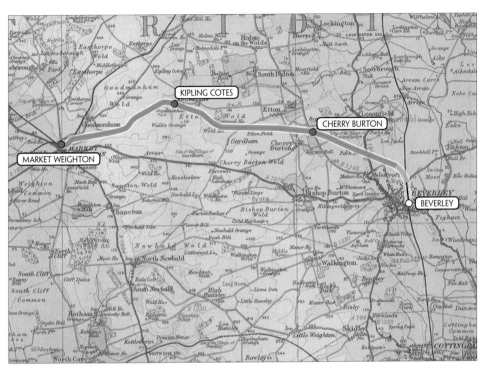

SCARBOROUGH →→→ WHITBY

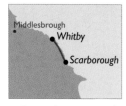

Scarborough
to Whitby
Rail Trail

ORIGINAL LINE
23½ miles

**LENGTH OPEN TO
WALKERS & CYCLISTS**
21 miles

ORIGINAL ROUTE OPERATOR
North Eastern Railway

LINE OPEN TO PASSENGERS
1885-1965

OS LANDRANGER
94/101

NATIONAL CYCLE NETWORK
Route 1

REFRESHMENT POINTS
Scarborough, Cloughton,
Hayburn Wyke, Ravenscar,
Robin Hood's Bay, Hawsker,
Whitby

CAR PARKING
Scarborough, Ravenscar,
Robin Hood's Bay, Hawsker,
Whitby

**NATIONAL RAIL
NETWORK STATIONS**
Scarborough, Whitby

HERITAGE RAILWAY
North Yorkshire Moors
Railway

The Yorkshire harbour town of Whitby was first served by a railway when the Whitby & Pickering Railway opened in 1836. It was a horse-drawn operation with inclined planes and was modernized by the York & North Midland Railway (Y&NMR) in 1845. A second railway reached Whitby with the opening of the Esk Valley line from Middlesbrough by the North Eastern Railway (NER) in 1863.

To the south, Scarborough had already been reached from York by the Y&NMR in 1845 and, a year later, the company opened its route to the town from Hull via Bridlington. The Y&NMR merged with three other railway companies in 1854 to form the North Eastern Railway (NER). Linking Whitby and Scarborough along the coast the final railway to serve this area was the Scarborough & Whitby Railway – construction work on this steeply-graded meandering single-track route started in 1872 but financial difficulties slowed progress. Featuring the graceful 120ft-high Larpool Viaduct over the River Esk at Whitby and worked from the outset by the NER, the line eventually opened in 1885. Trains had to reverse directions at Whitby West Cliff station to reach the lower terminus of the line in the town. Since 1883, West Cliff station had also been served by trains on the Whitby, Redcar & Middlesbrough Union Railway, and this was also worked by the NER. It was taken over by the NER in 1889, as was the Scarborough & Whitby Railway in 1898.

This highly scenic coastal route was heavily promoted by the NER which included it in circular tours for holidaymakers during the summer months. Introduced in the 1930s at intermediate stations, camping coaches remained popular until the line's closure. While the coastal route north of Whitby closed in 1958, diesel multiple units were introduced on the Whitby to Scarborough route in the early 1960s, but the 'Beeching Report' of 1963 brought bad news for Whitby as all its remaining railway routes were recommended for closure. In the event, the Esk Valley line was reprieved, the line to Pickering was closed and then reopened as a heritage railway by the North Yorkshire Moors Railway. The Whitby to Scarborough line was not so lucky and, despite strong protests, it closed completely on 6 March 1965.

Since closure much of this steeply graded scenic coastal route has been reopened as a footpath and cycleway (much of it in the North York Moors National Park) known as the Scarborough to Whitby Rail Trail. The start in Scarborough is at Sainsbury's supermarket car park and there is much of interest to lovers of lost railways along the 21-mile route: a café in an old railway carriage at restored Cloughton station; platforms at Hayburn Wyke; Staintondale station now a private residence; summit of line at Ravenscar where there is a visitor centre and tearoom; Robin Hood's Bay station now holiday accommodation; Hawsker station with its railway carriages, now a cycle hire centre and café; far-reaching views from Larpool Viaduct down the Esk Valley to Whitby. A superb day out for walkers and cyclists!

WHITBY

HAWSKER

ROBIN HOOD'S BAY

FYLING HALL

RAVENSCAR

STAINTONDALE

HAYBURN WYKE

CLOUGHTON

SCALBY

SCARBOROUGH

175

BATTERSBY JUNCTION
➤➤➤
ROSEDALE

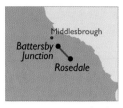

Rosedale Rail Trail

ORIGINAL LINE
15 miles

LENGTH OPEN TO WALKERS & CYCLISTS
14 miles

ORIGINAL ROUTE OPERATOR
North Eastern Railway

LINE OPEN TO PASSENGERS
1858/1861/
1865-1928 (freight only)

OS LANDRANGER
93/94

REFRESHMENT POINTS
Blakey Ridge, Rosedale Abbey

CAR PARKING
Bank Foot (south of Battersby), Blakey Ridge, Rosedale East, Rosedale Abbey

NATIONAL RAIL NETWORK STATION
Battersby

OPPOSITE TOP:
At 1,375ft above sea level the views from the top of the mile-long Ingleby Incline of North Yorkshire are superb on a clear day.

Now a tranquil, rural dale in the North York Moors National Park, Rosedale was an important iron-ore mining centre during the 19th and early 20th centuries. However, transporting the high-grade refined ore from this remote and elevated part of North Yorkshire to the ironworks of Teesside only became possible with the advent of the railways. In 1858, the North Yorkshire & Cleveland Railway (NY&CR) had opened its line to what is now known as Battersby Junction. The railway also bought an existing 3-mile narrow-gauge tramway that ran south from Battersby to the foot of the mile-long Ingleby Incline, serving ironstone mines high in the hills operated by the Ingleby Mining Company. In 1859 the NY&CR was taken over by the North Eastern Railway (NER), as were the mining company's mineral lines. Two years later the NER rebuilt the tramway from Battersby and up the incline to standard gauge. From the top of the incline it also opened a new 11-mile railway across the moors to mines at Rosedale West. Loaded wagons of refined iron ore were hauled from here by ageing steam locomotives to the incline where they were lowered and then transported in trainloads to ironworks on Teesside.

In 1865 the NER opened a 4½-mile branch line from remote Blakey Junction, over 1,000 ft up in the moors, to new mines at Rosedale East. The mining operations remained profitable through the rest of the 19th century, but falling demand and prices, worked-out mines and labour disputes after the First World War threatened their future. The mines closed in 1925, but the railway continued to operate, hauling calcine dust from the slag heaps, until 1929 when it was closed.

Nearly 90 years have elapsed since the incline and the mineral lines to Rosedale closed, but much of their route can be followed on foot, horseback or mountain bike today. At Bank Foot, about 1 mile south of Battersby Junction station, the trackbed of the lower level railway can be followed along a forestry track to the foot of the incline. From here the route to Blakey Junction is a public bridleway although the climb up the final stretch of the incline is very steep, it is rewarded by far-reaching views, 1,375 ft above sea level. From here the railway trackbed meanders across the moorland for 7 miles to the remote site of Blakey Junction, just half a mile from one of Britain's loneliest pubs, the Lion Inn. From Blakey Junction the branch line to Rosedale East winds around the head of Rosedale to the site of High Baring East Mines where there are remains of miners' cottages, workshops and calcine kilns where ironstone was heated to reduce its weight.

The 'main line' from Blakey Junction continues along Blakey Ridge to Bank Top, high above the pretty village of Rosedale Abbey. Here there are remains of more calcine kilns although the engine shed, which once stood here, has been moved stone by stone to Hutton-le-Hole where it was used to build the village hall.

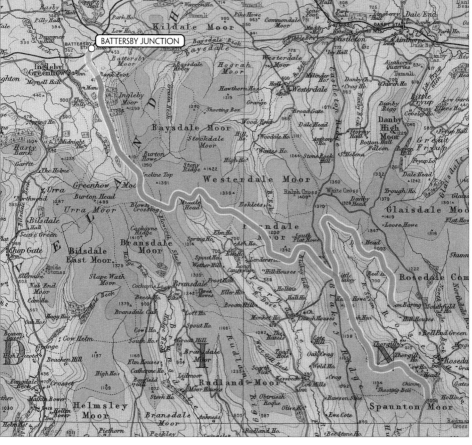

BATTERSBY JUNCTION

HARTLEPOOL →→ SUNDERLAND

Hart to Haswell Countryside Path

ORIGINAL LINE
21½ miles

LENGTH OPEN TO WALKERS & CYCLISTS
15¼ miles

ORIGINAL ROUTE OPERATOR
Hartlepool Dock & Railway/
Durham & Sunderland
Railway

LINE OPEN TO PASSENGERS
1835/1836–1952

OS LANDRANGER
88/93

NATIONAL CYCLE NETWORK
Routes 1 and 14

REFRESHMENT POINTS
Castle Eden, Wingate,
Haswell, South Hetton,
Murton, Ryhope

CAR PARKING
Hesleden, Castle Eden,
Haswell, Murton, Ryhope

NATIONAL RAIL NETWORK STATIONS
Hartlepool, Sunderland

By the end of the 18th century there were a whole network of primitive waggonways transporting coal by way of gravity, inclined planes and horsepower from the collieries of East Durham to staithes on the River Wear. The first use of steam power came in 1822 when the Hetton Coal Company bought locomotives from George Stephenson to haul coal trains between Hetton and Sunderland. Meanwhile, the Hartlepool Dock & Railway was seeking to develop what was then a small fishing harbour into a major coal shipment port and building a railway to link it with inland collieries. Engineered by George Stephenson, the 12¼-mile line between Hartlepool and Haswell opened via Hesleden and Castle Eden in 1835.

From the north, the Durham & Sunderland Railway opened its 9¾-mile line from Sunderland to Haswell via Seaton and South Hetton in 1836. At Haswell there was no physical connection between the two railways until they were amalgamated with the North Eastern Railway (NER) in 1857. Through passenger services between West Hartlepool and Sunderland were introduced, and this remained the only rail link between the towns until the shorter, coastal railway was completed in 1905. After this date, the route via Haswell was relegated to secondary status. While coal was the lifeblood of the line – steam-hauled empty coal trains battled up Seaton Bank until 1967 – passenger services were withdrawn on 9 June 1952.

Since closure, almost the entire length of the Hartlepool to Ryhope via Haswell railway route has been reopened as a footpath and cycleway. From Hart to Haswell it forms part of National Cycle Network (NCN) Route 14 and is known as the Haswell to Hart Countryside Path. The path starts at the site of Cemetery North Junction north of Hartlepool, reached along a signposted route from the centre of the town. En route to Haswell the path passes through the villages of Hesleden, Castle Eden and Wingate where it links up with NCN Route 1 and the Castle Eden Walkway, which have followed an old railway trackbed from Stockton-on-Tees. The path continues northwards through Edderacres Plantation before entering a long cutting near the site of Shotton Colliery where the station platform and road overbridge have survived.

The Countryside Path ends at the former mining village of Haswell where there is a car park between the Oddfellows Arms and The Wayfarers pubs. From here NCN Route 14 heads off west to Durham while the railway path and NCN Route 1 continue northwards through South Hetton where the Yellow Brick Road railway path heads off east to follow the route an early waggonway to Seaham. The main railway path continues northwards to Murton where a large semi-circular sculpture made of pit winding gear is a reminder of the once-important coal industry. Beyond Murton the path passes through a long cutting to emerge at the top of Seaton Bank. Following the downhill stretch through Seaton, the path ends at Ryhope from where the centre of Sunderland can be reached via designated tracks and side roads.

SUNDERLAND

RYHOPE

SEATON

MURTON

SOUTH HETTON

HASWELL

SHOTTON BRIDGE

THORNLEY

WELLFIELD

CASTLE EDEN

HESLEDEN

HART

HARTLEPOOL

SEA

SUNDERLAND

SEAHAM HARBOUR

PETERLEE

WEST HARTLEPOOL

179

CONSETT ⇢ SUNDERLAND

Consett & Sunderland Railway Path

ORIGINAL LINE
34 miles

LENGTH OPEN TO WALKERS & CYCLISTS
26 miles

ORIGINAL ROUTE OPERATOR
Stanhope & Tyne Railway/
North Eastern Railway

LINE OPEN TO PASSENGERS
1896-1955

OS LANDRANGER
88

NATIONAL CYCLE NETWORK
Route 7

REFRESHMENT POINTS
Consett, Annfield Plain, Stanley, Beamish, South Pelaw, Washington, Monkwearmouth, Roker

CAR PARKING
Lydgetts Junction (Consett), Annfield Plain, Stanley, Beamish, South Pelaw, Washington, Monkwearmouth, Roker

NATIONAL RAIL NETWORK STATIONS
Chester-le-Street, Sunderland

One of Britain's earliest railways, the Stanhope & Tyne Railway (S&TR) was formed in 1832 to transport lime from kilns at Stanhope in Upper Weardale and coal from collieries in the Consett area down to the River Tyne at South Shields. The 34-mile railway opened throughout in 1834, but journey times were painfully slow due to a wagon lift at Hownes Gill and numerous inclined planes with the sections in between being worked by horses – only the last 9 miles from Annfield Plain to South Shields were worked by steam locomotives. There was a big flaw in the formation of this railway as it was built without an Act of Parliament, instead paying an annual rent, or wayleaves, to the landowners along the route. This was its undoing as the company became bankrupt and was dissolved in 1841.

The eastern section of the S&TR between Leadgate, near Consett, and South Shields was incorporated into the Pontop & South Shields Railway (P&SSR) in 1842, and the western section from Stanhope to Leadgate was sold to the Derwent Iron Company which used the line to transport limestone to its ironworks at Consett. All these railways eventually became owned by the North Eastern Railway, which had been formed in 1854, but

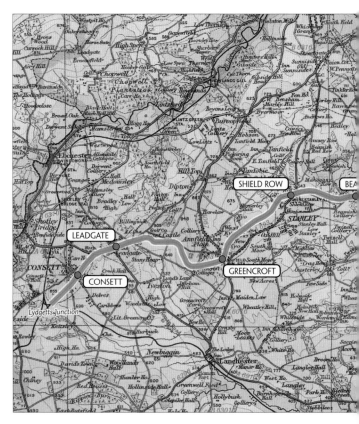

the Consett to South Shields route remained stuck firmly in the past until its inclined planes were bypassed by new deviations – that at Annfield Plain was opened in 1886 while the deviation at Beamish opened in 1893. A new station was opened at Consett in 1896 and through passenger services introduced to Newcastle via Annfield Plain, Beamish and a new junction with the East Coast Main Line at South Pelaw.

Passenger traffic on this steeply graded line was of secondary importance and the stopping passenger service ceased on 23 May 1955. Despite this, the line was an important route for iron ore trains from Tyne Dock to the steelworks at Consett until 1980 when the steelworks closed. The sight and sound of the steam-hauled trains struggling up the 1-in-36 gradient to Annfield Plain was a memorable experience until they were replaced by diesels in 1966.

Since closure, the route of the Stanhope & Tyne Railway between Lydgetts Junction at Consett and Washington has been reopened as a footpath and cycleway known as the Consett & Sunderland Railway Path. Also forming part of the C2C cycle route, the railway path continues eastwards from Washington along the north bank of the River Wear to end on Roker beach at Sunderland. Of interest along the route are a series of large modern sculptures commissioned by Sustrans in the 1990s, the most famous being Tony Cragg's 'Terris Novalis' which features a theodolite and an engineer's level at 20 times life size, on heraldic feet. At Beamish, the Open Air Museum with its reconstructed Edwardian town, colliery, tramway and railway station is well worth a visit, as is the Wildlife & Wetlands Trust Centre at Washington which is a haven for overwintering migratory water birds.

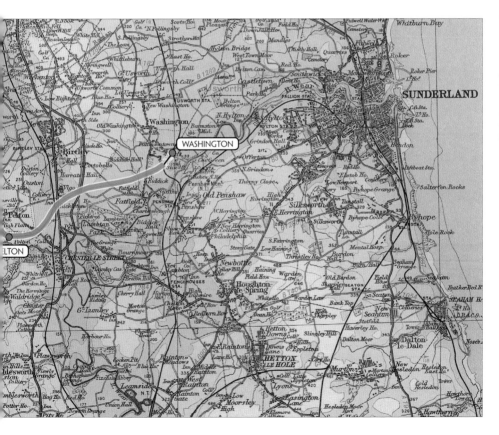

CONSETT ⇝ DURHAM

Lanchester Valley Railway Path

ORIGINAL LINE
14 miles

LENGTH OPEN TO WALKERS & CYCLISTS
12 miles

ORIGINAL ROUTE OPERATOR
North Eastern Railway

LINE OPEN TO PASSENGERS
1862-1939

OS LANDRANGER
88

NATIONAL CYCLE NETWORK
Route 14

REFRESHMENT POINTS
Lanchester, Langley Park

CAR PARKING
Lygetts Junction, Lanchester, Langley Park, Broompark (disabled only)

NATIONAL RAIL NETWORK STATION
Durham

By the mid-19th century local supplies of iron ore were running out, so the Derwent Iron Works at Consett was forced to look further afield. Thirty miles to the southeast the iron ore deposits in the Cleveland Hills were soon to play an important part in keeping the blast furnaces running at Consett.

Transporting the ore from Middlesbrough to Consett via existing circuitous routes was time consuming, so the North Eastern Railway (NER) built a 14-mile single-track line along the Browney Valley between Durham and Consett. The main engineering features were three stone bridges over the river between Durham and Lanchester and a 700-ft-long timber viaduct to the east of Knitsley. Other intermediate stations were provided at Lanchester and Witton Gilbert. The line opened in 1862 and within a few years had been doubled to serve four new collieries along the valley. A new station was opened at Aldin Grange in 1883 (later renamed Bearpark).

The line between Durham and Consett lost its passenger service on 1 May 1939 although Durham Miners' Gala excursion trains continued to call at the stations during each July until 1954. Local goods traffic continued until 5 July 1965 while mineral traffic to Consett continued until complete closure of the line on 20 June 1966.

Since closure, around 12 miles of the trackbed has been reopened as a footpath and cycleway known as the Lanchester Valley Railway Path (NCN Route 14). The path starts at Lydgetts Junction, south of Consett, a crossroads of railway paths with NCN Route 14 continuing northwards through Consett and down the Derwent Valley to end near Newcastle's Metro Centre. NCN Route 7 heads northeast from Lydgetts Junction through Annfield Plain, Stanley and Washington to Sunderland (see page 180) while in the opposite direction it uses the trackbed of the line to Tow Law and Crook as far as Rowley.

The Lanchester Valley Railway Path heads due east from Lydgetts Junction along the valley of Backgill Burn for 1½ miles to Knitsley station where the North Eastern Railway (NER) station building and eastbound platform survive as a private residence. Another 1½ miles west, the path crosses the 70-ft embankment that was built in 1915 to replace the original timber viaduct. After another 1½ miles, the path reaches the village of Lanchester where the eastbound platform and station building – built in a typical NER style with stepped gable ends – is a private residence. Continuing southeasterly, the path runs alongside the River Browney for 3 miles to reach Witton Gilbert station where the substantial NER building is identified by a cast-iron trespass notice in its drive.

From here the railway path soon crosses the river twice in quick succession followed by another 2 miles to the site of Bearpark station. The path then heads south for a further mile (NCN Route 14 heads off east into Durham) before reaching the B6302 at the Broompark picnic site, adjacent to the East Coast Main Line south of Durham. From here the railway path continues southwards to Bishop Auckland (see page 184).

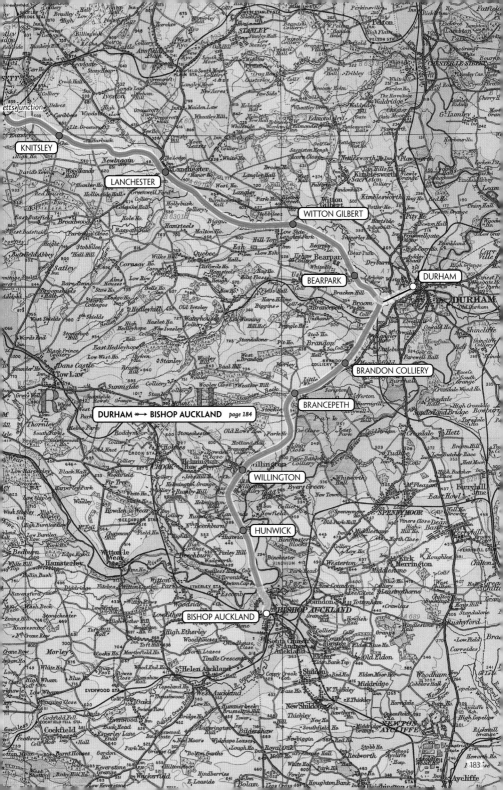

KNITSLEY

LANCHESTER

WITTON GILBERT

BEARPARK

DURHAM

BRANDON COLLIERY

BRANCEPETH

DURHAM ⟶ BISHOP AUCKLAND page 184

WILLINGTON

HUNWICK

BISHOP AUCKLAND

Newcastle

Durham

Bishop
Auckland   Middlesbrough

Brandon to Bishop Auckland Railway Path

ORIGINAL LINE
10 miles

**LENGTH OPEN TO
WALKERS & CYCLISTS**
9 miles

ORIGINAL ROUTE OPERATOR
North Eastern Railway

LINE OPEN TO PASSENGERS
1857-1964

OS LANDRANGER
88/92/93

NATIONAL CYCLE NETWORK
Route 20

REFRESHMENT POINTS
Broompark (disabled only),
Brancepeth, Hunwick, Bishop
Auckland

CAR PARKING
Lygetts Junction, Lanchester,
Langley Park, Broompark
(disabled only)

**NATIONAL RAIL
NETWORK STATIONS**
Durham, Bishop Auckland

*For route map see pages
182–183*

*For route map see pages
182–183*

ABOVE RIGHT:
*Ex-North Eastern
Railway Class 'Q7' 0-8-0 No
63460 hauls a RCTS/SLS
railtour near Brancepeth on 28
September 1963.*

DURHAM ↠→ BISHOP AUCKLAND

In 1854, four railway companies – York, Newcastle & Berwick, York & North Midland, Leeds Northern and Malton & Driffield Junction – merged to form the North Eastern Railway (NER) which, at its peak in 1922, controlled nearly 5,000 miles of railway.

One of the earliest railways built by the NER was the 10-mile line between Bishop Auckland and Durham, which opened to goods in 1857 and to passengers a year later. Intermediate stations were provided at Hunwick, Willington and Brancepeth. The major engineering feature was the 11-arch Newton Cap Viaduct north of Bishop Auckland which carried the railway 100 ft above the Wear Valley.

Serving numerous collieries along its route, this coal-carrying line also provided a link to the outside world for the coal miners and their families. A fourth intermediate station was opened at Brandon Colliery, north of Brancepeth, in 1861. In addition to locally generated passenger traffic, the line was also used by through trains in the summer months that operated between Newcastle and Blackpool via Barnard Castle, Stainmore and Tebay. Diesel multiple units were introduced on the line in 1959, but the through holiday trains to Blackpool ended in September 1961 and the

Stainmore route via Barnard Castle closed early in 1962. Recommended for closure in the 'Beeching Report', the line lost its passenger service on 4 May 1964 and goods facilities at intermediate stations ceased 3 months later. Despite this, the line remained open for through freight trains and locally generated coal traffic until 1968.

Since closure, 9 miles of the Durham to Bishop Auckland railway route have been reopened as a footpath and cycleway known as the Brandon to Bishop Auckland Railway Path. At its northern end the path starts at the Broompark picnic site on the B6302, 1 mile to the southwest of Durham, adjacent to the East Coast Main Line. From the north it is joined by the Lanchester Valley Path from Consett (see page 182). Heading southwards, the path soon reaches the former coal-mining village of Brandon where the railway cutting has been infilled and the station demolished. One mile southwest of Brandon the path reaches the small village of Brancepeth where there is a car park for walkers and cyclists and where the station building is a private residence.

From Brancepeth the path enters open country and winds around the contours for 2 miles before reaching the former coal-mining village of Willington. The last coal mine closed in 1967, but the village is still home to six pubs and a microbrewery. From here it heads south for 1½ miles into the valley of the meandering River Wear to reach the village of Hunwick – a car park for path users is located here while the station building is a private residence.

Edging ever closer to the River Wear, the path ends at the magnificent Grade II-listed Newton Cap Viaduct on the northern outskirts of Bishop Auckland. After crossing the viaduct, now a road bridge, it is a short walk into the town.

RICCARTON JUNCTION
⇶
REEDSMOUTH JUNCTION

Kielder Forest Border Railway Trail (part)

ORIGINAL LINE
42 miles

LENGTH OPEN TO WALKERS & CYCLISTS
8¼ miles

ORIGINAL ROUTE OPERATOR
North British Railway

LINE OPEN TO PASSENGERS
1862-1952

OS LANDRANGER
79/80

REFRESHMENT POINTS
Kielder

CAR PARKING
Kielder

The North British Railway (NBR) completed its long cross-border route across inhospitable terrain between Edinburgh and Carlisle in 1862. Thirteen miles south of the market town of Hawick, the Waverley Route, as the line became known, served Riccarton Junction, one of the loneliest and remotest railway outposts in Britain. With no road access, its inhabitants – railway workers and their families – depended entirely on the railway for all their needs. On 1 July, the same day that the Waverley Route opened, the 42-mile Border Counties Railway (owned by the NBR) opened between Riccarton Junction and the town of Hexham in Northumberland where it connected with the Newcastle & Carlisle Railway. Serving only scattered rural communities along its route, the railway was lightly used, occasionally coming to life for troop trains, rambler's specials and on market days when large numbers of sheep were transported to livestock sales at Bellingham and Hexham.

Following nationalization of Britain's railways in 1948, the Branch Lines Committee took a long and close look at loss-making rural lines such as

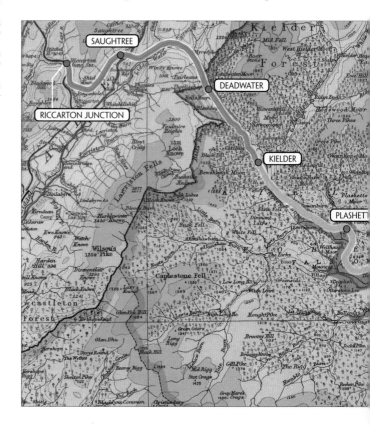

the Border Counties line. Closure had already looked likely as the bridge over the Tyne at Hexham was badly damaged during flooding in 1948 and, despite temporary repairs, it was considered too costly to rebuild. The line finally closed to passengers on 15 October 1956 although an infrequent goods service continued until 1958. The line was then closed completely between Riccarton and Bellingham with the latter town still seeing freight trains until November 1963. The end had come for the Border Counties line just over 100 years since it had opened, and the end also came for the Waverley Route through Riccarton Junction on 6 January 1969.

Accessible only along forestry tracks, Riccarton Junction is today an eerily silent place. Set deep in the forest, all that remains is the curving island platform, a replica station nameboard and a red telephone box. Two miles north, the Waverley Route Heritage Association is very slowly relaying track from its base at Whitrope Sidings towards

Riccarton. In the meantime the trackbed is still used for forestry operations but it can be accessed on foot to reach Riccarton. Much of the route of the Border Counties Railway from here to Deadwater station can be followed along a forestry track, en route passing the restored station at Saughtree where a short length of track has been relaid. Deadwater station is now a private residence, and from here to Kielder the trackbed is a 3-mile footpath and cycleway known as the Kielder Forest Border Railway Trail. On the approach to Kielder, the path crosses a viaduct before ending at the car park where there is a café and cycle hire shop. To the southeast of Kielder much of the route including Plashetts station now lies submerged beneath the massive Kielder Reservoir that was completed in the early 1980s. Further down the North Tyne valley the station buildings at Falstone, Thorneyburn, Tarset and Bellingham have all survived, the latter home to the Bellingham Heritage Centre.

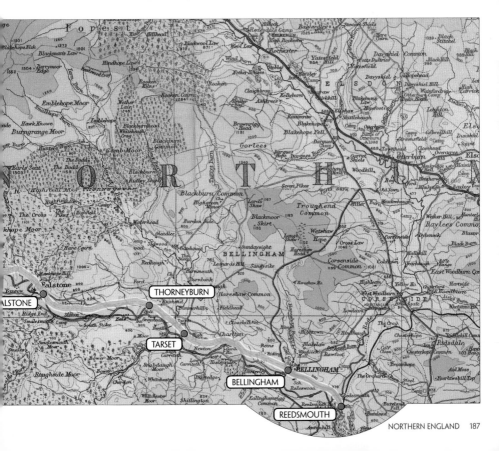

SCOTLAND

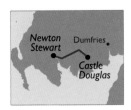

CASTLE DOUGLAS ⇢ NEWTON STEWART

The 'Port Road'

ORIGINAL LINE
29¾ miles

LENGTH OPEN TO WALKERS & CYCLISTS
12 miles

ORIGINAL ROUTE OPERATOR
Portpatrick Railway

LINE OPEN TO PASSENGERS
1861–1965

OS LANDRANGER
83/84

NATIONAL CYCLE NETWORK
Route 7 (part)

REFRESHMENT POINTS
Creetown

CAR PARKING
New Galloway
Station (Mossdale),
Big Water of Fleet Viaduct,
Creetown

Known as the 'Port Road', the single-track railway across the hills of Galloway between Castle Douglas and Newton Stewart was opened by the Portpatrick Railway in 1861 and was once an important route for traffic to and from Northern Ireland via the port of Stranraer. Also served by an overnight sleeper train to and from London Euston, the line featured several imposing viaducts and a bridge over Loch Ken. By the 1950s traffic was in decline and, steam-worked until the end, the entire route from Dumfries to Challoch Junction, east of Stranraer, closed on 14 June 1965, an early victim of Dr Beeching's 'Axe' in Scotland.

Since closure, two sections of the 'Port Road' between Castle Douglas and Newton Stewart have become accessible to walkers and mountain bikes. Reached along the A713, 4½ miles to the northwest of Castle Douglas, the 3-span bowstring bridge carried the railway westwards across Loch Ken although access to the rusting structure is blocked by a padlocked gate. The road journey to the other side is a ten-mile detour via the village of New Galloway.

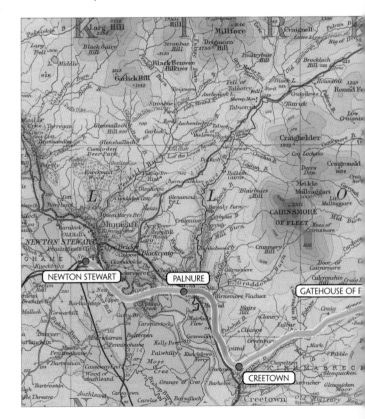

Five miles south of the village it served, New Galloway station (now a private residence) lies alongside the A762, where there is a car park – 1 mile to the east, the western end of Loch Ken bridge can be reached along a narrow lane. Westwards from the car park, the trackbed of the 'Port Road' is now a forestry track, which can be followed on foot or mountain bike for ten miles to Gatehouse of Fleet station. After crossing the River Dee on Stroan Viaduct, the track continues for 3 miles around the lower slopes of Airie Hill to reach Loch Skerrow. Trains once stopped at this lonely railway outpost to fill up with water fed from the nearby loch, but all that remains today are the disintegrating westbound platform, concrete fencing posts and cast iron pipes.

Heading off from Loch Skerrow in a southwesterly direction, the track sweeps through a vast area of forest for the next 4 miles. En route it passes the site of the Little Water of Fleet Viaduct which was blown up by the Army as a training exercise following closure of the line. Fortunately, the next 20-arch viaduct across the Big Water of Fleet survived and still stands in all its glory today. Once over the viaduct, the old railway route can be followed along a forestry track for 2 miles to Gatehouse of Fleet station, 12 miles north of the village it served.

The old railway route west of Gatehouse of Fleet is not passable, but National Cycle Network Route 7 passes through here along a country road and down the valley to the fishing village of Creetown (film location for 'The Wicker Man') where the station and goods shed survive. NCN Route 7 heads north along a country road before rejoining the old railway route up the valley of the River Cree to Palnure where the former station is now a private residence. The cycle route reaches Newton Stewart along country roads from here.

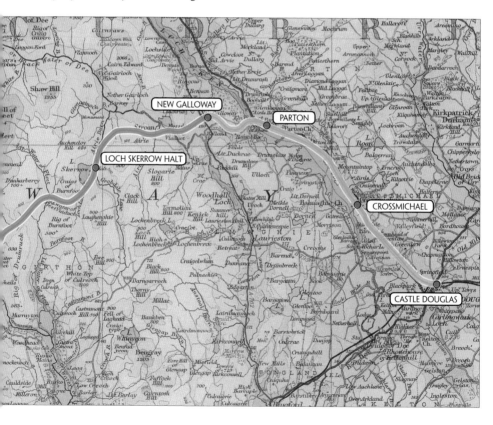

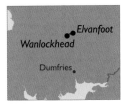

ELVANFOOT
⇒ WANLOCKHEAD

Leadhills & Wanlockhead Light Railway

ORIGINAL LINE
7¼ miles

LENGTH OPEN TO WALKERS & CYCLISTS
4 miles

ORIGINAL ROUTE OPERATOR
Caledonian Railway

LINE OPEN TO PASSENGERS
1902–1939

OS LANDRANGER
78

NATIONAL CYCLE NETWORK
Route 7 (part)

REFRESHMENT POINTS
Leadhills, Wanlockhead

CAR PARKING
Leadhills, Wanlockhead

HERITAGE RAILWAY
Leadhills & Wanlockhead Railway

Built as a Light Railway by 'Concrete Bob' McAlpine to serve the lead mining industry in the Lowther Hills, the Leadhills & Wanlockhead Railway opened between the West Coast Main Line at Elvanfoot and Wanlockhead in 1902 – the latter station, at 1,498 ft above sea level, was the highest standard-gauge station in Britain. Operated from the outset by the Caledonian Railway, the main engineering feature of the line was the concrete, curving, 8-arch Rispin Cleugh Viaduct that was faced with terracotta bricks.

Although the railway was built primarily to serve the mining industry at Leadhills and Wanlockhead, this *raison d'être* was not to last very long. The lead smelter at Wanlockhead closed in 1928 and by 1934 all the mines had also closed. With little passenger traffic, the line struggled on for a few more years until closure on 2 January 1939. Elvanfoot station closed in 1965 and the communities of the Lowther Hills were once again cut off from the outside world.

Despite closure nearly 75 years ago, much of the trackbed of the Leadhills & Wanlockhead Railway can still be traced today. Much of the railway's route up the Elvan Water Valley can be followed on foot – the best starting point is 1 mile west of Elvanfoot on the B7040 where the railway once crossed the road on the level. From here, the old trackbed can be seen winding back down the valley to Elvanfoot where its course is now blocked by a large electricity sub-station.

With the original ballast still visible, the trackbed can be followed up the valley on foot to Leadhills, a distance of 4 miles. En route there are magnificent views of the surrounding Lowther Hills although it is sad that the railway's engineering feature, Rispin Cleugh Viaduct, was demolished 25 years ago – the only reminder is a small plaque on the roadside.

The small village of Leadhills provides basic amenities such as a shop and the Hopetoun Arms, but pride of place must surely go to the 2-ft-gauge Leadhills & Wanlockhead Railway (the highest adhesion railway in Britain) which carries passengers for 1½ miles southwards as far as Glengonnar Halt. The railway opened in 1988 and has since been gradually extended to its current length. Future plans include extending southwards to a new terminus at Wanlockhead and also eastwards for ½-mile from Leadhills station to the B7040. Trains are usually hauled by diminutive diesel locos and normally operate on weekends and Bank Holidays from May to September.

At 1,531 ft above sea level, Wanlockhead is Scotland's highest village (it also has the highest pub) and consequently has a much higher than average rainfall. The station has long gone with its site now covered by agricultural buildings but everywhere there are traces of old mine workings and the narrow-gauge feeder lines that once transported ore to the village. One of these can be followed up the Wanlock Water Valley where there are still visible remains of mine workings and their buildings.

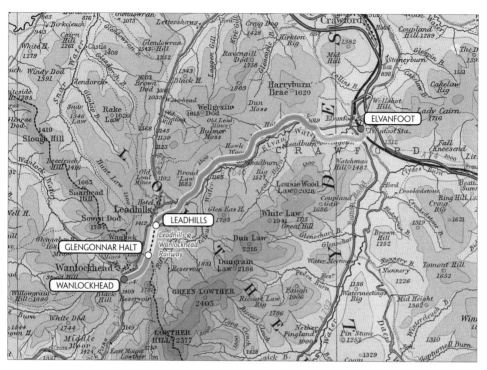

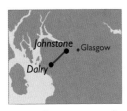

Johnstone · Glasgow

Dalry

Lochwinnoch Loop

ORIGINAL LINE
13 miles

LENGTH OPEN TO WALKERS & CYCLISTS
10¾ miles

ORIGINAL ROUTE OPERATOR
Glasgow & South Western Railway

LINE OPEN TO PASSENGERS
1905–1966

OS LANDRANGER
63/64

NATIONAL CYCLE NETWORK
Route 7

REFRESHMENT POINTS
Castle Semple Visitor Centre

CAR PARKING
Leadhills, Wanlockhead

NATIONAL RAIL NETWORK STATIONS
Johnstone, Lochwinnoch, Glengarnock

OPPOSITE TOP:
Southwest of Lochwinnoch the well-surfaced footpath and cycleway crosses the River Calder on this double-track stone bridge.

JOHNSTONE
⇒
DALRY

Completed in 1840, the Glasgow, Paisley, Kilmarnock & Ayr Railway's 33-mile line linked the Scottish industrial city with the port of Ayr along the Black Carr Water and Garnock valleys, for nearly 5 miles skirting the eastern shores of three small lochs – Castle Semple Loch, Barr Loch and Kilbirnie Loch. The company merged with the Glasgow, Dumfries & Carlisle Railway in 1850 to form the Glasgow & South Western Railway. The Glasgow to Ayr route had become increasingly congested by the end of the century, but doubling the line's capacity was not possible due to the cramped confines of the valleys. The G&SWR's answer to this was to bypass the section between Elderslie Junction, near Johnstone, to Brownhill Junction, north of Dalry, by building a new double-track line on the western side of the lochs. Serving intermediate stations at Johnstone North, Kilbarchan, Lochwinnoch and Kilbirnie, the 13-mile line opened for business on 1 June 1905. A feature of the new stations was that they all had one wide island platform, with a substantial, attractive wooden waiting room, connected to the road below by a subway and stairs at the platform end.

For the whole of its short life, the line was served by a frequent service of trains running between Glasgow St Enoch and Ayr, Largs or Kilmarnock. At weekends or Bank Holidays in the summer, the station at Lochwinnoch could be very busy handling hordes of daytrippers heading for Castle Semple Loch. Competition from road transport started to bite in the 1950s and, with falling passenger numbers, cost-effective diesel multiple units were introduced in the early 1960s. This was all to no avail and the line was recommended for closure in the 'Beeching Report' – closure to passengers came on 27 June 1966 although freight services continued until 1971 when the line north of Kilbirnie closed completely. The section from Brownhill junction to Kilbirnie remained open to serve a steelworks until the late 1970s.

Since closure, 10¾-miles of the Lochwinnoch Loop line between Johnstone and Kilbirnie has been reopened alongside the three lochs as a level, well-surfaced, traffic-free footpath and cycleway – it also forms part of National Cycle Network Route 7. Still popular with Glaswegians, Castle Semple Loch now has a modern visitor centre with car parking, café, bike hire, water sports and fishing facilities. The path can be accessed from the railway stations at Johnstone, Lochwinnoch and Glengarnock that are served by trains on the Glasgow to Ayr line that still operates along the other side of the lochs. Apart from cuttings, embankments, overbridges and the stone bridge across the River Calder near Lochwinnoch, little now remains of the railway infrastructure. While the old wooden waiting rooms with their wide awnings have long gone, the island platform at Kilbirnie has survived while the railway bridge, street entrance and remains of the island platform can be seen at Kilbarchan.

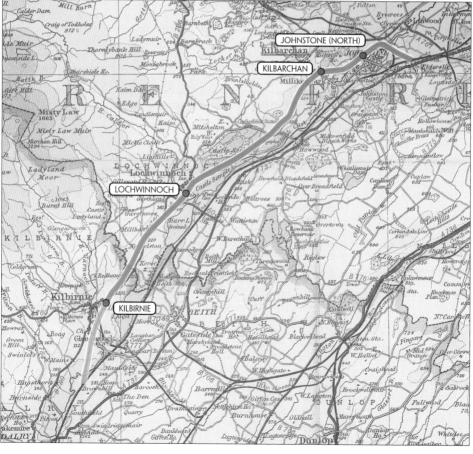

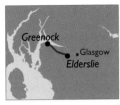

Greenock
Glasgow
Elderslie

Paisley & Clyde Railway Path

ORIGINAL LINE
15¾ miles

LENGTH OPEN TO WALKERS & CYCLISTS
13 miles

ORIGINAL ROUTE OPERATOR
Bridge of Weir Railway/
Greenock & Ayrshire Railway

LINE OPEN TO PASSENGERS
1864/1869–1965/1983

OS LANDRANGER
63/64

NATIONAL CYCLE NETWORK
Route 75

REFRESHMENT POINTS
Bridge of Weir, Kilmacolm, Greenock

CAR PARKING
Bridge of Weir, Kilmacolm, Greenock

NATIONAL RAIL NETWORK STATIONS
Paisley Canal, Johnstone, Port Glasgow, Cartsdyke, Greenock Central

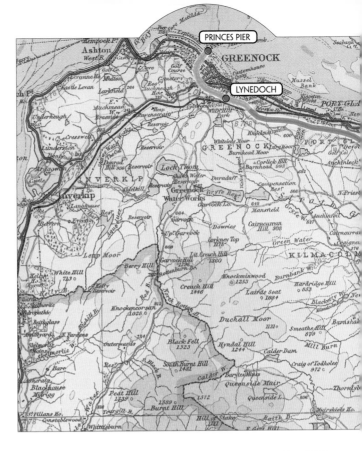

ELDERSLIE ⇢ GREENOCK

Getting away from industrial Glasgow 'doon the watter' to resorts along the Firth of Clyde had been a favourite pastime for Glaswegians since the early 19th century. The success of Henry Bell's 'Comet', the first successful steamboat service in Europe, which started operating between Glasgow and Greenock in 1812, soon led to hundreds of Clyde steamers operating up, down and across the river. Railway companies soon latched on to this lucrative traffic with the Glasgow, Paisley & Greenock Railway (GP&GR) opening from Glasgow Bridge Street to what is now Greenock Central station in 1841. Passengers for the steamers had a ¼-mile walk from this station to Custom House Quay. The GP&GR became part of the Caledonian Railway (CR) in 1847.

For more than two decades the CR had a stranglehold on this lucrative traffic until its rival, the Glasgow & South Western Railway (G&SWR), invaded its territory. The G&SWR did this by backing the Greenock & Ayrshire Railway (G&AR) which had been authorized in 1862 to build a 11¾-mile line from Bridge of Weir to Greenock. The former station had already been served from Glasgow by the Bridge of Weir Railway since 1864, the latter being absorbed by the G&SWR a year later. The G&AR

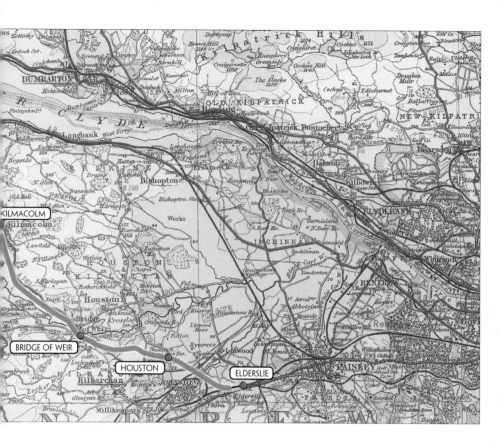

opened in 1869 and was worked from the outset by the G&SWR, the latter absorbing the former in 1872. The opening of this new route to Greenock from Glasgow St Enoch started a vicious price war between the GSWR and its arch-rival, the Caledonian. Despite increasing their Clyde passenger traffic, neither of the companies really won although the G&SWR had the edge as its station at Princes Pier in Greenock allowed passengers to board the steamers directly from their train. In the end the two companies came to an agreement to fix their fares and share the revenue from the two routes.

Nationalization of the railways and Clyde steamer services in 1948 finally ended the competition. Following the withdrawal of Clyde steamers from Princes Pier, local passenger services were withdrawn between Kilmacolm and Greenock on 2 February 1959 although the route continued to be used for trans-Atlantic liner passengers to and from Glasgow St Enoch until late 1965. The rest of the line between Elderslie and Kilmacolm closed on 3 January 1983.

Since closure almost the entire route of the railway has been reopened as part of a 21-mile footpath and cycleway known as the Paisley & Clyde Railway Path (P&CRP). The path starts at Paisley Canal station and shares the route of National Cycle Network Route 7 as far as Johnstone where the latter branches off westward along the railway path to Lochwinnoch (see page 194). The P&CRP heads northwest to Bridge of Weir where it crosses the River Gryfe on a stone viaduct. Heading up the Gryfe Valley into open countryside, the path reaches Kilmacolm where the station is now a pub. Beyond here it continues through cuttings and along embankments to Port Glasgow from where the traffic-free railway section ends and the P&CRP continues to Greenock and Gourock along public roads.

ST LEONARDS BRANCH

EDINBURGH
St Leonards
Branch

Innocent Railway Path

ORIGINAL LINE
1¾ miles

**LENGTH OPEN TO
WALKERS & CYCLISTS**
1¾ miles

ORIGINAL ROUTE OPERATOR
Edinburgh & Dalkeith Railway

LINE OPEN TO PASSENGERS
1831–1847

OS LANDRANGER
66

NATIONAL CYCLE NETWORK
Route 1

REFRESHMENT POINTS
Edinburgh (St Leonards),
Duddingston, Brunstane

**NATIONAL RAIL
NETWORK STATIONS**
Edinburgh Waverley,
Brunstane

One of Scotland's first railways, the Edinburgh & Dalkeith Railway (E&DR) was built to a gauge of 4 ft 6 in and opened in 1831. The main engineering feature was the 556-yd St Leonards Tunnel which carried the line under Arthur's Seat and was excavated out of volcanic rock. The 1-in-30 inclined plane up through the tunnel to the terminus at St Leonards was initially rope worked by a stationary steam engine. Other features along the route were a cast iron bridge over Braid Burn at Duddingston and the 65ft-high arched stone Glenesk Bridge over the River North Esk at Dalkeith – all these features from one of Scotland's earliest railways survive today. Passengers were catered for in a converted horse-drawn stagecoach laid on by an enterprising local businessman in 1832. The E&DR took over the service in 1836, and although still horse-drawn it carried more passengers than the Liverpool & Manchester Railway.

The railway was taken over by the North British Railway (NBR) in 1845 which then rebuilt it to the standard gauge, introduced steam haulage and opened a new connecting line from the NBR's new station at Waverley to Niddrie. While passenger services were then introduced from Waverley to Dalkeith, the St Leonards line, now effectively a branch line from Niddrie, lost its passenger service in 1847. Nicknamed the 'Innocent Railway' because of its exemplary safety record, the 1¾-mile branch line from Duddingston Junction (on the Edinburgh outer suburban line) to St Leonards remained steam-worked until the early 1960s with ancient ex-NBR Class 'J35' 0-6-0 goods locos struggling up the 1-in-30 gradient through St Leonards Tunnel with their trains of coal. The branch finally closed to all traffic on 5 August 1968.

Since closure, the 1¾ miles of trackbed of this pioneering railway between St Leonards and Duddingston have been reopened as a footpath and cycleway known as the Innocent Railway Path. Forming part of National Cycle Network Route 1, the path continues beyond Duddingston along paths to Brunstane where there is a rail connection to either Waverley station or Newcraighall. Since September 2015, this line has also been served by trains on the reopened Borders Railway to Galashiels and Tweedbank.

Accessed from St Leonards Lane in Edinburgh, the original 1830-built goods shed in St Leonards goods yard is a remarkable survivor and is now used as a vegetarian restaurant. From here, the railway path dives into the well-lit sandstone-lined tunnel (Scotland's oldest rail tunnel) on a downhill gradient of 1-in-30 before emerging into a green corridor through the pleasant surroundings of Holyrood Park and the Bawsinch Nature Reserve. Immediately to the north looms the 823-ft peak of Arthur's Seat and its ancient fort. Nestling below is the natural freshwater Duddingston Loch, once used for ice skating and curling and now owned by the Scottish Wildlife Trust as an important breeding site for overwintering wildfowl. At Duddingston, the railway path uses the original E&DR cast-iron bridge, made by the Shotts Iron Company in 1831, to cross over the Braid Burn.

OPPOSITE LOWER:
The Innocent Railway Path
descends through the 1-in-30
St Leonards Tunnel before
emerging in Holyrood Park.

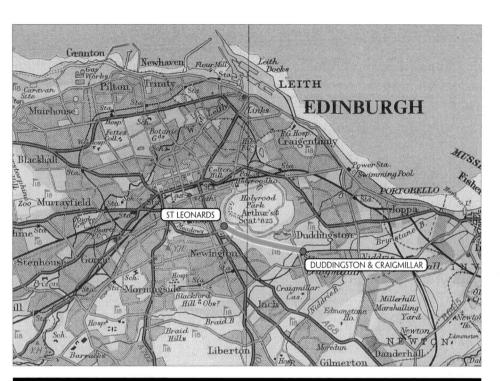

ST LEONARDS

DUDDINGSTON & CRAIGMILLAR

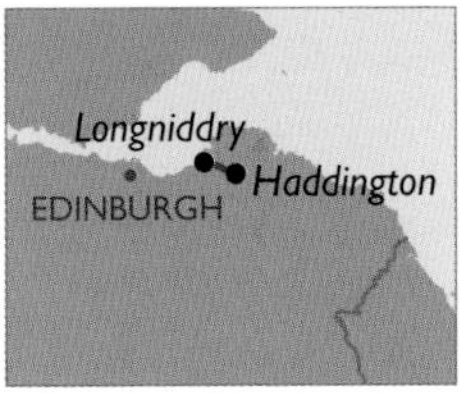

LONGNIDDRY → HADDINGTON

Haddington to Longniddry Railway Path

ORIGINAL LINE
4¾ miles

LENGTH OPEN TO WALKERS & CYCLISTS
4¾ miles

ORIGINAL ROUTE OPERATOR
North British Railway

LINE OPEN TO PASSENGERS
1846–1949

OS LANDRANGER
66

NATIONAL CYCLE NETWORK
76

REFRESHMENT POINTS
Haddington

NATIONAL RAIL NETWORK STATIONS
Longniddry

If the fledgling North British Railway had had enough funds it would have built its main line from Edinburgh to Berwick-on-Tweed via the town of Haddington, and this historic Royal Burgh would today be served by trains on the East Coast Main Line. But this wasn't to be as this shorter route across the hills of southeast Scotland would have been heavily engineered and costly to build. Instead, the company built its main line around the North Sea coast via Drem and Dunbar with the townsfolk of Haddington being given the less palatable option of a branch line. Both the main line and the 4-mile branch line from Longniddry to Haddington opened on 4 July 1844 – the latter was also built to main line standards with bridges wide enough to accommodate double track although only single track was laid. For just over a century Haddington was served by ten to eleven branch trains on weekdays and Saturdays to and from Longniddry, with trains taking 8-9 minutes for the short journey – at Longniddry passengers changed trains for the journey to Edinburgh.

All went well for the Haddington branch line until Britain's railways were nationalized at the beginning of 1948. Seeking to weed out loss-making services, the new British Railways (BR) was soon looking closely at rural branch lines up and down the country. By then the Haddington branch had seen a decline in its fortunes through increasing competition from road transport. It became one of the first to be closed by BR with passenger services ceasing on 5 December 1949. Despite this, freight traffic continued to reach Haddington by rail until the line closed completely on 30 March 1968.

Ten years after closure, the trackbed was bought by East Lothian Council and reopened as a well-surfaced traffic-free footpath, cycleway and bridleway known as the Haddington to Longniddry Railway Path. The council has provided interpretation 'signal posts' along the route with information on each site's human and natural significance. The railway path has also become a wildlife corridor rich in wildflowers, small mammals and, at Coatyburn, even bats.

For cyclists it is a useful commuter route to and from Edinburgh, either by taking the bike on the train to and from Longniddry or using the bike racks at the latter station. There are several stone road overbridges along the route, all of which were built to accommodate double track while at Haddington the platform and brick station building survive uneasily amidst a small industrial estate. Hopes of reopening the line may come to naught as the A1 dual carriageway now bisects the trackbed on the western outskirts of the town.

OPPOSITE LOWER:
A pleasant 4¼-mile walk or cycle ride, the Haddington to Lonniddry Railway Path, seen here at Coatyburn, is also an important wildlife corridor.

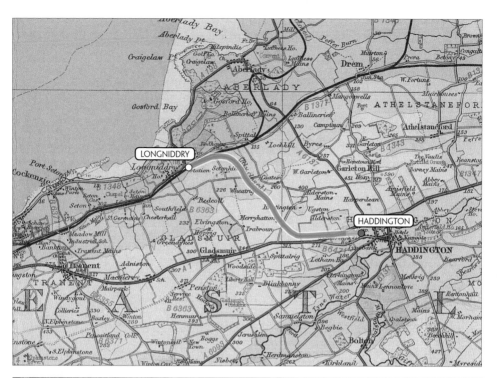

LONGNIDDRY

HADDINGTON

Stirling
Dunfermline
EDINBURGH

West Fife Way/ Alloa to Dunfermline Link

ORIGINAL LINE
13¾ miles

LENGTH OPEN TO WALKERS & CYCLISTS
8 miles

ORIGINAL ROUTE OPERATOR
Stirling & Dunfermline Railway

LINE OPEN TO PASSENGERS
1850–1968

OS LANDRANGER
58/65

NATIONAL CYCLE NETWORK
Route 764

REFRESHMENT POINTS
Dunfermline, Clackmannan

CAR PARKING
Dunfermline, Slack, Clackmannan

NATIONAL RAIL NETWORK STATIONS
Dunfermline Queen Margaret, Dunfermline Town

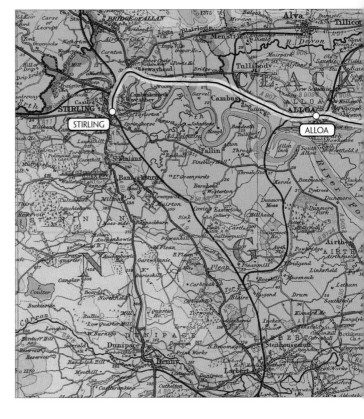

STIRLING ⇢ DUNFERMLINE

Built to serve the coalfields of West Fife, the Stirling & Dunfermline Railway opened westwards from Dunfermline to Alloa and Stirling in stages between 1850 and 1852. The fairly level double-track route featured the 8-arch Comrie Dean Viaduct and served intermediate stations at Oakley, East Grange, Bogside, Forest Mill, Alloa, Cambus and Causewayhead. The railway was absorbed by the Edinburgh & Glasgow Railway in 1858, which was then taken over by the North British Railway in 1865. A short branch line was opened from Oakley, home to an ironworks and colliery, to serve Comrie Colliery and the Rexco smokeless fuel works– this line became much busier in the 1930s when the Fife Coal Company started extracting coal from a large underground seam between Comrie village and Dollar.

Coal remained the lifeblood of the railway for its entire life, and passenger services were of secondary importance even though most trains along the route started or ended their journeys at Edinburgh. This route would have taken trains across the Forth Bridge to Dunfermline Lower station and then on a 2½-mile trip around the town to Dunfermline Upper station, all very time consuming and probably perplexing for passengers! Steam

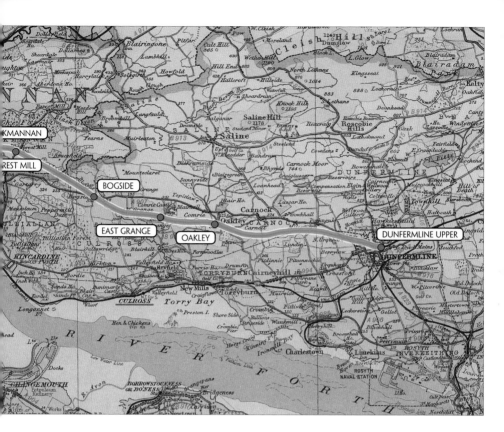

haulage on these trains was replaced by diesel multiple units in the early 1960s, but by then many of the intermediate stations had already closed. Facing increased competition from road transport and with an alternative route available between Edinburgh and Stirling, the passenger service between Dunfermline Upper and Stirling was withdrawn on 7 October 1968. The line remained open for freight until 1979 when it was closed west of Oakley, with the connection from Dunfermline staying open until the closure of Comrie Colliery in 1986. At its western end, Alloa was served by freight trains from Stirling until 1988. This section reopened in 2008 not only for merry-go-round coal trains destined for Longannet power station, but also for passengers to a new station at Alloa.

Since closure, the 8-mile section of trackbed between Dunfermline Queen Margaret station and the eastern outskirts of Clackmannan, via the site of Dunfermline Upper station, has been reopened as a mainly traffic-free footpath and cycleway known as the West Fife Way. Sadly nothing remains today of the extensive station and sidings at Dunfermline Upper, despite it surviving fairly intact until demolition in 1990. Just to the west of the station site, a remarkable survivor is a cast-iron lattice footbridge that once crossed the railway but now faces an uncertain future. Apart from a number of double-track width road bridges and the Comrie Dean Viaduct, the rest of the route to the outskirts of Clackmannan is sadly virtually devoid of any surviving railway infrastructure apart from one shining example at Bogside – here the signal box still stands in a wooded cutting, complete with imitation painted windows.

KILLIN

KILLIN JUNCTION

GLENOGLEHEAD CROSSING

BALQUHIDDER

KINGSHOUSE PLATFORM

STRATHYRE

LAGGAN FARMHOUSE

ST BRIDE'S CROSSING

CRAIGNACAILLEACH PLATFORM

CALLANDER

CALLANDER EAST

DRUMVAICH CROSSING

DOUNE

DUNBLANE ⇢ KILLIN

Callander & Oban Railway

ORIGINAL LINE
34½ miles

LENGTH OPEN TO WALKERS & CYCLISTS
25½ miles

ORIGINAL ROUTE OPERATOR
Scottish Central Railway/
Caledonian Railway

LINE OPEN TO PASSENGERS
1858/1886–1965

OS LANDRANGER
51/57

NATIONAL CYCLE NETWORK
Route 765/Route 7

REFRESHMENT POINTS :
Callander, Strathyre,
Kingshouse Hotel, Killin

CAR PARKING
Callander, Pass of Leny,
Strathyre, Lochearnhead, Killin

NATIONAL RAIL NETWORK STATION
Dunblane

What was to become the Caledonian Railway's route to Oban started life in 1858 when the Dunblane, Doune & Callander Railway opened. Financially backed and worked by the Caledonian Railway (CR), the Callander & Oban Railway (C&OR) then took over and opened its route up through Glen Ogle to Crianlarich and then through the Pass of Brander in 1880. A branch line was opened from Killin Junction to Loch Tay in 1886. Although the Dunblane to Crianlarich section and the Killin branch were recommended for closure in the 1963 'Beeching Report', the end came sooner than expected after a rockfall closed the line in Glen Ogle on 27 September 1965 and it never reopened.

Since closure, much of the route of this scenic railway has been reopened as a footpath and cycleway; the section between Callander and Killin forms part of National Cycle Network Route 7.

While the old railway route immediately to the west of Dunblane has been severed by the A9, there are plans to reopen it as a footpath and cycleway beyond here to Doune and Callander. In the meantime, a 1-mile section to the east of Doune now forms a footpath and cycleway known as the Doune Trail. West of Doune the old railway route closely follows the A84 and for the last 3 miles from Drumvaich into Callander has been reopened as a footpath and cycleway.

The railway path restarts at Callander Meadows and heads west into the Pass of Leny – the nearby Falls of Leny are a popular tourist attraction, and this section of the route can be muddy in the winter. It then follows the tranquil west shore of Loch Lubnaig for 5 miles to reach the village of Strathyre. North of Strathyre, the cycle route departs from the old railway route through the village of Balquhidder where it crosses the River Balvag to head east to Kingshouse Hotel on the A84. It then continues north, for a short distance following the trackbed of the Lochearnhead, St Fillans & Comrie Railway, before rejoining the C&OR trackbed via a steep zig-zag at Craggan, half a mile south of Lochearnhead.

From Craggan the C&OR's dramatic climb up Glen Ogle is the most spectacular part of this cycle route with magnificent views of what Queen Victoria called 'Scotland's Khyber Pass' and General Wade's military road from the viaduct about 2 miles way up the glen. The railway path ends alongside Lochan Lairig Cheile on the A85 and, after crossing this road, makes a detour along forest tracks for a mile before joining the trackbed of the Killin branch line in Glen Dochart.

The route of the Killin branch is followed for 2 miles to the attractive village of Killin, en route passing over the River Dochart near the Falls of Dochart on a 3-arch stone viaduct. A footpath continues from Killin along the last section of railway, via an old rusting girder bridge over the River Lochay, to Loch Tay where the station building is now a private residence.

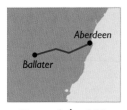

Aberdeen

Ballater

Deeside Way

ORIGINAL LINE
43¼ miles

**LENGTH OPEN TO
WALKERS & CYCLISTS**
27 miles

ORIGINAL ROUTE OPERATOR
Deeside Railway/Great North
of Scotland Railway

LINE OPEN TO PASSENGERS
1853/1866–1966

OS LANDRANGER
37/38

NATIONAL CYCLE NETWORK
Route 195

REFRESHMENT POINTS
Peterculter, Drumoak, Milton
of Crathes, Banchory,
Kincardine O'Neil, Aboyne,
Dinnet, Cambus O'May,
Ballater

CAR PARKING
Peterculter, Drumoak, Milton
of Crathes, Banchory,
Kincardine O'Neil, Aboyne,
Dinnet, Cambus O'May,
Ballater

**NATIONAL RAIL
NETWORK STATION**
Aberdeen

HERITAGE RAILWAY
Royal Deeside Railway

RIGHT:
*Room with a view alongside
the Deeside Way near Cambus
O' May – once patronized by
royalty, the railway closed
in 1966.*

ABERDEEN ⇥ BALLATER

Patronized by royalty visiting nearby Balmoral Castle, the 43¼-mile railway along the Dee Valley from Aberdeen to Ballater was opened in three stages between 1853 and 1866, but a planned extension to Braemar was thwarted by Queen Victoria. The eastern section also featured an intensive suburban commuter service to and from Aberdeen that was introduced at the end of the 19th century. Despite the regular passage of royal trains and the introduction of a unique battery-operated railcar in 1958, the line became a victim of Dr Beeching's 'Axe' and closed to passengers on 28 February 1966. Freight traffic continued for a little while longer, but by the beginning of 1967 the line had closed completely.

Since closure, much of the Deeside line from Aberdeen to Ballater has been reopened by Aberdeenshire Council as a footpath and cycleway known as the Deeside Way. With a few deviations en route, the first section uses the trackbed of the railway from Duthie Park, close to the site of the former Aberdeen Ferryhill engine shed, to Banchory, a distance of around 16 miles. From Banchory the Way temporarily leaves the old railway route, which loops inland through Lumphanan, instead following a route through Blackhall Forest to the south of the Dee. The railway route

is rejoined at Aboyne for the next 11 miles before terminating at Ballater station.

There is much to interest lovers of lost railways along this long route, most of which is closely paralleled by the A93 to the north and the River Dee to the south. The first significant remains can be found at Culter station where the eastbound platform has been graced by a reproduction station name board mounted on original concrete posts. At Milton of Crathes, the Way runs alongside the Royal Deeside Railway which has relaid nearly 2 miles of track to the eastern outskirts of Banchory. The Deeside Way ends its first section at Banchory where only the former engine shed has survived, albeit with a different use.

The Way now leaves the old railway route, rejoining it in the town of Aboyne where the restored station building is now used by a range of shops. Continuing westwards for 4½ miles, the Way reaches Dinnet station where both platforms have survived, albeit hidden in the encroaching woodland, while the station building is now used as an estate office. Continuing westwards along the heavily wooded Dee Valley for another 2½ miles, the Way reaches the beautifully restored and secluded station of Cambus O'May where road, rail and river converge through a narrow pass. Complete with platform, this remote station is now used as a holiday cottage while a graceful suspension pedestrian bridge, built across the river in 1905, gains access to a riverbank path.

Leaving Cambus O'May behind, the Deeside Way continues its westward journey for another 4 miles before ending at Ballater station. Sadly, the station building, once home to a royalty exhibition, restaurant and tourist information centre, was almost totally destroyed in a fire in May 2015.

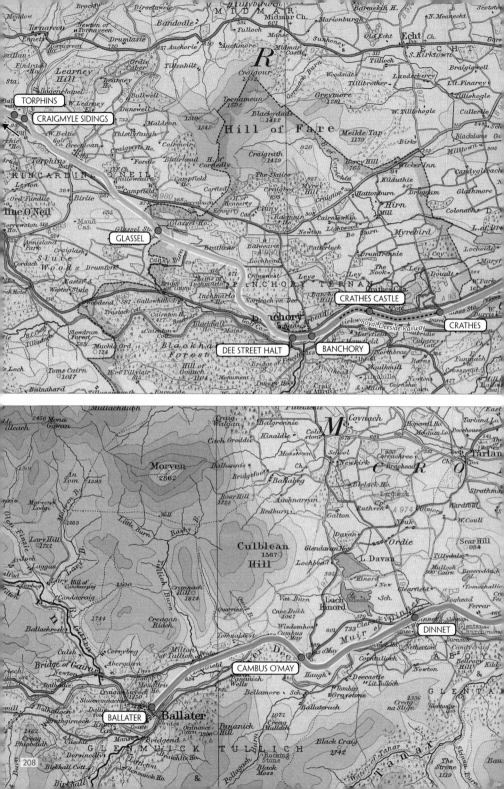

ABERDEEN

ABERDEEN

RUTHRIESTON

HOLBURN STREET

PITFODELS HALT

BIELDSIDE

CULTS

WEST CULTS

MILLTIMBER

MURTLE

DRUM

CULTER

MILLS OF DRUM

PARK

LUMPHANAN

TORPHINS

CRAIGMYLE SIDINGS

DESS

ABOYNE

ABOYNE CURLING POND PLATFORM

GLASSEL

DYCE »→ PETERHEAD

Formartine & Buchan Way

ORIGINAL LINE
38 miles

LENGTH OPEN TO WALKERS & CYCLISTS
38 miles

ORIGINAL ROUTE OPERATOR
Great North of Scotland Railway

LINE OPEN TO PASSENGERS
1862–1965

OS LANDRANGER
30/38

NATIONAL CYCLE NETWORK
Route 1 (part)

REFRESHMENT POINTS
Dyce, Udny, Ellon, Maud, Peterhead

CAR PARKING
Parkhill, Newmachar, Udny, Ellon, Auchnagatt, Maud, Old Deer, Mintlaw, Longside,

NATIONAL RAIL NETWORK STATION
Dyce

The Great North of Scotland Railway (GNoSR) was incorporated in 1846 to build a line from Aberdeen to Huntly, but shortage of capital delayed construction work which eventually started in 1852. The line opened between Kittybrewster and Huntly in 1854, and a new station was opened at Aberdeen (Waterloo) in 1856. There then followed several unsuccessful proposals to build a line from Dyce, north of Aberdeen, to the fishing ports of Peterhead and Fraserburgh before the GNoSR-backed Formartine & Buchan Railway (F&BR) received authorization in 1858 to build it. Construction was held up by severe weather in February 1860 when the viaduct across the River Ythan at Ellon collapsed; the line eventually opened between Dyce and Mintlaw in July 1861. Peterhead, 38 miles from Dyce, was reached one year later, and a branch line to the important fishing harbour was opened in 1865. The 16-mile line from a junction at Maud, on the Peterhead line, to the fishing port of Fraserburgh opened in 1865. Both lines were worked from the outset by the GNoSR, which went on to absorb the F&BR in 1866.

Two branch lines were built by the GNoSR: the 15½-mile line from Ellon to Boddam opened in 1897, primarily to serve the company's new hotel and golf course at Cruden Bay; the 5-mile branch from Fraserburgh to St Combs was built as a Light Railway and opened in 1903. The former closed to passengers as early as 1932 but remained open for freight until 1945.

For the next 100 years both 'main lines' were served by through passenger trains from and to Aberdeen with most of them splitting or joining at Maud Junction. Fish traffic was the lifeblood of both lines with fish catches landed at Peterhead and Fraserburgh being despatched to distant markets such as Billingsgate in London in overnight refrigerated trains. Diesel multiple units were introduced in 1959, but with declining passenger numbers both routes were recommended for closure in the 1963 'Beeching Report'. The Maud Junction to Peterhead line, along with the St Combs branch, lost its passenger service on 3 May 1965. The rest of the route from Dyce to Fraserburgh lost its passenger service on 4 October of that year. Freight trains continued to serve Peterhead until 7 September 1970 and to Fraserburgh until 8 October 1979.

Following closure, the 54-miles of trackbed of both lines was purchased by what is now Aberdeenshire Council and reopened as a footpath and cycleway known as the Formartine & Buchan Way. Much of the infrastructure such as bridges, viaducts and stations has survived, the latter mainly used as private residences.

The main route from Dyce to Peterhead heads north from Dyce station which is still served by trains operating between Aberdeen and Inverness. The first station to be reached is at Parkhill which closed in 1950 and where the platforms and the viaduct over the River Don have survived. Further north the screened-off Newmachar station is a private residence while a short distance further on is a deep cutting at the summit of the line. Descending from here, the Way passes through Udny, Logierieve and

MAUD JUNCTION

MINTLAW

LONGSIDE

NEWSEAT HALT

INVERUGIE

PETERHEAD

AUCHNAGATT

ARNAGE

ELLON

ESSLEMONT

LOGIERIEVE

UDNY

NEWMACHAR

PARKHILL

DYCE

Esslemont stations which are all now private residences. At Ellon, the Way passes over the River Ythan on a substantial 4-arch viaduct before continuing north past Arnage and Auchnagatt stations (both private residences) to arrive at Maud Junction.

There are well-preserved station, platforms and a turntable pit at Maud Junction, where the Fraserburgh section of the Formartine & Buchan Way heads north (see below), while the route to Peterhead now turns eastward. En route, the Way first passes the ruins of Mintlaw station followed by the stations at Longside and Newseat which are both private residences. Not much remains now of the penultimate station at Inverugie and nothing at all remains of the once-extensive station site at Peterhead which was completely bulldozed and redeveloped in the 1970s.

MAUD JUNCTION
⇼⟶
FRASERBURGH

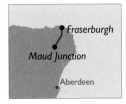

Formartine & Buchan Way

ORIGINAL LINE
16 miles

LENGTH OPEN TO WALKERS & CYCLISTS
16 miles

ORIGINAL ROUTE OPERATOR
Great North of Scotland Railway

LINE OPEN FOR PASSENGERS
1865–1965

OS LANDRANGER MAP
30

REFRESHMENT POINTS
Maud, Strichen, Fraserburgh

CAR PARKING
Maud, Strichen, Fraserburgh

ABOVE RIGHT:
After closure Maud Junction station was once home to the Maud Railway Museum.

The 16-mile Fraserburgh section of the Formartine & Buchan Way continues north from the well-preserved station at Maud Junction. The first station en route was at Brucklay which is now a private residence. On the approach to the village of Strichen, the Way winds eastward over the tall girder bridge across the North Ugie Water, while the station building and two platforms in the village have all survived. Now heading northeast, the Way passes the stations at Mormond, Lonmay and Philorth all of which have platforms and are now private residences – the latter station was built for the use of the eighteenth Lord Saltoun, a Scottish Representative Peer who lived at nearby Philorth House. The Way ends near to the site of Fraserburgh station, but apart from the goods office building and engine shed, the rest of the once-extensive site here has been demolished to make way for a road and commercial redevelopment.

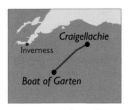
Craigellachie
Inverness
Boat of Garten

Speyside Way

ORIGINAL LINE
33½ miles

**LENGTH OPEN TO
WALKERS & CYCLISTS**
19¾ miles

ORIGINAL ROUTE OPERATOR
Great North of
Scotland Railway

LINE OPEN FOR PASSENGERS
1863/1868–1965

OS LANDRANGER
28/36

REFRESHMENT POINTS
Nethy Bridge, Grantown-on-
Spey, Aberlour, Craigellachie

CAR PARKING
Nethy Bridge, Grantown-on-
Spey, Ballindalloch, Aberlour,
Craigellachie

HERITAGE RAILWAYS
Strathspey Railway, Keith &
Dufftown Railway

BOAT OF GARTEN
≫→
CRAIGELLACHIE

Serving numerous distilleries along its 33½-mile route up the picturesque Spey Valley from Craigellachie, the Strathspey Railway initially had problems reaching its goal of Boat of Garten. Worked from the outset by the Great North of Scotland Railway, the single-track line led a fairly quiet life and despite the introduction of cost-cutting railbuses and the opening of new halts in the late 1950s, it was recommended for closure in the 'Beeching Report'. Closure to passengers came on 18 October 1965 although parts of the line remained open to serve whisky distilleries until 1971.

Since closure, several sections of the railway along the Spey Valley have been reopened as a footpath, forming part of the Speyside Way Long Distance Path. Walkers can join the Speyside Way at Nethy Bridge where the former station building now provides bunkhouse accommodation. From here, the trackbed of the railway is followed northwards to Grantown-on-Spey where the Speyside Way diverts across the river before rejoining the railway route further on at Cromdale station. Following the course of the Grantown to Forres railway, the 24-mile Dava Way footpath and cycleway can also be joined at Grantown. At Cromdale, where there is

RIGHT
*A popular destination for
fishermen, the former station at
Blacksboat is conveniently
located very close to the
River Spey.*

OPPOSITE:
*Ivatt Class 2 2-6-0 No 46512
waits to depart from Aviemore
with a train for Broomhill – the
railway is being extended to
Grantown-on-Spey where it will
connect with the Speyside Way.*

plenty of railway ephemera and a restored carriage, the station building has been superbly restored as a private residence.

From Cromdale station, the Speyside Way continues to follow the old railway route for about a mile before diverting along forest tracks and side roads to rejoin it about 2 miles to the west of Ballindalloch station, the latter now a hostel. Immediately north of Ballindalloch station, the Way crosses the River Spey on a steel latticework girder bridge before continuing northward down the valley to Blacksboat station. A haunt of fishermen in this beautiful riverside location, the goods shed, platform and station building have been lovingly restored, the latter being used as holiday accommodation. Following the meandering river down the wooded valley, the railway path reaches Knockando station which has been restored by the adjacent Tamdhu Distillery – only the track is missing from this delightful station with its two platforms and signal box. Following the bends in the river, the Way reaches Carron station, adjacent to the once rail-served but now mothballed Imperial Distillery. The station building here survives complete with rusty clock and cast iron drinking water fountain.

From Carron, the railway path crosses over the Spey again and follows it for 3½ miles to Aberlour, en route passing the lovingly restored railway halt at Dailuaine. The restored station and platform at Aberlour now house a café while the former station site and goods yard have been landscaped as a riverside park.

Beyond Aberlour the Way passes through the 68-yd Taminurie Tunnel, the only tunnel on the Speyside Line, before reaching Craigellachie – here all that remains of the junction station is one platform and a road overbridge while the station site is now a car park for users of the Speyside Way. From Craigellachie, the 4-mile railway route southwards along the valley of the River Fiddich to Dufftown is also a footpath.

CROM

CROMDALE

GRANTON-ON-SPEY-EAST

BALLIFURTH FARM HALT

NETHY BRIDGE

BOAT OF GARTEN

Strathspey Railway

River Spey

River Dulnain

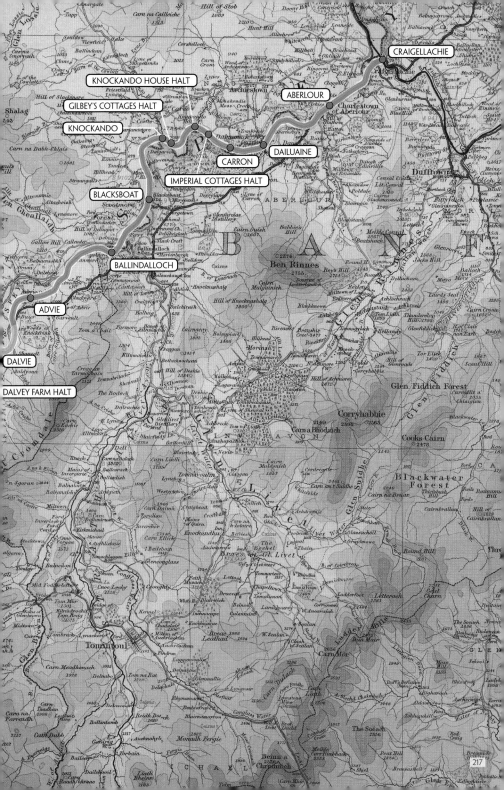

CRAIGELLACHIE

KNOCKANDO HOUSE HALT

ABERLOUR

GILBEY'S COTTAGES HALT

KNOCKANDO

DAILUAINE

CARRON

IMPERIAL COTTAGES HALT

BLACKSBOAT

BALLINDALLOCH

ADVIE

DALVIE

DALVEY FARM HALT

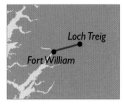

Loch Treig
Fort William

Lochaber Narrow Gauge Railway

ORIGINAL LINE
21 miles

LENGTH OPEN TO WALKERS & CYCLISTS
18 miles

ORIGINAL ROUTE OPERATOR
British Aluminium Company

OS LANDRANGER
41

REFRESHMENT POINTS
Fort William

CAR PARKING
Fort William,
Torlundy, Fersit

NATIONAL RAIL NETWORK STATIONS
Fort William, Tulloch

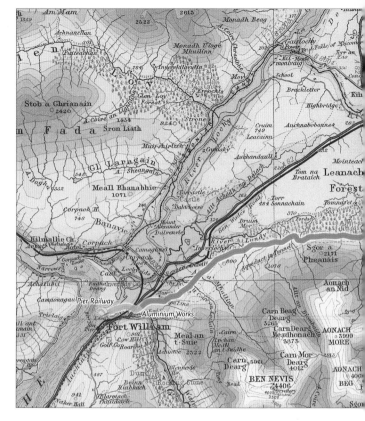

FORT WILLIAM ⇢ LOCH TREIG

While not a public railway, the most extensive narrow-gauge line to operate in Scotland was the Lochaber Narrow Gauge Railway which was built by Balfour Beatty in connection with the construction of a hydro-electric scheme to power a new aluminium smelter being built at Fort William. With no road access on the lower slopes of the Nevis range of mountains, the contractors built a 21-mile 3ft-gauge railway to carry men and materials to numerous construction sites between Fort William, Loch Treig and Loch Laggan. Construction of this enormous civil engineering project started in 1925 and was only completed during the Second World War, but the railway, known as the Upper Works Railway, remained in use for maintenance work until it was severed following a landslip in 1971. Although the break was not repaired, the two surviving sections on each side remained in use until complete closure in 1976. A separate 1¾-mile 3-ft-gauge line that connected the aluminium smelter with jetties on Loch Linnhe survived until the early 1960s.

Its route still marked on Ordnance Survey maps, the trackbed of the Upper Works Railway can still be followed on foot today while many of its 53 bridges with track still in situ survive intact. A note of caution to

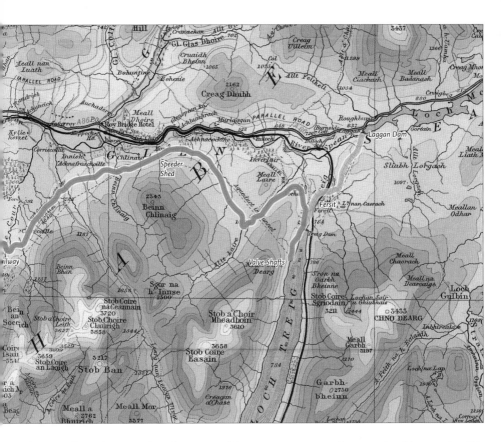

walkers: in places the ground can be very muddy and boggy, especially after heavy rain, and crossing the trestle bridges on foot is definitely not recommended as many of them are dangerous structures.

At its western end, the trackbed can be accessed alongside the aluminium works in Fort William where there is a small car park. From here, it crosses several rebuilt bridges (Nos. 51 and 50) before reaching a car park at Torlundy provided for mountain bikers using the trails in Leanachan Forest – in fact, the section from Fort William to this point is also used by mountain bikes. Two miles east of here is the Nevis Range Mountain Resort from where the trackbed can also be accessed. From here, it hugs the contours through the Leanachan Forest before arriving at Bridge No. 15 – complete with track, this dangerous structure once carried the railway over one of the many mountain streams that often become raging torrents after periods of heavy rain. This point on the railway can also be reached on foot from Spean Bridge via Corriechoille and a steep forestry track. Further east, two intact American-style trestle bridges (Nos 10 and 9) can also be accessed on foot by continuing along the lane through Corriechoille to Insh and then up another steep forestry track, passable by 4-wheel drive vehicles, to a small parking place. From here, high above the Monessie Gorge, the trackbed can be followed eastwards to the two bridges, both of which still have track in situ but are not safe to cross.

The eastern end of the railway can be accessed by road to Fersit, near Tulloch station on the West Highland Line, where there is another car park. From here, the railway route can be followed to the Treig Dam and the valve intakes on Loch Treig.

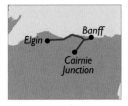

ELGIN ⤳ BANFF
AND CAIRNIE JUNCTION

Speyside Way (part)

ORIGINAL LINE
39¼ miles
(Banff branch: 6 miles)

LENGTH OPEN TO WALKERS & CYCLISTS
13¼ miles

ORIGINAL ROUTE OPERATOR
Banff, Portsoy & Strathisla Railway/Great North of Scotland Railway

LINE OPEN FOR PASSENGERS
1859/1886–1964/1968

OS LANDRANGER
28/29

NATIONAL CYCLE NETWORK
Route 1

REFRESHMENT POINTS
Garmouth, Buckie, Cullen, Banff

CAR PARKING
Garmouth, Buckie, Cullen, Banff

For route map see pages 222–223

PAGES 222–223:
From Garmouth the coastal footpath and cycleway crosses the Spey Estuary on the 950ft long Spey Viaduct, completed in 1886 to carry the Great North of Scotland Railway on its route from Elgin to Cairnie Junction.

A latecomer to the railway scene in northeast Scotland, the Great North of Scotland Railway's (GNoSR) route along the Morayshire coast between Elgin and Cairnie Junction was finally completed in 1886. Featuring curving viaducts on the coast at Cullen and a magnificent bridge across the River Spey, the line offered speedy transport for fish catches from the many coastal villages and an alternative route for passengers between Elgin and Aberdeen. Opened in 1859, the branch line to Banff was served by a shuttle service of trains connecting with the 'main line' at Tillynaught.

By the 1930s, increasing competition from road transport had started a decline in both passenger and goods traffic along the coastal route – the all important fish traffic from the coastal harbours was also being lost to lorries. Further decline followed the Second World War, and the introduction of unreliable diesel locos in the late 1950s probably made the situation worse rather than better. The 1963 'Beeching Report' brought bad news for the vast majority of the former GNoSR lines in northeast Scotland including the Elgin to Cairnie Junction route and the Banff branch. Both were recommended for closure with the steam-hauled Banff passenger service being withdrawn on 6 July 1964. The coastal route and goods traffic to Banff continued until 6 May 1968 when both these lines were closed completely.

In the near-50 years since closure, several scenic coastal sections of this railway have been reopened as footpaths and cycleways, which all form part of National Cycle Network Route 1. The railway path starts at Garmouth where there is car park for walkers and cyclists. Heading east the path soon crosses the River Spey on an enormous steel latticework bridge which was saved from demolition by Moray District Council and reopened in 1981. On the east bank of the Spey, the station and platforms at Spey Bay survive as a private residence. From here, NCN Route 1 diverts away from the old railway to follow side roads into Portgordon.

The railway route is rejoined east of Portgordon, following a straight stretch along the coastline with magnificent views across Spey Bay before there is another diversion around Buckie. Despite this, there are still reminders of the railway here where a steel latticework footbridge across the overgrown trackbed is open to pedestrians. The old railway route is rejoined to the east of the town to follow it in a straight line to the village of Findochty. After a short diversion through the village, the railway route is rejoined again for 1½ miles to Portknockie.

From Portknockie, the path passes through a cutting before emerging high above the coast on an embankment to sweep over the rooftops of Cullen on a series of magnificent curving viaducts. At the moment Cullen is the end of the road for walkers and cyclists along this superb railway coastal route. Further west at Banff, the last mile or so of the railway route behind rows of former fishermen's cottages is also a footpath.

ELGIN ⇢→ LOSSIEMOUTH

Lossiemouth
Elgin
Inverness

For route map see page 222

Serving the harbour town of Lossiemouth and with no intermediate stations, the 5¾-mile branch line from Elgin was built in a more-or-less straight line across low-lying land, en route crossing the moribund Spynie Canal. It was opened by the Morayshire Railway in 1852, and opening day on 10 August was a close-run thing as the two locomotives needed to run the line were delivered to Lossiemouth by sea from Glasgow only a few days before the event. The railway eventually became part of the Great North of Scotland Railway which heavily promoted the scenic attractions of the Morayshire coast, dubbing it the Scottish Riviera on posters and other promotional material.

Once served by a through sleeping car to and from London King's Cross, the railway fell on hard times in the years following the Second World War, and despite the introduction of diesel multiple units in the late 1950s, it was recommended for closure in the 'Beeching Report'. Passenger services were withdrawn on 28 March 1966 although Elgin East station remained open until 6 May 1968 when the remaining GNoSR lines to Cairnie Junction via Cullen ad Craigellachie were closed.

Since closure, 3¾ miles of the northern section of the Lossiemouth branch line has been reopened as a footpath and cycleway. The harbour town of Lossiemouth was the birthplace of Britain's first Labour Prime Minister, Ramsay MacDonald. It is once again a popular resort with fine sandy beaches, sand dunes, bracing sea air and a championship golf course, but is still heavily dependent on the nearby RAF station which contributes millions of pounds to the local economy.

While the railway station in the town has been demolished to make way for a leisure park, a short section of line can still be seen embedded in the nearby harbour quayside where an old warehouse has taken on a new life as café and bar. The railway path starts close to the Mercat Cross from where a tarmac path leads south out of the town before crossing the B9103. From here, the unsurfaced railway path – it can be muddy in winter – heads south for 3 miles in a dead-straight line, en route crossing the disused Spynie Canal and skirting the ruins of Spynie Palace. A good view of the railway's imprint on the landscape can be seen from the roof of the palace when it is open to the public. The railway path proper ends about 1 mile south of the palace where there is a minor road into Elgin. South of here, the trackbed is a very muddy farm track and is not recommended for walkers or cyclists.

The railway's approach to Elgin via a bridge over the River Lossie and a long embankment has survived the ravages of time, and it is hoped that they will one day be incorporated into the railway path. Floodlit at night, Elgin East station building with its magnificent booking hall has been superbly restored and is now a business centre.

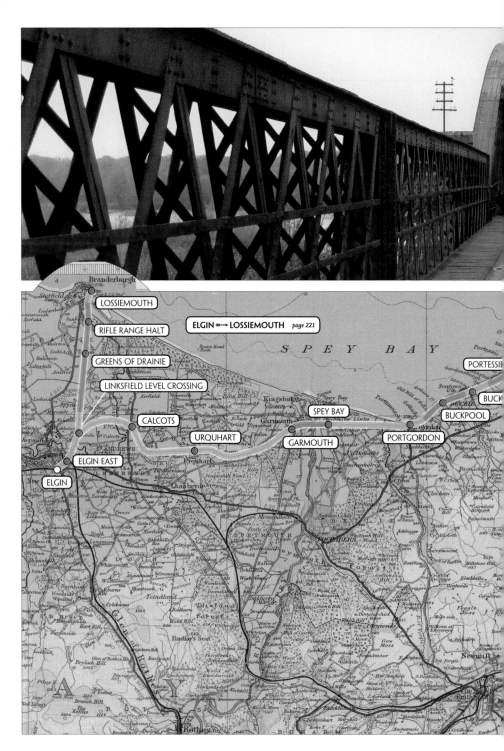

LOSSIEMOUTH

RIFLE RANGE HALT

GREENS OF DRAINIE

LINKSFIELD LEVEL CROSSING

ELGIN ➟ LOSSIEMOUTH   page 221

S P E Y   B A Y

PORTESSIE

SPEY BAY

CALCOTS

URQUHART

GARMOUTH

PORTGORDON

BUCKPOOL

BUCK

ELGIN EAST

ELGIN

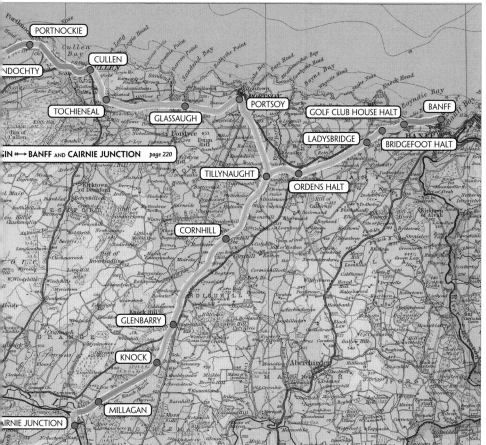

PORTNOCKIE

CULLEN

NDOCHTY

TOCHIENEAL

GLASSAUGH

PORTSOY

GOLF CLUB HOUSE HALT

BANFF

LADYSBRIDGE

BRIDGEFOOT HALT

IN ←→ BANFF AND CAIRNIE JUNCTION   page 220

TILLYNAUGHT

ORDENS HALT

CORNHILL

GLENBARRY

KNOCK

MILLAGAN

AIRNIE JUNCTION

PHOTO CREDITS

p7 Henry Casserley; **p8** Andrew Swift; **p11** Julian Holland; **p15** Andrew Swift; **p18** *top* Julian Holland; **p18** *lower* Julian Holland; **p21** (SS) jennyt; **p23** Mike Jones; **p25** Julian Holland; **p27** Paul Townsend; **p33** (CC) Stewart Black; **p37** Richard Casserley; **p39** Julian Holland; **p40** Julian Holland; **p46** Julian Holland; **p47** Henry Casserley; **p53** Julian Holland; **p57** Julian Holland; **p62** Mike Esau; **p65** (CC) Peter O'Connor; **p67** Tony Harden; **p69** Julian Holland; **p71** (CC) Mick Baker; **p75** Julian Holland; **p76** Henry Casserley; **p81** Julian Holland; **p82** Julian Holland; **p85** Julian Holland; **p92** *top* (CC) Paul Stainthorp; **p92** *lower* (CC) Paul Stainthorp; **p94** Henry Casserley; **p97** (CC) bazzadaram-blerimages; **p99** (CC) Matt Buck; **p101** (CC) Peter Broster; **p103** (SS) David Hughes; **p110** *top* Julian Holland; **p110** *lower* (CC) Ingy The Wingy; **p114** *top* (CC) Stevep2008; **p114** *lower* (CC) Chris Morriss; **p118** *top* (SS) Simon Geig; **p118** *lower* (SS) Elena Schweitzer; **p123** *top* (CC) chrispd1975; **p124** (CC) Ashley Van Haeften; **p127** Julian Holland; **p129** Tony Harden; **p131** Julian Holland; **p135** (CC) Hefin Owen; **p137** (SS) Stephen Rees; **p141** (CC) Ben Salter; **p145** (CC) Richard Szwejkowski; **p147** Henry Casserley; **p149** Andrew Swift; **p150** (CC) Ashley Van Haeften; **p157** (CC) Chris Sampson; **p158** Henry Casserley; **p161** (CC) Tim Green; **p163** Tony Harden; **p165** (CC) Xerones; **p166** Julian Holland; **p173** Julian Holland; **p177** Brian Sharpe; **p183** Mark Bartlett; **p185** Colour-Rail; **p188** (CC) Detroit Publishing Co; **p193** Julian Holland; **p195** Julian Holland; **p199** (CC) Ben Heathwood; **p201** Julian Holland; **p206** (CC) Ted and Jen; **p212** (CC) Freetalk1; **p214** Julian Holland; **p215** (SS) Philip Bird LRPS CPAGB; **p222** (CC) Ted and Jen

CAPTIONS FOR IMAGES INTRODUCING CHAPTERS

PAGES 8–9: *The Somerset & Dorset Railway station at Highbridge was at right-angles to the GWR main line – in the background is the railway works. (Evercreech Junction to Burnham-on-Sea)*

PAGES 40–41: *Highgate station with a Great Northern Railway train in the early 20th century. The tunnels at the station are now bricked up and home to colonies of bats. (Finsbury Park to Alexandra Palace)*

PAGES 76–77: *A Midland & Great Northern Joint Railway Beyer-Peacock 4-4-0 departs from Norwich City station with a train for Melton Constable in the 1920s. Today this is a footpath and cycleway known as Marriott's Way. (Norwich to Reepham)*

PAGES 94–95: *An ex-LMS Class '4F' 0-6-0 heads a mixed freight on Headstone Viaduct across the River Wye in the 1950s. Today this is a footpath and cycleway known as the Monsal Trail. (Buxton to Matlock)*

PAGES 124–125: *An early 20th century view of Barmouth Bridge and Cader Idris – opened in 1867, the 764-yd-long structure carries the railway and a footpath across the Mawddach estuary to Morfa Mawddach (for the Mawddach Trail). (Barmouth to Dolgellau)*

PAGES 150–151: *Robin Hood's Bay was once served by trains on the scenic Scarborough to Whitby line. (Scarborough to Whitby)*

PAGES 188–189: *Completed in 1894, the Italianate railway station at Prince's Pier in Greenock gave the Glasgow & South Western Railway's customers easy access to the company's Clyde steamers. (Elderslie to Greenock)*

MAPPING

Maps courtesy of:

© Collins Bartholomew: back cover, p4, all location maps

All historical maps are from Bartholomew's Half Inch Series from the 1950's and 1960's publications, © HarperCollins Publishers and the National Library of Scotland (NLS). With thanks to Chris Fleet at the NLS.

Thanks also to Gordon Edgar for his assistance.